The Technology of Political Co

The Technology of Political Control

Carol Ackroyd, Karen Margolis,
Jonathan Rosenhead, Tim Shallice

Second edition

Second revised edition first published 1980
by Pluto Press Limited, Unit 10 Spencer Court,
7 Chalcot Road, London NW1 8LH

First edition published by Penguin Books Limited, 1977

Copyright © Carol Ackroyd, Karen Margolis,
Jonathan Rosenhead and Tim Shallice 1977;
Introduction and Afterword to second edition, Copyright ©
Karen Margolis, Jonathan Rosenhead and Tim Shallice 1980

ISBN 0 86104 307 3
Cover designed by Graeme Murdoch
Printed in Great Britain by Lowe & Brydone Printers
Limited, Thetford, Norfolk

Contents

Preface ix
Introduction xi

Part One: The New Technology Comes of Age: Lessons from Northern Ireland
1. Old and New Traditions of Violence 19
2. The Tory Offensive 26
3. Maximum Repression 32
4. Sophisticated Counter-Insurgency 38
5. The Significance of Northern Ireland 43

Part Two: The British Road to the Strong State
6. Capitalism in Crisis 49
7. The Fascist State 52
8. Military Intervention in Politics 57
9. Steps to the Strong State 68
10. 'Small Steps' in the Law 78

Part Three: The Strong Arm of the Strong State
11. From Counter-Insurgency to Internal Defence 89
12. Low-Intensity Operations in Britain 115

Part Four: The Technology of Political Control
13. Watching and Waiting 151
14. Monitoring Militant Action 182
15. Riot Control 197
16. Torture and Interrogation 229
17. Scientific Interrogation 247
18. Prisoners of the Strong State 254

Conclusions 287
Afterword 293
References 301
Index 327

It would be possible to write quite a history of the inventions, made since 1830, for the sole purpose of supplying capital with weapons against the revolt of the working class.

> Karl Marx

Preface

This book stems from a series of investigations organized by the British Society for Social Responsibility in Science. The views expressed are those of the authors, but the book would have been neither started nor finished without the active support of BSSRS. Many other organizations have assisted us, including the American Civil Liberties Union (through John Shattuck); NARMIC (and especially Eric Prokosch); the National Council for Civil Liberties (particularly Catherine Scorer); Science for the People; the staff of *Time Out*; the Center for Research on Criminal Justice, Berkeley (publishers of *The Iron Fist and the Velvet Glove: An Analysis of the US Police*); the Counter Measure Security Systems of Ann Arbor, Michigan; and the Communication Control Corporation of New York.

We have been fortunate in the help we have received from so many comrades – information and technical advice, critical reading, and practical and personal support of all kinds. All our attempts to construct a list of who helped us with what have collapsed, because so often the help straddled all boundaries. So we would simply like to express our thanks, for their shares in our collective enterprise, to: Pat Arrowsmith, Tony Bunyan, Patrick Camiller, Alan Campbell, Sherman Carroll, Burt Cohen, Stan Cohen, Gillian Elinor, Fred Fletcher, Tom Gilmore, Nelson Heller, Deborah Hodgkin, Rachel Hodgkin, Farooq Hussein, Judy Kelly, Sarah Litvinoff, Moshe Machover, Laura Margolis, Ann Morris, Anna Murch, Petter Nore, Tim Potter, Steven Rose, John Shirley, Myra Siskind, Vic Siskind, Andy Solandt, Laurence Sparham, Capt. Andy Sutor, Begonia Tamarit, Alan Wallace and Paul Walton. We are also most grateful for the help – both witting and unwitting – we received from employees of official agencies, whom it would hardly be appropriate to acknowledge here. We are particularly grateful to Patrick Camiller for preparing the index.

Since the main text of this book was completed in December 1975 a great deal of information has become available which both supports and extends our general thesis. This book records only a stage in the advance of these technologies. New developments can be expected in a continuing stream, and the end of this book cannot spell the end of our project. We at BSSRS (9 Poland Street, London W1) will be glad to receive and disseminate information from any source, as part of our activity to expose the implications of this growing technology.

March 1976

Introduction to Second Edition

The technology of political control is a new type of weaponry. It is the product of the application of science and technology to the problem of neutralizing the state's internal enemies. It is mainly directed at civilian populations, and it is not intended to kill (and only rarely does). It is aimed as much at hearts and minds as at bodies.

This new weaponry ranges from means of monitoring internal dissent to devices for controlling demonstrations; from new techniques of interrogation to methods of prisoner control. The intended and actual effects of these new technological aids are both broader and more complex than the more lethal weaponry they complement. Merely to catalogue their direct effects on their victims would be inadequate as a way of explaining what they are supposed to do. We must also explain why and in what circumstances they are used, and what tactical strength the state gains from their use, as well as what weaknesses are revealed by its need to use them.

Our approach, then, may seem a curious amalgam of technological exposé and political analysis. It is not a particularly familiar or apparently natural one. But it is an approach which is being used more and more by scientists who are becoming aware of the political implications of their work. When this book was first published in 1977, the 'neutrality' of science and the 'infallibility' of experts could still be invoked to shame and silence critics. Now, not only the lay public but scientists too are asking what the effects of their work will be on humans and our environment.

Why are more scientists coming to use this approach? To understand this it is necessary to look briefly at how scientists have faced the political effects of their work. In the years leading up to the Second World War there was an influential movement among scientists which regarded science as an inherently progressive force, and stressed the benefits which would spring naturally from the application of science to social problems. The atomic bomb ended all that. At the same time the war-time flirtation with science by the military became a marriage of convenience. Science grew from a small esoteric speciality to an industry, much more directly tied to military and economic applications. Most scientists retreated from political involvement to a profitable tending of their own subject area, conveniently claiming that scientists were in no way responsible for how their work was used. After all, science was 'neutral'.

The Vietnam war demonstrated how bogus was that claim. After the failure of a CIA-controlled counter-insurgency campaign, and then of massive conventional military intervention, the Pentagon turned increasingly to the scientists. Scientists responded with anti-personnel weapons, such as the fragmentation bomb (designed to kill as many unprotected people as possible), with the laser-controlled bomb, and with defoliants and herbicides to destroy crops and forests. The culmination was the electronic battlefield, conceived by the top scientific advisors of the Pentagon, the Jason division of the Institute for Defense Analyses – described by MacNamara, then US Secretary for Defense, as 'the cream of the scholarly community in technical fields'. The group of forty-seven eminent scientists included three Nobel Prize winners.

The Vietnam war led to an increasing realization among scientists all over the world that their occupation was not something remote from politics. In Britain a major conference on preparations for and use of chemical and biological warfare by the USA in Vietnam led to the founding of the British Society for Social Responsibility in Science (BSSRS).

BSSRS was founded in May 1969. In August came the Battle of Bogside, where a whole section of the Northern Ireland city of Derry was deluged with CS gas by the Royal Ulster Constabulary. The fledgling society, with its knowledge of the use of CS gas in Vietnam, was inevitably drawn into the controversy over its use in Derry. But as one new technological weapon followed another in the attempt to fill the political vacuum in Ireland, BSSRS found that the approach 'proper' to scientists, epitomized by the submission of detailed technical memoranda to government inquiries, had little or no influence when those scientists were challenging state policy. By 1971, rubber bullets had established themselves as a complement to CS in riot control; and 'depth interrogation' of interned IRA suspects revealed a new application of psychology: sensory-deprivation torture.

Under pressure of these events, the ineffectiveness of a purely technical response to a highly political question became more and more evident. BSSRS began to look for other ways to bring these fruits of military-technological collaboration to public attention.

The first result of this new approach was a pamphlet 'The New Technology of Repression' published by BSSRS in 1974. Its authors were scientists active within BSSRS, together with members of the Troops Out Movement. The pamphlet analysed not just the technical characteristics of the weapons, but also the political use made of the technologies in the Irish campaign. It was addressed not to the government but to the technology's actual and potential targets.

The aim of this book is to carry the analysis further: to relate the whole range of political control technologies to the need of states to reduce internal dissent and to silence particular critics at different times in different ways. There is a chilling familiarity about the concepts underlying these techniques: they stem from the historic process, interrupted only by revolutions, whereby the small minority of rulers of societies have always tried to neutralize or destroy opposition. As we show, the 1980s Army-issue plastic bullet with its sophisticated aerodynamics is the descendant of the wooden stave. Paris police were using chemical weapons to subdue crowds in 1912. Electronic surveillance merely multiplies the possibilities of the ancient arts of tailing and eavesdropping. The white totality of isolation torture cells in German prisons is the exact modern counterpart of Galileo's pitch-black cell.

Yet despite this similarity, the technology of political control we describe is qualitatively different and specific to the latter half of the twentieth century. This is not just because it employs advanced scientific techniques. As important is that it is tailored to fit the political conditions of present-day states and, in particular, advanced capitalist states with a liberal democratic political structure.

This concentration on Western tools of political control drew criticism from a number of reviewers of the first edition of this book. Why concentrate on these mere puddles of undemocracy, they asked, rather than on the vast oceans of repression behind the barbed-wire borders of the East? This particular theme-song was accompanied by the busy noise of cold war axes a-grinding.

It is undoubted fact that many liberties vital to a genuinely socialist society are conspicuous by their absence in Soviet bloc countries. A wide range of inhuman and anti-democratic practices have been and are still present on a large scale. It is also true that barbarous methods and blatantly repressive political systems are in force in a depressingly large number of countries in Africa, Asia, South America (especially) and elsewhere. This is certainly not the place to attempt a league table of torture and repression. Such practices should be censured wherever they are carried out.

However, certain aspects of the Soviet–Western comparison so often made by apologists for our political system need to be examined more closely. One is that it simply is not good enough to say 'it's much worse over there'. Tendencies to curtail civil liberties should not be neglected because we still have liberties unavailable elsewhere. That is one sure way to lose them here too. Already senior police representatives are saying (for example, after the death of Blair Peach at the hands of the Special Patrol Group) that people on demonstrations must expect to get hurt. The right to demonstrate is under attack, and should be defended.

Another point is that the particular technology we discuss in this book is specially designed for, and peculiarly suited to, the circumstances of liberal democratic regimes under stress. There is an export trade to client dictatorships, but their use of the weaponry seems to be conditioned not by domestic political conditions, but by the need to present a 'clean' face to the television cameras of the United States and Western Europe. Certainly in most of the technical sectors discussed in this book the weaponry available in the West is far more sophisticated than the Soviet Union has seen the need to develop. In this particular branch of repression, the liberal democracies are in the lead.

From the 1950s cold war onwards, state repression has been carved in people's minds in the image of the totalitarian societies of Eastern Europe, to the point where there is a dangerous complacency about the condition of our own democratic rights and practices. We are bombarded with information on East European atrocities, but information on the inhumanities perpetrated by our own state apparatuses is much harder to come by. Let one extreme example stand for many. 'The Manchurian Candidate' was a successful and influential film of the 1960s. Its story concerns the victim of a communist brainwashing technique, who can be triggered by his control to act as a trained assassin and yet have total amnesia about his actions. A good yarn, but far-fetched? Perhaps more gullible viewers thought the communists might possess such a technique. What has recently been revealed is that an extensive research programme to develop such a mind-bending capability did in fact exist. Not however in China. Nor in Russia. The agency responsible was the CIA.

Why do we hear so little about Western state repression and its technologies? Modern capitalist states just like Eastern European ones are intensely secretive about their means of repression. Secrecy is becoming more and more endemic in Western government. To take a recent example, in November 1979 a Cabinet document leaked to the press showed that the Cabinet was so worried about opposition to its civilian nuclear programme that it intended to implement it secretly. And if this is true about issues like nuclear power, how much more true is it of a process like the state repression of dissent, which is only half supposed to exist and would lose much of its efficacy if known.

Secrecy is the reason there is still very little information about the repressive state apparatus in any country. In Britain, on many occasions since the first publication of this book, investigators have been prevented from exploring state secrets in this area, either by covert censorship (like the 'D' Notice system) or by open legal sanctions. At the end of every line of questioning is the blunderbuss of the Official Secrets Act. Labour and Tory governments alike have conducted persistent campaigns against journalists and state researchers.

Moreover Britain is one of the most secretive of all Western states. The contrast between the British Official Secrets Act and the United States Freedom of Information Act is stark, even though the US legislation still cannot protect citizens from covert action against them by the security forces. The Watergate scandal of the mid-seventies at least obliged the CIA and FBI to go through the motions of public accountability; individual US citizens were able to invoke the Constitution to attempt to guarantee their democratic rights against state infringement of civil liberties.

Secrecy is not, however, the only reason for general ignorance about Western state repression. The reporting of such repression is a delicate matter for all media. The British media in particular have a feeble record on these issues, either through managerial censorship or reporter/producer self-censorship. Take the war in Northern Ireland. The job of covering it on television, said Jonathan Dimbleby on BBC in 1976 'should not be baulked, and the reason it is baulked is because of the political institutions, BBC, IBA, British government, British Opposition'. And the press? 'The coverage of Ireland has been so distorted in this country that if I am going to be forced to contribute to that distortion, I may as well not go', said John Pilger of the *Daily Mirror*. At a quite different level, when Noam Chomsky wrote a monograph on the gross state terror of America's client regimes, he received very similar treatment. The parent company of the publisher insisted it be pulped, all 20,000 copies. It was 'unpatriotic'. One can hardly then expect much discussion of a state's technologies of political control in its national media.

What then does this book set out to do? First, we consider in the initial two parts the political situations in which the technology of political control is liable to be used. What distinguishes the circumstances in which use is made of the technology of political control, as opposed to conventional weaponry? They are situations in which the state's repression needs to be at least partially masked. The development of the technologies is therefore especially stimulated by major social conflicts which for political reasons cannot be 'solved' by open repression by the state – which needs a velvet glove to sheath the iron fist. Such conflicts are much more likely to occur in countries with a liberal democratic political structure, where the state has to respond to a greater or lesser extent to public opinion, than in countries such as Eastern European ones where open repression has fewer costs for the state.

In the first part we illustrate the thesis by examining a very special conflict, that in Northern Ireland, which saw a rapid development of the technology of political control. The special nature of this conflict is that it has occurred in a statelet specifically designed to curtail drastically the democratic rights of one-third of its population, the Catholics, while itself being within the territorial boundaries of a classic liberal democratic state. The crude nature of power relations in the statelet meant that the use of repression was needed to maintain them. The fact that Northern Ireland was territorially part of Britain meant that this repression had to be masked. The rapidly developing technology of political control provided the state with a subtler range of options than was previously available for damping down mass dissent.

Northern Ireland is, however, an exceptional case. In the second section we consider more typical liberal democratic states, and show that within them the technology of political control is likely to become more and more widely used. It is commonplace that the economic prospects of world capitalism, and especially of countries like Britain, are much less rosy than was generally believed even as little as ten years ago. It is even more obvious that economic decline and rising unemployment would stoke up political conflict within Western liberal democracies. How would capitalist states cope with widespread civil unrest?

At the time we wrote this book, in the aftermath of the 1974 miners' strike which toppled the Heath government, there were rumours (now confirmed) that a small group of officers had been prepared 'in an emergency' to 'rescue' Britain. In the same period the spectre of fascism was being raised as the likely consequence of economic collapse. Such openly 'strong state' forms of government as fascism or military dictatorship we consider most unlikely to arise in liberal democratic capitalist states. Instead we argue that major internal political conflict will not be met by abandoning the existing political structures. Instead they will survive, but real decision-making powers will move to agencies of the state which are relatively inaccessible and not subject to any democratic control.

How can we characterize these developments? What new kinds of states would these be, which seek to build an ever-stronger repressive apparatus to protect themselves from some of their own citizens? In this book, we distinguish a new state model, a form of 'strong state', different from either fascism or military dictatorship, yet increasingly authoritarian and contemptuous of human rights. Its principal features are an increasingly restrictive legal framework; a police and Army unaccountable to the population and largely concerned with internal political control; secret intelligence services engaged in covert operations against a wide range of dissidents both internally and internationally; a press and media too fearful or too self-interested to protest; and a prevailing consensus that the state should not be questioned. Such a state would have great need for a technology of political control, an assembly of weaponry whose development would be limited only by scientific ingenuity. An essential feature of this type of state is that, unlike other forms of authoritarian state, it can arise gradually through a series of small steps within the existing political framework.

Key elements in this process are the legal system and the users of the technology of political control: the Army, the police and secret intelligence services. In Part Three we show that already by 1975 many changes had occurred in the operation of the security services which fitted these trends well. The official rationale for these changes remains hidden. However, we can and do examine in this section the writings of those military theorists who advocated them, chief among whom is Frank Kitson, many of whose detailed proposals have now been incorporated into the Army Land Operations Manual on counter-revolutions operations (ALOM). Leaks of military manuals after the first edition of this book was published further confirmed that the Northern Ireland experience is being rapidly integrated into the Army's general doctrine and practice.

The final and longest part, dealing with the technology itself, is also the most straightforward. In the first subsection we look at the gathering of low-grade information on the activities of the enormous range of individuals and groups which the security forces feel might pose some future threat to the economic or political fabric. Crucial, too, is the analysis of this mass of information, which now means computerization. In the second and third sub-sections we consider more open conflict, and in particular the technology for the monitoring and control of demonstrations. The last two sub-sections are about political prisoners – their interrogation and imprisonment. This is the meat of the book, but it would be a mere list of technical information if not set within the context of the preceding parts.

The main text of this book was written during 1974–75. The publication of this second edition gives us a welcome opportunity to re-examine the argument presented and to see how well it holds up when confronted with more recent developments.

There have in fact been a number of quite dramatic corroborations of particular trends highlighted. One of these is the use of drugs in British prisons. Almost all the evidence we were able to discover of the use of drugs for prisoner control came from US sources. (See Chapter 18.) Since that time information leaked from the then secret *Prison Medical Journal* has revealed just how extensive the use of psychotropic drugs including major tranquillizers has become, to 'improve discipline' in British prisons. The cons themselves call this 'the liquid cosh'. In the five years to 1978 the Prison Department's drugs bill increased $3\frac{1}{2}$-fold.

An equally emphatic case of technology transfer, though this time largely from Ireland, has occurred in the field of riot control. The disorders resulting from the National Front's attempt in August 1977 to parade through areas of Lewisham with a high density of black residents were used a pretext for the Metropolitan Police to introduce their custom-designed plastic riot shields. Helmets with visors were added at the Notting Hill Carnival a few days later. Since then this riot gear has become standard issue, used in scores of confrontations round the country. Police use them as assault weapons, and injuries are now commonplace. Major demonstrations have their circling helicopters, equipped with 'heli-teli' camera with zoom lens. The camera is remotely operated from a mobile unit, and can be focused-in on any section of the crowd, or on individual demonstrators.

A third area of major development has been the police use of computers. Far more is now known about the type of information which the police maintain in their electronic data-files, and on the proportion of the population on whom intelligence records are kept. Examples of this kind, where new developments (or new information on earlier developments) have tended to substantiate the general thesis of the book, could be repeated almost indefinitely. There is no space here to do them full justice. We have therefore chosen instead to list in an Appendix some of the major sources of more up-to-date information on technological or organizational innovations in the areas covered by the book.

One major 'cause-célèbre' of the late 1970s, the Agee–Hosenball/ABC campaigns, is worth examining here in some detail.* In its tortuous history it illuminates at various points the state's reliance on the technology of political control, and its concern to keep this from the public view. In this respect it parallels the account of the Army's use of technology in Ireland, given in Part One. Except that, nearly ten years on, the arena is mainland Britain itself.

The saga starts with the deportation orders served on ex-CIA agent Philip Agee and American journalist Mark Hosenball by the then Home Secretary Merlyn Rees in 1977. Agee and Hosenball were working to expose secret agencies – particularly the CIA – and to reveal links between Western intelligence forces. Agee had not only defected from the CIA but had written a record of his work for the Agency, blowing details about covert operations. He had gone further, agitating against his former employers, speaking against the system that needed covert action to maintain social order, and naming CIA agents in countries such as Britain, Greece and Jamaica. He worked together with Mark Hosenball and a group of other left-wing journalists on

*See *State Research Bulletin* No. 9 (January 1979) for a fuller account.

articles about state security and intelligence usually published by the London magazine *Time Out*.

It is widely believed that the CIA put pressure on its British security allies to expel the two investigators. In 1975, Agee had published a list of 50 CIA agents at the US Embassy in London. A year later, Hosenball and Duncan Campbell of *Time Out* published 'The Eavesdroppers', an article explaining the work of Government Communications Headquarters at Cheltenham, the centre of British military intelligence operations. SIGINT is the codename for its operations for intercepting military and diplomatic communications. The article described how SIGINT spies not only on Eastern Europe but also on the Third World; it gave details too of the giant American National Security Agency (which controls the CIA) and its bases in Britain.

The deportation orders generated a formidable defence campaign. And as the campaign grew in strength and effectiveness the defence committee evidently became the subject of surveillance by MI5 and the Special Branch: mysterious break-ins to cars and thefts of documents, as well as phone tapping and mail-opening, were never explained. Eventually the surveillance paid off. When John Berry, a former Signals Intelligence Corps soldier, connected the 'Eavesdroppers' article with the Agee–Hosenball campaign, he arranged to talk to two *Time Out* journalists, Crispin Aubrey and Duncan Campbell, about his own knowledge of intelligence communications. They walked out of their meeting to find Special Branch officers delegated by MI5 to arrest them. The reason – the arrangements for the meeting had been made over a tapped telephone. Aubrey, Berry and Campbell ('ABC') were charged with offences under the Official Secrets Act.

The state made every effort to make an example of Aubrey, Berry and Campbell. 'Whistle-blowers' who expose state agencies from within for political motives, and the journalists who encourage them, are a real danger to the repressive apparatus. The more so in Britain, where as we have pointed out, secret restrictions agreed between governments and media usually effectively suppress sensitive information. The security and intelligence agencies were clearly bent on scaring-off potential investigators. That is why charges were laid under Section One of the Act (usually reserved only for spies, as we explain in this book) – against Duncan Campbell for 'collecting information of use to an enemy'. The Attorney-General had been directly influenced by Ministry of Defence intelligence and top security chiefs to press this charge, later dropped for lack of evidence.

Meanwhile, the *Guardian* discovered a further manipulation of justice: the jury had been vetted for political sympathies. Three of its members had signed the Official Secrets Act and the foreman was an ex-member of the elite Special Air Services. After these exposures, the jury was dismissed; the new jury selected was also vetted. Forced by public outcry to publish the guidelines for jury vetting, the Attorney-General produced figures to show that jury vetting had been carried out 25 times since 1975, including in 12 IRA cases, and two Official Secrets trials. (A subsequent case of jury vetting, for the 'Persons Unknown' trial of anarchists in late 1979, produced stark statistics on the scope of police computer files. The *Guardian* revealed that out of a panel of 93 potential jurors information was available on 19 of them – the majority of whom had never received a criminal conviction.)

The ABC case in its turn spawned a lusty and vocal defence campaign, which drew blood. It was able to demonstrate that large sectors of the British people no longer accepted the government's definition of state security. Three papers (*The Leveller*, *Peace News* and the *Journalist*, organ of the National Union of Journalists), were prepared to flout contempt of court laws by naming a secret Army witness known to the court as 'Colonel B'. By the time the trial was over, Colonel Johnstone, whose identity was so secret it could not be revealed to the public, was a mass media figure. These violations of the sanctity of the secret world of security themselves constituted a major defeat for the state, and for the secret services – the state within the state.

By the time the ABC trial ended, only three of the original nine charges remained. On the judge's direction, the jury found Berry guilty; he was sentenced to six months' imprisonment suspended for two years, and warned by the judge: 'We will not tolerate whistle-blowers'. Campbell for receiving information, and Berry, for abetting him, were given conditional discharges but ordered to pay penal costs.

Introduction xxiii

In the end, the secret state lost because it could not silence its critics without coming into the open. It could not prove that its critical investigators were undermining state security because it could not explain how the agencies themselves protected it. They could not justify their own existence. As *State Research* commented: 'the public now knows a great deal more about Signals Intelligence, the very thing the state sought to prevent'. The trial cost more than £250,000.

The ABC case illustrates in microcosm a number of themes from this book – the regular routine interception of international telecommunications, the harassment, surveillance and phone-tapping of oppositional groups, the building up and computer storage of masses of low-grade intelligence information on the population at large. It also illustrates two factors which were not perhaps sufficiently emphasized in the book. One is the crucial reliance of the state on secrecy, whose significance was discussed earlier. State secrecy is the cotton wool in which new technology for repression is nurtured until the right moment can be chosen for public exposure. As we try to challenge the state's use of new weaponry we must simultaneously struggle to multiply the breaches in the walls of silence and denial which are erected to keep it from view.

The second factor thrown up by the history of the ABC case is that there is no need to accept fatalistically that the power of the state machine must invariably carry the day. There remain vital elements of democratic practice and tradition in Britain which can carry great force. Juries may be vetted, but this cannot yet be kept secret. Juries may be vetted, and still decline to return the verdicts the state demands. Journalists are threatened, but some continue to probe. Journals are convicted and fined, but the exposures continue. Radical MPs can take advantage of parliamentary privilege. Whistle-blowers still emerge. Powerful coalitions can still be built against encroachments on civil liberties. Democratic practice is without doubt in a delicate condition in Britain, but its muscles are not yet atrophied, and will gain strength from repeated flexing. We discuss this dimension further in the new afterword (page 293).

Re-reading the original edition of the book with the advantage of hindsight there are a number of more general comments of this kind which we think may be of help to the 1980s reader. There has, for example, been at least one political development of the late seventies which might appear to run counter to certain strands in the book's argument; other developments, by contrast, seem to corroborate or lead to extensions of the argument. In drafting these comments, however, we have encountered an unexpected snag. The political analyses of four co-authors, never identical, have developed in different ways since the first edition, and now cover a wider spectrum. One of the authors feels that her politics have changed so much that it would not be possible for her to agree to a new collectively written introduction and afterword – so these have been written by three of the original four.

On re-visiting the book one factor which stands out is our dismissive attitude to the prospects for fascism in Britain. In fact the National Front and other fascist groups, while still failing dismally at the polls, have been able to sustain a malign influence on the British political scene out of proportion to their numerical support. It is evident that the existence of a fascist 'threat to democracy' has proved useful to the ruling-class in a number of ways – in swinging the political argument to the right, and in providing a pretext for strengthening state power (for example, moves to revise the Public Order Act) in ways which will then be turned against the left. Nevertheless our basic argument still seems to hold. This was that fascism as a *system of government* was not an attractive option as a solution to capital's problems; nor, for various reasons of social structure, was it likely to achieve the minimum level of popular support necessary to render it feasible. The experience of recent years, while unsavoury and saddening, is not in contradiction with this position.

The other openly anti-democratic alternative, the threatened coup from our military Bovver-boys, evident at the time of writing, was never of much substance, and evaporated rapidly as successive governments have found other ways of handling their 'internal security' problems. These 'other ways' have consisted in part of a multitude of small steps towards the creation of the strong state which we described. Some of these are legal innovations – for example, the Home Office-inspired clause outlawing any demonstrations held without seven days' notice to the police, which keeps popping inconspicuously into a series of local authority private bills going through Parliament. Others are organizational, such as the continuing militarization of the police, and the tempering of the Special Patrol Group (and its provincial counterparts) in confrontations like Grunwick and Southall, into a hardened shock-corps of riot police. The death of Blair Peach at the hands of truncheon- and riot-shield-wielding SPG thugs at Southall in April 1979 is one result of this policy.

One impact of fascist activity in recent years has been on the conduct of both police and demonstrators. Labour movement and left demonstrations have regularly adopted a ceremonial and passive style, in which large columns process slowly on pre-ordained routes. Confrontations with the police occur, if at all, when the column is blocked by police, or when police 'flying wedges' attempt to break up a stationary crowd. Fascist incursions into black neighbourhoods (Lewisham, Ladywood, Southall and the rest) have provoked a more fluid and activist style of demonstration from black youth. Set-piece confrontations at places of the police's own choosing are no longer the only form of conflict. Undoubtedly the emergence of this more mobile adversary has presented the police with some new operational problems; it has also been used as a pretext for accelerating the introduction of both crowd control hardware, and of techniques borrowed from the military. Many of the techniques used by the police at Lewisham, for example, were clearly the result of a close reading of the (secret) *Army Land Operations Manual* volume on 'Counter-Revolutionary Operations'. Snatch squads emerged through a line of riot-shields, which closed behind the returning squad and its chosen victim. The employment of vehicles driven into the crowd to make random arrests are also a (military) textbook operation. This process of convergence between police and military is proceeding at a rate faster if anything than we anticipated when the book was written.

Another aspect of the strengthening of the state which has proceeded apace in the last few years has been that of European cooperation on external security measures. Of course, both Germany and Italy have their own draconian anti-terror laws similar to those in force in Britain. The German Federal Republic police have discovered a new twist to demonstrators' rights: not only are they deluged with CS, suffering all the ill-effects we catalogue in this book, but they are then held responsible for the use of the gas. In 1979, several participants in an anti-nuclear march in Germany were sued by the police for the cost of using thousands of CS gas grenades. But West Germany in particular has insisted that a coordinated European anti-terror policy is needed.

Britain's entry into the EEC has given us a share not only in the butter mountain, but also in anti-terrorist policy and strategy. Annual ministerial meetings within the EEC have been taking place since 1975 on the subject of policing and law and order. Direct agency-to-agency cooperation began around the same time, sharing expertise in technology, weapons training, and exchanging personnel. In May 1979, senior police officers from 17 European countries met in London to discuss the problems of policing large cities: among topics covered were crowd control techniques and police riot equipment. West German computer surveillance experts and British Special Air Service Officers joined the Italian police in the hunt for Aldo Moro. SAS officers led the assault on the hijacked Lufthansa Boeing at Mogadishu in 1977. In March 1978, Britain launched an international training programme on counter-terrorist operations, open only to senior members of internal security forces. Should a 'strong state' with its suppression of democratic challenge establish itself firmly throughout Europe, the British security forces and Home Secretaries will be able to take credit for some of its most fearsome aspects.

As we explain in the book, the suppression of terrorism is only one aim of such activity. Real or imaginary threats from terrorism are seized on or inflated as public justification for measures which are equally directed against a much more significant enemy of the state – the organized left. And while the state has been preparing itself organizationally for coming conflicts, there has also been an attempt by the radical right to reclaim ideological ground lost to the left in the late sixties and early seventies. One manifestation of this was the Gould Report on the alleged conspiracy by marxists to take over British universities and so warp the minds of the rising generation of students. Even by the low standards of witch-hunts it was a botched job, and the stench of stale paranoia which surrounded the Gould Report has severely limited its influence. But other attempts have been more successful. There has, for example, been a determined attempt to impede the publication of left-wing books.

One instance of this surfaced with the publication by Penguin of the first edition of this book. Robert Moss (whose role as 'military theorist' is discussed in this book) reviewed it at inordinate length on the leader page of the *Daily Telegraph* in his fortunately inimitable style. (Moss, among his other accomplishments, has acted as speech writer for Margaret Thatcher. His name is often mentioned in connection with the CIA – an allegation he naturally denies.) Moss labelled this book 'a tedious sort of sub-marxist tract which would normally be left to gather dust among the manifestoes of the Black Transvestite Liberation Front and the Xhosa Squatters Commune'. Why then review it so prominently? The answer was that a good half of the article was an attack on Penguin Books 'which must by now have overtaken the Moscow State publishing house as the biggest purveyor of marxist literature'. The chairman of Penguin replied, not to stand by Penguin's judgement in bringing out this book, but to point out the mass of right-wing titles (by Solzhenitsyn, for example) published by Penguin. Penguin had previously been subject to a very similar onslaught from Bernard Levin in the pages of *The Times*. The effect of such attacks on the editorial policy of influential and establishment publishing houses should not be underestimated. Of recent years authors of non-academic left-wing books have been finding it much harder to gain acceptance by mainstream publishers.

Perhaps the major new factor to emerge since the book was written has been the state commitment to base the British economy for the foreseeable future on the twin high technologies of nuclear energy and the microprocessor. Both have serious implications for the issues discussed in this book.

Major nuclear energy programmes bring not only the well-publicized risks of radiation leaks, but also the danger of 'police state' security to protect installations and the movement of nuclear material. In March 1978, Mr. Justice Parker published his report on the Windscale Inquiry, in which he weighed the dangers of terrorism in a 'plutonium economy' against the erosion of civil liberties. His conclusion was that he could see 'no solution at all' except the strengthening of security, albeit at the expense of individual civil rights.

The development of nuclear power stations in Britain has been accompanied by the growth in size and powers of a police-force to guard the installations – the Atomic Energy Authority Constabulary. Under legislation passed in 1976, this force has the power to carry arms at all times; to engage in 'hot pursuit' of thieves of nuclear materials; to enter premises at will and to arrest on suspicion. The AEA Constabulary is accountable only to the Atomic Energy Authority – a non-elected body.

Mass surveillance is also deemed necessary to protect nuclear plants. All the workers in the industry, their families, friends and 'known associates' are 'vetted' under the direction of MI5. But the largest group to be placed under surveillance are those whom MI5 and the Special Branch consider 'potential terrorists'. The Department of Energy, when asked to define this category, stated that nobody would be put under surveillance 'unless there was reason to believe that their activities were subversive, violent or otherwise unlawful'. The Department of Energy was basing its definitions on a speech made by Lord Harris, Minister of State at the Home Office: 'Subversion is defined as activities threatening the safety or well-being of the state and intended to undermine or overthrow parliamentary democracy by political, industrial or violent means'. Justice Parker concluded that if terrorism is to be checked, 'innocent people are certain to be subject to surveillance, if only to find out whether they are innocent or not'.

As we write, the potential impact of the widespread introduction of microprocessor-based systems into the country's workplaces hangs threateningly over the heads of the British working class. Blue-collar, white-collar and even middle-management jobs will be lost by the million in the coming decade unless the trade union movement can find an effective counter-strategy. And this at a time when the national and world economies will

Introduction xxix

offer little if any scope for alternative employment. It is inevitable that industrial relations in this country will be shaped decisively by this new situation. Employers and the state will try to take advantage of this opportunity to break the power of particular trade unions, and of the trade union movement as a whole. The outcome of such a struggle is impossible to predict, but it is quite on the cards that an extended period of economic, political and social upheaval lies ahead. In this case, the technology of political control would approach much nearer the centre of the political stage.

The micro-chip revolution is significant for a second reason. This is that microprocessor development will give a direct boost to the effectiveness of the technology of political control itself. This applies particularly in the field of surveillance. The possibility of electronic tracking and monitoring of an individual's movements, of the use of electronic identity cards to deny access to particular areas or establishments, is clearly coming out of the realm of science fiction and into the arena of practical politics. Computer technology as a whole is undergoing a related revolution, which will augment the state's information-handling capacity, especially at the local level. The prospects for automatic word or voice identification will improve, and so facilitate mass telephone tapping.

So the latest technologies, and by no means coincidentally, will once again be turned to the purpose of strengthening the state. This is, in a sense, a historical inevitability. What is not inevitable is that this armoury of the state must necessarily prevail. Some of the possibilities and strategies for opposition are discussed in the new Afterword.

January 1980
                K.M.
                J.R.
                T.S.

Part One
The New Technology Comes of Age: Lessons from Northern Ireland

1
Old and New Traditions of Violence

Technological developments transform warfare with murderous regularity. In this century the First World War brought the tank and the aeroplane, the Second World War brought radar and the atomic bomb and the Cold War has brought the guided missile. The Vietnam war saw the introduction of laser-guided 'smart' bombs, and the first rehearsal of the electronic battlefield.

For the Americans in Vietnam, the cure for the 'creeping disease' of communism was the technological fix. Refined technology could enter where their ideology feared to tread. The British, far more experienced as an imperialist power and far less advanced in the realm of technology, have adopted a different approach in the numerous colonial wars they have fought since the Second World War. The British Army, which has played the colonial role since the seventeenth century, treated its campaigns as political wars. Their basic tactic was to try to break popular support for the guerrillas, not just by physical repression, but also by political and economic reforms, by means of propaganda and by blanket control of the media. This was the doctrine of 'Mao minus Marx'.

Some of the technology* the British Army began to utilize in these campaigns was very different from that used by the USA in Vietnam. Riot-control agents like CS gas can disperse a demonstration nearly as effectively as bullets and at much lower political cost. 'Depth interrogation' extracts information as easily as physical tortures, but leaves no external scars. In Britain's colonial campaigns, the balance between military and

*Throughout the book we use the term 'technology' very broadly to apply to any device or method which exploits knowledge from any of the sciences from physics through to psychology.

political effectiveness was gradually swung in favour of the latter. New developments and uses of military technology began to reflect this change of emphasis. In the Northern Irish campaign – the most important, most costly and most politically complex colonial campaign the Army has been involved in – these technologies have been developed and their uses refined. The rubber bullet, for instance, created specially for the Northern Ireland conflict, was designed to wound but not to kill, and to sound much more innocuous than it really is. The aim of these technologies is not primarily the physical elimination of opponents. Their target is the thoughts of opponents and potential opponents as much as their bodies.

This book is about such technologies, developed to wage a campaign which is neither conventional war nor policing operation. We have gathered together technical details of what these weapons are, how they work and what they have been designed to do. Equally important, we aim to show that the development of this more novel technology – the technology of political control – is the result of powerful social and political processes, and is itself part of these processes. To understand the weapons, we must look at the way in which the apparatus of the state, especially the Army and police, is transforming itself. These changes have their origin in fundamental conflicts within society and in the new forms in which they are being expressed.

Why is the technology of political control worth all this attention? Aren't these new weapons just the fruits of normal technological progress? Aren't they, in any case, humane technologies which prevent violence in the least harmful way? And after all, isn't it necessary that 'violence' be put down? Questions like these are raised wherever this technology is discussed. Against them, we would argue, firstly, that technology does not just *happen*. In warfare, as in industry and other activities, there is nothing autonomous about the development of technology. Developments occur when they serve the purposes of those who control the resources which can put the technology to use, rather than when the basic scientific knowledge becomes available. This is as true of the Industrial Revolution as of the rubber bullet. Technological 'progress' is a thoroughly social

Old and New Traditions of Violence 21

process. We will see how the technology of political control fits the requirements of the counter-insurgency programme of the security forces, at particular phases of their operations.

Secondly, the motives behind the technology of political control are not humanitarian. These technologies are used by states to achieve specific political goals. Sometimes only relatively low levels of force are applied, but on other occasions higher levels are involved. What they have in common is that the level of force is masked. To those not directly concerned they seem much less brutal than they really are. The state's need to justify their use publicly controls their design.

Thirdly, the 'violence' which is being put down is itself a response to another form of violence – repression by a state which is the instrument of sectarian and class interests. This type of violence is all the more effective because it is hidden behind sentiments such as 'national interest' and 'law and order'.

Once these answers are accepted, the importance of the implications of this new technology are apparent. But for the moment our answers can only be assertions. These assertions are substantiated and documented in the rest of this book. They can be vividly demonstrated, however, by considering how the factors we have outlined come together in Northern Ireland. The lessons of this campaign may be quite as crucial, especially for advanced capitalist countries, as those of Vietnam. It is the first major counter-insurgency campaign in a developed, urbanized society which is technically part of a liberal democracy. The conflict occurred at a time when some of the new technology had been developed but not yet refined – and had certainly never been used on a large scale in urban guerrilla warfare. Its use gave the British Army an experience which has been gained by no other army. And although these weapons were used so close to home, the release of knowledge about their effects was managed in such a way as to minimize outcry. The awareness of the British public about their nature and use has thus been blunted by the Northern Ireland conflict, which makes it all the more possible for the Army to use them inside Britain at some future date. For all these reasons, the use of the technology in Northern Ireland is worth looking at in some detail. By examining the situations which led to the introduction of the four main political control technologies used in the Irish campaign – CS gas, rubber bullets, depth interrogation and the intelligence computer – we aim to show, with the minimum of technical detail, the interaction between technology and politics.

Throughout the fifty years of the existence of the Northern Ireland statelet, the Catholics had been heavily discriminated against in jobs, in housing and through the operation of both the law and the security forces. By the 1960s, though, the priorities of British capitalism had changed. In the North, once the major industrial area in Ireland, the traditional industries were in decline, while the South had become Britain's third largest market. So Britain began to pressure the Northern Irish government to make their state more acceptable in the South, and this policy was verbally echoed even by Prime Minister O'Neill.

The government's hints of reforms acted like a spark to the tinder of the age-old Catholic grievances. The year 1968 saw the emergence of a new movement onto the streets of Northern Ireland – the Civil Rights Movement. It adopted new forms of political action used with some success in other parts of the world – non-violent protest marches and civil disobedience. The first such march, on 14 August 1968, was ignored by the Northern Ireland government and the media. But the second, on 5 October 1968, in Derry, was answered by the traditional violence of the Royal Ulster Constabulary (RUC) against the Catholics: seventy-seven people were injured.

There was one novel factor in the RUC response – the use of a water cannon* to soak the crowd with a fierce jet of water. This was the first of a range of riot-control weapons which were to be introduced into Northern Ireland over the years. In fact, water cannon proved to be of only very limited effectiveness. Against a determined crowd they could anger but not disperse.

*A primitive version had in fact been used some years previously in Belfast.

Old and New Traditions of Violence 23

So the first technological innovation of the campaign proved to be something of a damp squib.

But if water cannon were too weak, the RUC baton charges were altogether too strong. (Sir Arthur Young, later Chief Constable of the RUC, described the charges as 'each man taking out his baton and using it to thump the nearest member of the public'.) At another period the violence might have achieved its desired effect of teaching the Catholics a lesson. But in the political climate of late 1968 the effect of the brutality was not to suppress the campaign but to enlarge it. Massive demonstrations took place in the following weeks. Even the naked violence at Burntollet Bridge when a protest march from Belfast to Derry was first harassed by Paisleyite gangs, and then waylaid by an organized mob of 200 Protestants (half of them B Specials*) only swelled the movement. Too much violence was as bad as too little.

It was clear that the Civil Rights Movement had the potential to grow into a movement challenging the very existence of the Northern Ireland statelet. This threat forced Prime Minister O'Neill to appeal in December 1968 for 'a truce on the streets'. But the Catholics gave less weight to O'Neill's promises of reform than to the continuing brutality of the police. Repeated incursions by the RUC into the Catholic Bogside area of Derry (as well as repression elsewhere) demonstrated the reality of political power. And it was one of these police raids which led, in August 1969, to the third, and best-known, Battle of Bogside. This was to be the attack which precipitated British Army intervention in Northern Ireland.

The trouble started during the traditional demonstration of the Protestants' ascendancy over the Catholics – the Apprentice Boys' March, along the old city walls of Derry and past the Catholic Bogside area. The RUC, backed up by gangs of Protestant youths, took advantage of the predictable stone-throwing by the Catholics to launch an attack on the Bogside. The attack was resisted; barricades were thrown up, stones and

*The B Specials were a part-time reserve force which no Catholic could join. It was described by the *Manchester Guardian* at the time of its introduction as 'the instrument of a religious tyranny'.[1]

petrol bombs used in defence, and the RUC advance was halted. Fighting continued throughout the night, as the Catholics repulsed charge after charge by the RUC. In preparation for the demonstration, the RUC had been well supplied with CS gas – which had only just been made available to them by the British Ministry of Defence. But they had received no instruction or training in how or when to use it until about 11 p.m. that evening. At 11.50 p.m., they began to use CS gas – the first time it had been used in the United Kingdom.

Why was this more powerful riot-control technology introduced? The overriding reason was the political crisis faced by the Stormont government. They needed something to enable them to suppress the Catholic revolt without calling on the British for help – which would inevitably carry a political price. The British government, in turn, was anxious to avoid direct military involvement in Ireland (with incalculable domestic political consequences) if a little extra technology would enable Stormont to do the job itself. The use of CS gas was an attempt to expand the options open to Stormont and Westminster. Naked repression such as Burntollet Bridge and the RUC attack on the Bogside had failed to stem the rising tide of demonstrations. So had water cannon. What was needed was a weapon more finely adjusted to the pressing need to disperse crowds without generating powerful political backlash. CS had already proved its worth in the British campaign in Cyprus in 1956 (as well as in the US campaign in Vietnam). It was brought into Northern Ireland as a technological aid to govern the 'ungovernable'.

For a day and a half, the RUC kept up a constant barrage of CS over the few streets of the Bogside. By mid-afternoon of 14 August, more than a thousand cartridges had been fired. But the resistance of the Catholics proved too much for the RUC. They were being forced inexorably out of the Bogside. And throughout Northern Ireland the RUC was stretched to breaking point by Catholic demonstrations in support of the Bogsiders. Chichester-Clark was about to launch the armed and undisciplined B Specials, 8,500 of whom had been mobilized on that day. If the B Specials had invaded the Bogside the result could have been a bloodbath on a scale large enough to force decisive action by the British government – even the end of the nearly fifty years of Stormont government. The British government wanted this no more than the Protestants. The Army was sent in.

That night the disturbances spread to Belfast, where a Protestant mob, including many uniformed B Specials, swept into the Catholic areas in the wake of an RUC armoured car firing bursts of automatic fire. Ten people were killed and 145 injured, mainly unarmed Catholics. In the aftermath of these Belfast pogroms the introduction of the Army was widely seen as a peace-keeping operation to separate the warring communities. In reality, the attacks of the RUC had evoked a response in the Catholic community which threatened to endanger British state rule west of the River Bann. There was also the need to protect British interests in the South of Ireland, which were threatened by an upsurge of Republican sentiment. There was even the danger of an invasion from the south. Both states in Ireland were put at risk by this unrest. The arrival of the British Army helped the Southern government to hold the line and damped down the disturbances in the North.

So the attempt to find a solution to the Catholic resistance in the technological fix of CS gas ended in failure. The British were forced to send in the Army. CS failed because by the time it was introduced the situation had already escalated beyond the small-scale or isolated confrontations which it might have been able to contain. In the new, cooler political environment resulting from the entry of the Army, CS gas was to prove its value, though now in the hands of the British Army. It enabled the Army to break up demonstrations without resort to gunfire – which would have had enormous repercussions both in Northern Ireland and further afield. Yet, as we shall see, this 'graduated response' which is designed to lessen confrontation can in fact end by causing an escalation of violence. The Catholics met each new and more powerful riot control weapon with a more determined response.

2
The Tory Offensive

After the introduction of the Army, the British government followed a policy of containment of the Catholic revolt together with a few reforms of the worst aspects of discrimination. They disbanded the B Specials, but made no attempt to reduce overall Unionist control. Meanwhile, both Protestants and Catholics were discovering what Army 'peace-keeping' meant. As General Freeland, the Army GOC, had said earlier, 'Soldiers in riot situations must carry guns and show they mean business' – though the constraints on the use of full firepower remained. As the real role of the Army and its collusion with the Unionists became more obvious to the Catholics, it became clear that the Labour government's policies in Northern Ireland were failing. But it was the victory of the Tories in the British General Election of June 1970 which drastically shifted the British Army into its more traditional activity in Northern Ireland – that of repressing the Catholics.

The threat of reform had pushed the Protestant working class to the right, as they saw the possibility of their traditional advantages over the Catholics being reduced. The Unionist Party thus put concentrated and successful pressure on the newly elected Tory government to stop the programme of reform. This naturally meant that the Army would need to suppress the Catholic revolt rather than contain it until it died away.

Within days of the election, the Army moved into the Lower Falls to conduct a massive search and curfew operation, in which four civilians, none connected with the IRA, were killed. The area was deluged to choking point with CS gas – canisters broke through roofs and filled houses with smoke. With the new political line, the use of CS in this blanket fashion – which amounted to a form of community harassment – became a standard feature of Army operations.* Some idea of the effects this had can be gauged from the following eye-witness account of an operation in the Springfield Road:

> The riot squad was charging down the street arresting rioters ... all of a sudden we found ourselves in the middle of CS gas actually in the house. A soldier had kicked the door and fired this CS gas bomb into the house. My wife and I were almost immediately overcome and we were pretty sick and half collapsing trying to get out to the back door. My wife was almost at the door when I remembered we still had the children upstairs. I tried to make my way upstairs. I got as far as five or six steps when I collapsed and almost fell down the stairs.

Use of the gas in this way is deliberate. It serves as a means of collective punishment for *all* the people in an area where political activity, whether 'violent' or otherwise, is taking place. The goal is to make the community politically ineffective by inducing them to withdraw their support for the activists. Gas is very useful for producing demoralization, because, as we shall show later, it singles out for its worst effects the weakest members of the community.

The use of CS as a weapon of harassment was only one of a number of measures designed to intimidate the population. The deaths in the Lower Falls operation showed that, if necessary, the Army was now prepared to use guns. The largest trackless Armoured Fighting Vehicles in the British Army had been used in squadron strength, so as to overawe the population. The curfew itself was another form of community punishment, restricting the movements of the Catholics.

Another sign of the new British government line was that, within a month of the election, it authorized the use of rubber bullets for the first time. They had been developed in a nine-month crash-research programme especially to meet the Army's needs for a weapon which would traverse the 'fifty yard gap' which so often separated demonstrators and stone-throwing

---

*Before the election of the Tories in June 1970, there was only one incident in which the Army fired more than 300 CS cartridges and grenades. In the three months from 27 June, there were eight such occasions, with a maximum of nearly 1,600 fired.

youths from the security forces in Northern Ireland. And CS had proved to have certain tactical disadvantages, such as being highly dependent on wind and weather.

So rubber bullets were tailor-made to a military specification. But their introduction was part of a concerted political–military policy. The new Tory line was to present Northern Ireland as a problem of 'law and order' – a purely technical problem, for which rubber bullets and other devices provided the appropriate 'technological fix'.

Most people outside Ireland seem to have the idea that the rubber bullet is some kind of squashy pea-sized pellet. This is far from the case. It is made of black rubber, rather harder than car tyres. The size and long blunt-nosed shape rapidly earned it the name of the 'Belfast dildo'. It has about the same weight and hardness as a cricket ball and leaves the muzzle at about twice the speed of a ball bowled by the fastest fast bowler.

Rubber bullets are not supposed to be fired at ranges below twenty-five yards. They are supposed to be fired at the ground in front of rioters so that they ricochet unpredictably (and lose some of their momentum). The objective is to 'deter' and disperse stone-throwers or unauthorized crowds – by actual impact or the fear of it.

There is much evidence that rubber bullets are misused by soldiers. They are often used at shorter than the permitted range. An investigation by surgeons from the Royal Victoria Hospital, Belfast, of victims brought to the hospital for treatment showed that more than half of those for whom information was available had been shot from a range of less than fifteen yards, and a third had been shot at less than five yards' range. One patient gave a description of a soldier pressing a gun against her, followed by a bang and a smell of fireworks. She fell to the ground with a severe pain in her side. She had a massive bruise on her lower ribs and a rubber bullet to prove her story. And unofficially officers will admit that soldiers prefer to aim rubber bullets directly at targets rather than at the ground in front of them – a practice which violates all their other weapons training. There have been repeated allegations that rubber bullets are stiffened by the insertion of objects, torch batteries in particular, to make them more painful on impact – and more dangerous. Four deaths are known to have resulted from injuries due to rubber bullets in Northern Ireland. The following eye-witness account relates the incident which resulted in the death of Francis Rowntree, aged 11½, in 1972:

Frank and I ... approached the corner of Whitehall Place. As we rounded this corner, we could see the back end of a Saracen sitting jutting out from the corner. Frank walked straight out down the wee path to reach the Falls Road. The next thing I heard was a bang, Frank fell backward, his feet sticking out at the corner. As the bang came, I noticed splinters, this object whatever it was, disintegrated. I think it was a battery, because the stuff looked like the black carbon that is inside a battery.

It seems a curious coincidence that a visitor to the Army barracks in the Creggan in early 1974 noticed that rubber bullets and electric batteries were stored right next to each other there.

One does not even have to be on the street to become a victim. Emily Groves, mother of eleven children, was standing at the window of her Andersonstown house when she was blinded by a rubber bullet fired at 8 yards range by a paratrooper. Her apparent offence – playing a Republican song on the gramophone. Ms Groves was awarded £35,000 damages from the Ministry of Defence. Her comment: 'I'd still rather take a four-penny bus-ride into town and see Belfast for myself.'

When CS was used in the Battle of Bogside, the public reaction in Britain was immediate and intense. The government felt the need to appoint an official investigating committee under Sir Harold Himsworth to damp down the furore. But the introduction of rubber bullets was achieved with barely a protest. Some of the reasons for the CS protest were fortuitous – CS was already in the public eye through its use in Paris in May 1968 and in Vietnam. It was brought into service in Derry in the middle of a headline-catching confrontation. And ever since the First World War the word 'gas' has produced strong gut reactions. But the way in which the lesson of the CS introduction was learnt by the government indicates their growing sophistication in the technology of political control. The new weapon (originally called a 'baton round' by the Army) was renamed and popularized as the harmless-sounding rubber bullet. It slid quietly into use with a total absence of fanfares. And the government has consistently made every effort to keep the public in ignorance about the true nature and effects of rubber bullets. One revealing example is the fate of the report by four Belfast surgeons cataloguing the widespread indiscriminate injuries, many severe and some fatal, which had been caused by rubber bullets between 1970 and summer 1972. This report was intended for publication in a medical journal. But the Army were sent an advance courtesy copy and slapped it between covers marked 'Restricted'. The information contained in that report might never have come to light if the *Sunday Times* had not published a leaked story on it in May 1973.

The Tory offensive against the Catholic population demonstrates how the use of the technology of political control was becoming part of an overall strategy developed by the security forces. CS gas used for community harassment, rubber bullets and curfew operations were backed up by legal measures such as the Criminal Justice Act – introduced a fortnight after the Tories returned to power – which made it an offence punishable by six months' imprisonment to swear at a soldier or chalk slogans on walls. Rising Catholic resentment against the Army was reinforced by searches aimed much more at Catholic than at Protestant areas, even though the Ulster Volunteer Force as well as the IRA was officially illegal.

Any successes of riot-control technology in containing street disorders only had the effect of pushing protest to more violent expressions. The IRA had split in December 1969 into two wings – the Officials and the Provisionals. Up to the Tory election victory even the Provisionals were involved in virtually no shooting or bombing incidents. However the hard line of the British Army led to widespread support for the Provisionals, and they rapidly built up their organization. After the death of the first British soldier in February 1971, Major Chichester-Clark declared that 'Northern Ireland is at war with the IRA'. The explosion of planted bombs became a feature of the struggle. By early August 1971, ten British soldiers were dead.

It was now no longer a case of lead or rubber bullets – it was now lead *and* rubber bullets.

To use the terminology of Major-General Kitson, the Army's major counter-insurgency theoretician, this stage may be characterized as the end of the 'non-violent' phase of operations against a colonial population. This is the phase when civil law-enforcement activity takes place alongside the use of riot-control technology to prevent the development of a mass movement of protest aimed against the government. Kitson writes of this phase: 'Although with an eye to world opinion and the need to retain the allegiance of the people, no more force than is necessary for containing the situation should be used, conditions can be made reasonably uncomfortable for the population as a whole in order to provide an incentive for a return to normal life and to act as a deterrent towards a resumption of the campaign.'[1]

The 'non-violent' phase had come to an end for two reasons. Firstly, riot control and legal measures combined had not succeeded in persuading Catholics to trust in the government. Secondly, the Tory offensive had led to an escalation of the struggle and encouraged the growth of the IRA. The Army now had to adopt the counter-insurgency strategy of separating the guerrillas from their base of support in the population.

3
Maximum Repression

The Provisionals' bombing campaign grew to over fifty major explosions in June 1971 alone. The rightward move of the Protestant working class caused by this intensification of the war led to the replacement of Chichester-Clark as Prime Minister by Brian Faulkner. By July 1971, even Faulkner's parliamentary majority was under strain.

Faulkner had long been an advocate of internment (administrative detention without trial), which he saw as having been a basic factor in the defeat of the IRA campaign of 1956–62. The Army too had experience of internment from a number of its recent colonial operations. Internment would permit a short, sharp campaign – two months, estimated GOC General Tuzo, somewhat optimistically. Enough of the IRA would be interned, their chain-of-command discovered by interrogation and the organization smashed. Internment had become necessary to save Faulkner. The Tory Cabinet approved it on 5 August 1971.

In the early hours of 9 August, 342 men were arrested (though 116 of them, presumably arrested in error, were released within forty-eight hours). Not only IRA members were interned, but also those thought most likely to organize mass protest movements against internment. Thus, of the 160 men initially interned in Crumlin Road gaol, not more than half had anything to do with the IRA.[1] Within six months, 2,357 people had been arrested, of whom 1,600 were released after 'interrogation'. The Tory government had embarked on a policy as intense as the fabric of a liberal democratic state could bear – a policy of maximum repression.

Interrogation was the area which saw the major innovation in political control technology during the period of maximum repression. Many of those interned were subject to cruel and exhausting pre-interrogation treatment. However, one group of twelve of the initial 342 was further subjected to a set of procedures* which were clearly a modern form of torture designed to break them.

During their six days at the interrogation centre, apart from periods when they were actually being interrogated, they were forced to remain in what the KGB call the 'stoika' position – hands spreadeagled high on a wall, legs apart and a fair amount of weight on the fingers. If they moved they were beaten. When they collapsed, their limbs would be massaged and then they would be replaced at the wall. The room was filled with a loud monotonous sound 'like the escaping of compressed air' or 'the constant whirring of a helicopter blade'. Their heads were hooded in black bags of tightly woven cloth which cut out all light. They were dressed in loosely fitting boiler-suits. The hood, the masking noise, the fixed position and the boiler-suit were designed to produce highly stressful sensory deprivation by preventing nearly all changes in sensory input to the brain. In addition no sleep was allowed for the first two or three nights and diet was restricted to bread and water.

This sophisticated torture based primarily on sensory and sleep deprivation produced a state of temporary insanity in the victims, who were often left with a severe persisting personality disorder. It is this state of temporary insanity which the interrogations are able to exploit. This is how one of the victims experienced it:

The hood was put on my head again and I was put against the wall for a short time. They beat my head on the wall. I was then taken into a copter; taken a journey of one hour, put in the lorry and back into the room with the noise. I was put against the wall and left. I was beaten when I could not stand any longer, taken away for questioning, taken back to the wall, back for questions – 'God when will it stop?' Time meant nothing. I was only a sore aching body and a confused mind. After a time I was only a mind. Think about my wife, think about the babies, think about the

*Fuller details can be found in J. McGuffin, *The Guinea Pigs*, Penguin Books, 1974.

martyred dead, think about my friends. I prayed for God to take my life. I can remember being handcuffed to the heating pipes. I remember being in a room and seeing one cigarette and one match. I looked at them, felt them and eventually smoked them. I remember singing 'Four Green Fields'. I remember praying to God. I remember thinking that martial law had been declared and that they were going to shoot me. I had given up all hope. I think then I asked for a priest. I would have liked to have seen my wife and children before I died.

Why were such techniques used by the Army? Firstly, a prime necessity for any Army trying to break a guerrilla movement is information, and interrogation is an important source of information. Brutal physical torture, the standard method of obtaining information, would in this case have produced an outcry, not only in Northern Ireland, but also in Britain and even farther afield. The sensory-deprivation method, since it appears to most people to be relatively harmless and leaves no obvious physical after-effects, was therefore preferable as a means of extracting information. But there is reason to believe that information was not the sole rationale for its use. Unless one presupposes that security-force intelligence was so bad that twelve IRA men could not be pre-selected from the internment scoop (which, after all, netted 342 suspects), it becomes very difficult to explain away the fact that some of the hooded men were released very quickly, and could therefore not have been suspected IRA members.

As McGuffin has pointed out, the use of this torture could well have been an experiment – the twelve men were 'guinea pigs' for the British Army's new and sophisticated torture methods (though the same or closely related methods had been used in *ten* previous campaigns by the Army). But if we look at these methods in the context of the Army's needs in the counter-insurgency war against the IRA, we can see that they served additional functions. Knowledge of these methods in the Irish Catholic community would make it much easier to conduct interrogations in the future. Other internees were indeed threatened with 'the horror treatment'. The tortures would also serve to generate a climate of fear in the 'insurgent' population which would discourage further recruits to the IRA and so help to isolate them from their base of support. Further, since these were novel methods of torture which left no physical external scars, it would be possible to contain full knowledge about them to the immediate community from which the victims came, and to cover up their real effects from the eyes of world opinion. In fact it was a full two months, which could have been decisive for the Army's campaign, before the *Sunday Times* gave the British public the first information about what had been carried out in its name. And the process of government secrecy and attempted mystification was carried on by two official commissions headed by ex-ombudsman Sir Edmund Compton and former Lord Chief Justice Parker.

Both reports (with the single dissenting opinion of Lord Gardiner) glossed over the real purpose of the techniques and rejected allegations that they were harmful. Compton said that 'brutality' was not involved, Parker, recommending the continuing use of the methods, blandly stated 'in a small minority of cases some mental effects may persist for up to two months', blatantly ignoring expert evidence of probable long-term damage. Three years later, when the psychiatric evidence of very long-lasting personality damage had become overwhelming, the government agreed to pay damages of £10,000 or more to each of four victims.[2]*

When maximum repression results in an escalation of conflict, the struggle is likely to take novel forms. The immediate response of the Catholic community to internment was the rent and rates strike which grew at its height to 90 per cent effectiveness throughout the Catholic areas. But just as the police and Army responded to the new forms of political expression of the Civil Rights Movement, such as non-violent protest marches, with new riot-control technology, so the Stormont government responded to the rent and rates strike with a new form of administrative repression. The Bad Debt Act was a pioneering effort in the use of the Welfare State as an agent of social control. The Act enabled the Stormont government to withhold

* In August 1976 the European Commission unanimously denounced the techniques as 'a modern system of torture'.

social-security benefits from anyone with debts to central or local government, and potentially to private creditors as well. The Act was draconian in its severity. Such legislation, in a region of profound social distress caused by years of heavy unemployment and exacerbated by the present conflict, can only be described as barbaric.

The importance of internment, interrogation and the resulting rent and rates strike was that it brought virtually the entire Catholic community, and not just an activist minority, into direct opposition to the Stormont government. Under military and administrative siege, the community continued to give shelter and support to the IRA. Another opportunity to demonstrate their opposition to Stormont came with the series of anti-internment marches, which started in late December 1971. To the British government and Stormont the danger was clear that, if these demonstrations were successful, then the policy of trying to separate the IRA 'fish' from the 'water' of the Catholic community would fail. When it was announced that a major Civil Rights demonstration was to take place in Derry on 30 January 1972, a decision was taken which can only have been made at the highest level: that this demonstration must be stopped. The objective was to scare enough people to keep them off the streets.

The march, which was in contravention of a government ban, developed into a typical Derry confrontation. A crowd of a few hundred, separated from the main march, threw stones and bottles in front of an Army barricade, and the Army replied with rubber bullets, CS gas and a water cannon spraying purple dye. Then at about 4.15 p.m. soldiers of the 1st Battalion of the Parachute Regiment deployed out from behind their barricades. When the Army stopped shooting, thirteen unarmed people lay dead, shot at close range by Army bullets.

Civilian unarmed non-combatant deaths from Army operations were never rare events.* What distinguished Bloody Sunday was that the Army seem knowingly to have accepted the

*Of the first 500 people to die in the Northern Irish campaign, as many (seventy) died as 'casual victims of security force operations' as died from explosions.[3]

Maximum Repression 37

risk of civilian casualties. The presence of General Ford, Commander of Land Forces in Northern Ireland, at the scene of the shooting, suggests that the Army was prepared for no ordinary confrontation. And so does the fact that Ford rejected the advice of the local RUC chief to make no attempt to stop the demonstration.

There is at present no way of knowing the precise policy considerations which led to the Bloody Sunday massacre. It is certain that Faulkner needed to produce drastic action against the anti-internment marches. Doubtless it was thought that strong measures would frighten people off the streets. Also it has been argued (and backed up by some evidence) that the Army hoped to provoke the IRA into a shoot-out on terrain of the Army's choosing, which the IRA would certainly lose. But one thing is clear. If Bloody Sunday represented an attempt to crush the Catholics by yet more open repression, then it too failed.

The results of Bloody Sunday were politically a disaster for the British government. The effect was to bring into reality what had long been a nightmare of those in Britain responsible for the Irish war – a growth in the South of Ireland of massive anti-British reaction which threatened to endanger Britain's economic interests there. The solidarity movement in Britain also showed signs of developing into a mass political force. The popular upheavals following Bloody Sunday demonstrated, by contrast, the advantages of the Army's reliance since 1969 on the new riot-control techniques. This had enabled them to repress dissent routinely, without the outcry and publicity backlash to which Bloody Sunday gave rise.

4
Sophisticated Counter-Insurgency

The aftermath to Bloody Sunday put an end to the British government's 'get tough' policy, brought in by the Tories in June 1970. In March 1972 Stormont was abolished and replaced by direct rule from Westminster. The previous British policies had foundered on the twin rocks of Protestant resistance to even minimal reforms and Catholic solidarity with the IRA. The new policy of the British government and Army recognized this. The reliance on the simple technological-fix of riot control, or on maximum repression, was abandoned in favour of a policy crudely characterizable as 'carrot and stick'. Under the new policy the Catholics were to be offered political concessions (the 'carrot') backed up by a continuation or even intensification of population harassment (the 'stick'). There were two objectives. First, to defuse the mass movement – the possibility of political openings would prevent the effect of the 'stick' from being counter-productive as it had in the past. Second, to isolate the IRA from its support in the Catholic community, so that it could be defeated.

In the more militant Catholic areas, the harassment of the population was intense. Forts were set up from which the Army conducted house-to-house searches and the repeated arrest and interrogation of the younger inhabitants. As a parachute lieutenant told the *Guardian*: 'You know when we were in Ballymurphy we had the people really fed up with us, terrified really. I understand what the refugees must feel like in Vietnam ... after every shooting incident we would order 1,500 house searches ... 1,500!'[1] The number of house searches rose from 17,292 in 1971 and 36,614 in 1972, to 71,914 in 1974.

In contrast to its frequent counter-insurgency operations in Catholic areas, the Army was only occasionally active in Protestant areas. It made little response to sectarian assassinations. Most of the killings were the work of the Protestant paramilitary groups. But, as the *Daily Telegraph* wrote in November 1974: 'Many of those involved in Protestant killer gangs are well known to the security forces. Why aren't they pulled in? Because if that happened the Protestant majority would immediately be in an uproar.' The Army on occasions gave the Ulster Defence Association tacit support, because they had a common enemy, the IRA – a tactic common in counter-insurgency wars.

Harassment of the Catholic areas was however much more localized in time and in place than it had been before direct rule. It was now a component of a much more sophisticated political–military campaign. Once the IRA had been weakened in an area, the aim of the Army was to 'win over the people'. As Major-General Clutterbuck argued in his book *The Long Long War* this could never be done effectively 'unless there was better co-operation among the three arms of government – civil, police and military – not only from the top level but right down into every district'. Co-operation at the highest level had been established since the start of the Irish campaign by regular meetings of a security committee which included the Secretary of State for Northern Ireland, the Chief Constable, the General Officer Commanding and the head of the Northern Ireland Civil Service. Below this level, co-ordination was far from satisfactory. In late 1970, Kitson, then commander for the Belfast Brigade, after establishing links with the local police, had asked for closer links with the Civil Service at local level, but had met with no response. By the end of 1972, after the disaster of internment and with the new policy of direct rule, he had achieved a civil representative for each police division.[2]

The civil servant – called Mr Fixit by the Army – has a function which is well known from previous counter-insurgency campaigns. Vietnam and the various American-inspired campaigns in Latin America have publicized the role of military-backed civic-action programmes in attempting to gain the confidence of disaffected populations. Mr Fixit's task was to solve the day-to-day problems caused by the breakdown in local authority facilities and services as a result of the prolonged campaign in Northern Ireland. While he organizes holidays for children and repairs of drains, he keeps an ear open for anything going on in the community which can be handed on to Army intelligence. One senior officer with direct experience of this type of operation in Northern Ireland, extolling Civil Affairs as 'a weapon in CRW (counter-revolutionary warfare)', pointed out: 'As experience in Malaya, Kenya and Vietnam has shown ... information begins to flow.' This 'benefit' he claimed is 'the key to the whole campaign'.

RUC intelligence about the Catholic community had been totally out-of-date, as the internment operation had shown. So, for the Army, intelligence became a high priority. Every soldier is now trained in intelligence work before his unit is sent to Ireland. Once there, one of his major tasks is to find out as much as possible about the people in the area in which his unit operates. Sometimes as many as one-fifth of each battalion are engaged in full-time plain-clothes intelligence or covert surveillance operations.

The type of covert surveillance activities undertaken by the Army is well illustrated by the experience of Joseph McKearney, who found three soldiers, having smashed an entry-hole in the wall of his attic, keeping watch on the Falls Road Sinn Fein headquarters. Mr McKearney was promptly arrested for discovering soldiers engaged in surveillance activities in his own home! This operation was entirely legal, being covered by Section 17 of the 1973 Emergency Powers Act.

The law had in fact been closely tied to the Army's intelligence-gathering activities in other ways too. If intelligence runs low in an area many people may be arrested at random and interrogated. Although the statistics for the number of arrests made by the Army has been concealed carefully from public view since direct rule, it is known that very large numbers of arrests have been made using the four-hour provision of the 1973 Emergency Powers Act. According to the NCCL, 2,000 people were arrested between March and July 1973 in Derry alone, one person being arrested twenty-eight times. In Belfast the story was similar. And according to the *Observer*, 'Most young men in areas like the Falls Road assume that if they are picked up by soldiers, they can expect to be kicked and punched.'[3] This type of operation constitutes intense harassment of the population as well as providing the Army with ample opportunities to collect large quantities of low-level information.

While the propaganda machine continued to assert that the battle was against a small minority of men of violence, in reality a large proportion of the Catholic population was hostile to the Army. The Army recognized this and have treated the Catholic community accordingly, amassing a vast amount of information on it. Everyone who has an actual, historical or suspected connection with the IRA seems to have been arrested, on average, every nine months. The Army also conducts routine four-monthly checks on the occupants of each house in selected areas. Even minute details such as the colour of the wallpaper are recorded. All this information is stored on card-indexes at local battalion level. It has been estimated that by mid-1974 the Army had details on between 34 and 40 per cent of the adult and juvenile population of Northern Ireland.

The information stored at battalion level is duplicated on central files at Army headquarters at Lisburn. But the volume of information required for effective intelligence operations on this scale cannot be adequately handled by a manual card system. It takes too long to find any one piece of information. This need led to the development of the major technological weapon of the post-direct-rule period in Northern Ireland – the Army computer. According to Robert Fisk of *The Times* the Army computer system in Northern Ireland is 'the most advanced to be adopted by the security forces in Northern Europe'.[4]

It has already been publicly admitted that the computer is being used to keep track of vehicle movements in the Province, especially near the border. Twelve computer links have been installed near the border and there are others on main roads out of Belfast, in Derry and Down and near Newry. When the computer receives a car's registration number it sends back details about the licence holder and any information about the car's movements which appear 'suspicious'. Some of these details are probably held in the computer's own memory store; for others it will provide an index to a manual file.

Fisk also suggested that the computer is used for other kinds of intelligence work. This was officially denied by Merlyn Rees. However, according to Leslie Huckfield, M.P., who investigated the *Times* story, it is substantially correct: by December 1975 the computer system was ready, the punch cards prepared, and 'half the population of the Province' would go on the computer. It is likely that the computer will be used to act as a rapid index to the existing manual files. However, given the technical difficulties involved, it will probably be some time before the system is fully operative. It does not at present seem technically feasible to store in the computer all the information at present on manual files.

While by no means the last technological innovation of the Northern Ireland campaign, the development of the Army computer may be seen as logically completing the process of change which the security forces have undergone since 1968. The initial infatuation with technological gimmicks of CS gas, rubber bullets and sensory-deprivation interrogation has been tempered. The Army has relearnt the lessons of its colonial experience – the importance of great quantities of low-level information and the need for intimate civil–military co-ordination. Only now the campaign will increasingly rely not on the spy, the gun and physical torture, but on the new technology of political control. The Army is now capable of waging counter-insurgency war in the tighter constraints of domestic political circumstance.

5
The Significance of Northern Ireland

We began by considering three basic questions about the new technology which is available to the state to deal with internal dissent. The excerpts we have presented from the Irish struggle do not in themselves provide complete answers, but they do at least offer powerful support for our initial assertions. We have shown, firstly, that technologies, far from being introduced because of scientific advances, have been introduced to meet the needs of the state in times of crisis and to fit the general needs of the security forces. CS gas, which was first used by the British Army in 1956, was brought into the Northern Ireland conflict, not from the start, but when the Civil Rights Movement threatened to grow beyond the possibilities of containment. Rubber bullets, on the other hand, were specially developed in the space of nine months when it became clear that new weaponry would be necessary to supplement and overcome some of the tactical disadvantages of CS. And they were introduced as part of a political campaign by the new Tory government. A similar conclusion can be drawn for every new technological development which has been introduced into the Northern Ireland campaign.

Secondly, we have shown that the technologies do not operate simply to prevent violence with minimum force. They are in fact a variable in a political equation. Most commonly the objective is to maximize repression, subject to a constraint that any political backlash must be kept to manageable proportions. Backlash depends not on how harmless the technologies are, but on how harmless they *seem*. 'Humanitarianism', then, is not an objective, but a propaganda claim. When CS gas was first used, for example, official sources argued that, if the Army were not using gas, they would have to use guns. In fact, the Army has used gas alone only in situations where gunfire would have been politically unacceptable – against unarmed crowds. It has not been gas *or* guns but gas *and* guns. This combination had enabled the Army to exercise maximum repression. The ugly face of governmental callousness is revealed by the use of sensory-deprivation torture. Its crippling effects must have been known to any competent scientific advisor. It was adopted for its combination of high local impact with low visibility to the wider public. It was abandoned when the political heat generated proved counter-productive. Humanitarian motives never entered the equation.

The mystery and ignorance surrounding the use of the technology of political control in the Irish campaign has been particularly useful from the point of view of minimizing backlash. Since information about the testing and effects of rubber bullets was suppressed, it became very difficult for those people concerned about their use to mount an effective campaign to alert the public. Similarly, the government tactic of setting up official committees to investigate complaints about the use of these technologies has often achieved its intended purpose of diffusing public protest. The Himsworth report on CS gas was very successful in this respect. The Compton report on torture failed to put public opinion to sleep largely through its own ineptitude; but the majority Parker report was clearly designed to repair this damage, and might well have succeeded in giving the government a freer hand if government policy itself had not outdated the report before it was published.* Had relevant and timely information on these technologies been available, the possibilities for a mass movement in Britain to bring the troops of occupation out of Northern Ireland would have been strengthened.

The use of the technology of political control gave the government and security forces greater flexibility in dealing with the Catholic upsurge. Yet each phase of the campaign led, at worst, to an escalation in the level of violence, and at best to deadlock for the state. Why have successive governments at Stormont and Westminster been unable to resolve the situation

*The report was published less than a month before the introduction of Direct Rule.

The Significance of Northern Ireland 45

since 1968? And why did Northern Ireland find itself the first testing ground for this new technology? This raises our third question concerning the source of the violence. Violent confrontations have been a sporadically occurring feature of the Northern Ireland statelet ever since its inception. The very persistence of the conflict suggests that the key to understanding must lie in the fundamental nature of the state.

When riot-control technologies became a political issue in Northern Ireland, the state had basically the same form as when it was set up in 1920. Partition had cut six out of the thirty-two counties of Ireland in such a way that the Protestants could control as much Catholic area as they could dominate 'in perpetuity'. The Catholics, 34 per cent of the population of the North, never considered 'Ulster' to be legitimate. Even Lloyd George, the Prime Minister who fathered partition, was forced to admit that: 'The majority of people of two counties prefer being with their Southern neighbours to being in the Northern Parliament ... if Ulster is to remain a separate community, only by coercion can you keep them there.'[1]

The creation of this artificial statelet benefited directly only the ruling classes of Britain and of Northern Ireland. However, the relative material and social advantages which the Protestant working class had over the Catholics caused them to identify with the interests of their own ruling class. To retain this support the marginal economic benefits had to be maintained. So, to ensure the maintenance of the Union, two complementary strategies were adopted: monolithic political organization of the Protestants and discrimination against the Catholics.

Northern Ireland thus developed many characteristics of what we shall call a 'Strong State'. The security forces, the RUC and the B Specials were shaped to defend the state against any possible Catholic resistance. No Catholic was allowed to become a B Special. The law was moulded to assist in this task. The 1922 Special Powers Act has been envied by Prime Minister Vorster of South Africa, who once declared that he would 'willingly swap' his anti-communist powers in their entirety for this one law. In the sphere of local government, there was widespread gerrymandering, Protestant control of the Civil

Service, job and housing discrimination. Fifty years of this situation lay behind the Catholic upsurge of 1969.[2]

Evidently, Northern Ireland has never been a liberal democratic state. As in South Africa, the entire state structure has been moulded in order to ensure the dominance of those who benefit from the ascendancy by the oppression of those who oppose it. But the level of explicit violence which can be used to maintain the state is far less in Northern Ireland than in, say, South Africa. This arises from the paradoxical fact that Northern Ireland – an oppressive statelet – is supposed to be an integral part of the United Kingdom – which is regarded as the model of a liberal democratic state. This puts tight limits of political feasibility on the visible violence. If the British government were seen to be engaged in brutal repression of a section of its population, it would face both internal dissent and external opprobrium as well as putting its economic interests in Southern Ireland at risk. On the other hand, effective democratization of the Northern Ireland statelet was also impossible, because its foundations rested on oppression of the Catholics and the resultant Protestant working-class allegiance. It was into this situation that the technology of political control was introduced, as a way of widening the options open to the government of Stormont and Westminster.

There are many lessons to be drawn from the use of the technology of political control in Northern Ireland. The paradox of being a strong statelet within a liberal democratic state has made it the first major testing ground for the technology of political control. It is for this reason that our examples have been drawn from there. But there is another reason for considering the lessons of Ireland. For we have seen how it is the state's need to manage conflicts arising out of unresolved and sharpening internal contradictions, but within politically acceptable limits, which calls the technology of political control into action. Ireland's problems are in many ways unique, but she has no monopoly of such conflicts and contradictions. Britain itself has its own, different but increasingly acute. It is natural to ask: 'Will the technology of political control be used in Britain?'

Part Two
The British Road to the Strong State

6
Capitalism in Crisis

In Ireland, repressive technologies were developed to help suppress the revolt of a partially subjugated caste. But the situation in Ireland is in many respects unique. Classically, the major internal threat to advanced capitalist countries has come from their own working classes. This threat has always taken its most intense form in periods of severe economic and social crisis such as the inter-war years in this century. These were years of sharp class conflict in Europe, particularly in Italy, Germany and Spain. In Britain, too, resistance to wage cuts led to the massive confrontation of the 1926 General Strike.

At the present time, the world is experiencing another period of economic crisis. Unless it can be resolved, capitalism may be facing a time of prolonged class conflict which could threaten its very existence.

Since the late 1960s the international capitalist system has been in disarray. There have been repeated crises in the arrangements for financing international trade; the increased inflation set in train by the US involvement in Vietnam spread round the world; and a wave of industrial militancy engulfed Western Europe, and even showed signs of affecting Japan and the United States.

The long post-war boom was over. During 1974–5 the real incomes of workers in the advanced capitalist countries fell as fast as they did at the start of the Depression. World capitalist production dropped sharply. Only inflation and unemployment went up and up.

In retrospect, it can be seen that the long post-war boom was bound to end. Capitalist economies have always been subject to periodic fluctuations, some of them of violent intensity. Periods of relative calm and prosperity are succeeded by periods of turbulence and crisis. Booms run out of steam when capital investment cannot produce an adequate rate of profit; depressions persist (with minor ups and downs) until capitalism can by-pass, crush or transcend the obstacles to its further development. Thus the Depression of the thirties was ended only by the economic stimulus of the Second World War. The crisis we are now experiencing is no transient phenomenon.[1] It was heralded (though largely unobserved by economists) by a slow steady squeeze on the profits of capitalist corporations in many countries during the 1950s and 60s. It is likely to be with us for many years to come. Weak national economies such as Britain's will suffer worst of all.

Some of the easier routes out of the recession which would have been possible in the fifties or sixties are now blocked. The increasing synchronization of national economies means that there are no longer booming economies which can revitalize the sagging parts of the system – internal and external demand fall together. And the growth in the size of the state arising from the need to prop up weakening private industry as well as to maintain a healthy, educated labour force has paradoxically limited its ability to restimulate the economy – the result would be to exacerbate inflation.

Whatever route capitalism eventually takes as it seeks an exit from its impasse, one thing is certain: the working class will have to pay for the solution. Big business will need to boost its profit levels by increasing the exploitation of the workers, and lowering their living standards. This can happen in many ways – through unemployment; through inflation coupled with a stringent wages policy; through cuts in the 'social wage' of welfare provisions; through attempts to rack up productivity and force wage cuts. Economists know this. Thus Professor Harry Johnson (until recently at LSE) predicts 'the likeliest changes [in British economic policy] are escalation of the class war, disguised as restraining the greed of the workers and punishing their ingratitude for the benefits of full employment conferred on them by their educated betters'.[2] And this although they are paid as much as a third less than their European counterparts.

As we write, this process is already well under way. The

early seventies have seen social polarization and industrial militancy manifest themselves in many new forms. If this crisis proves as long and as deep as that of the thirties, the strains on the social fabric will be intense. More workers could come to see the capitalist system itself as the root cause of their problems. Under such conditions the 'normal' techniques of persuasion – through party politicians, TUC leaders, the media, the educational system – might well no longer be sufficient.

What other strategies are available to capitalism to maintain its hold? Three have been mooted: military intervention, fascism or the use of existing political structures to move by indirect means towards a 'Strong State'. For reasons given later, the first two seem unlikely to occur in Britain in their 'pure' form. The third has the advantage that it does not require a complete restructuring of the state. It does not have to be a consciously planned process and yet it allows more direct political control by the capitalist class. It also has longer-term advantages. Although the three alternatives are by no means clearly distinct or mutually exclusive, they are sufficiently different to make it easier to discuss them separately.

7
The Fascist State

As the world economic crisis deepens, British commentators are once again reviving the spectre of fascism. It is wheeled out to provide an awful warning of the political consequences of hyper-inflation, and so lend weight to the pleas for wage restraint.* Indeed it is suggested that too militant a movement for any social or economic reform is less likely to lead to revolutionary socialism than to a right-wing backlash with fascism as its beneficiary. To assess the danger, it is necessary to look at the conditions under which fascism emerges and at the extent to which these conditions exist now in Britain or could arise in a deepening economic crisis.

The history of fascism also has important lessons for an understanding of the nature of the capitalist state. The Jeremiahs who bewail the perils of fascism are being disingenuous. Fascism, they would have us believe, arises because in a desperate crisis evil but charismatic demagogues sway the normally level-headed populace. This view ignores a good half of the story. The mass movements based on economic and social desperation did not lead to the fascist parties coming to power spontaneously. Behind the scenes, encouraging them, facilitating the taking of power and then benefiting richly, were the capitalist classes of Italy and Germany.[1] By using fascism to crush organized labour, big business rapidly restored their falling profits. The history of the rise of fascism in Italy and Germany shows that, in order to preserve the viability of capitalism, the capitalist class can encourage the most barbaric of political

*For example, *The Times* ran a series of articles in 1975 drawing the lessons of Weimar Germany, where rampant inflation preceded Hitler's rise to power.

regimes. It has done so before and it can do so again, although not necessarily in the same sort of way.

In both Italy and Germany after the First World War, the initial successes of violent fascist tactics won the support of powerful industrial concerns. In Italy in 1922 the Banca Commercial and the Federation of Industry provided Mussolini with more than 20 million lire. And in Germany powerful Ruhr business leaders engineered Hitler's coming to power. In Britain, though, the embryonic fascist movement was defeated by militant opposition, culminating in the 1936 Battle of Cable Street. So massive financial support for fascism in Britain was never forthcoming. But despite the full post-war revelations of the atrocities committed in the name of fascism, small fascist groups have continued to exist. In 1967, a number of these groups reconstituted themselves as the National Front.

Their ideology is a hotch-potch of patriotism, monarchism, racialism and economic nationalism. In line with the classical fascist movements, they stand for complete denial of civil liberty and democratic rights. But their tactics since 1972 have included working in the trade unions, even at times giving support to working-class industrial action. This type of tactic, together with exploitation of the immigrant issue, has earned them more support than any other post-war fascist group in Britain.

Could the National Front (or its rival National Party) be the basis for a fascist mass movement in Britain? They are still very tiny, and their electoral record is weak. But fascist parties have never relied primarily on parliamentary means, and they can grow very rapidly. In the 1928 German elections the Nazis received only 800,000 votes. But in the subsequent slump their strong-arm methods against socialist and working-class organizations appealed to large sections of the middle class, and by the July elections of 1932 Hitler commanded over 13·5 million votes. But the ability of the National Front or a similar organization to build a mass fascist movement depends on a number of crucial factors and these all seem to argue against fascism's chances of success.

Firstly, the economic, social and political crisis in Britain is

54 The British Road to the Strong State

not yet of anything like the same intensity – and is unlikely to be within the next few years – as those of Italy and Germany after the First World War. Secondly, to be successful, a fascist movement must be capable of crushing the strength of the working class. Employers and government must be able at times to confront the working class physically, without resorting to the use of regular state forces, which could stimulate a direct, united and overwhelming response. But here any fascist movement would encounter trouble. For the British working class is very strongly organized and militant in its tactics, and is in a good position to resist such attacks. Unlike the German and Italian working classes after the First World War, the British has not been defeated in any major confrontation with the government or employers for a generation. Its trade-union movement is not split between conflicting organizations. It is much larger than those of Italy and Germany in the period when fascism came to power; and it is growing fairly rapidly, with white collar and women workers entering its ranks in increasing numbers.

Classically fascist movements have relied on the divisions and weak leadership within the working-class organizations to ease their task. Certainly the leadership of the British trade-union movement is anything but revolutionary, and their tendency is to co-operate with any Labour government at the expense of the living standards of their members. But in reaction to this, a relatively strong movement has developed among the rank and file of many of the larger unions. In a crisis, new political organizations based on this movement could provide a more vigorously anti-fascist leadership. Even though it does some consistent work in unions, the National Front finds it very difficult to undermine the influence of the shop stewards. The only exception is on racial issues, where there is a real possibility of division.*

An aggressive policy against union militants is vital to any fascist group hoping to build itself into a mass movement.

* In 1974, the NF was successful in persuading groups of white workers in several disputes to scab on their immigrant fellow workers.

Without it, not only would it be unable to gain financial support from big business, it would also be unable to attract the small businessmen who have traditionally formed the mass base of fascist movements. Hitler and Mussolini both played on this layer of the population – the petty bourgeoisie – who felt threatened economically and psychologically both by the increasing standard of living of the working class and by the ability of larger competitors to squeeze them out. The disappearance of much of this layer in modern Britain provides yet another reason why fascism is unlikely to become a major threat. Indeed the only section of the petty bourgeoisie which retains any significance is the lower bureaucratic sector, which is rapidly unionizing into such unions as ASTMS and NALGO. Once unionized they are more likely to absorb the traditional anti-fascism of the Labour movement.

Finally, for a fascist movement to come to power, it must have the support of the dominant class in Britain. Big business and finance must decide that for the moment it can no longer afford parliamentary democracy. Yet, as we show in the next chapter, parliamentary democracy is an extremely stable form of government. It will not be lightly discarded. A severe crisis may considerably weaken all the indirect means of control, such as the media, the Welfare State system and the law, which we discuss later. But it may also strengthen the ties between the government and the leaders of the Labour movement, and thus would obviously be a variant preferable for the ruling class to violent street fighting and coercion of workers by force. The splitting of the traditional political parties could open the door for a fascist party to step in to restore 'law and order', but it could equally lead ultimately to development of a revolutionary socialist party, capable of leading the working class.

So, in summary we do not consider that British capitalism will resort to a fascist solution. But the argument is not conclusive. For the ruling class, fascism is always in the last resort preferable to socialism, because it allows for the preservation of capitalism and the suppression of the working class. In 1932, Trotsky, with remarkable perceptiveness, had already identified the appeal of fascism for the ruling class:

Fascism is not merely a system of reprisals, of brutal force and of police terror. Fascism is a particular governmental system based on the uprooting of all elements of proletarian democracy within bourgeois society. The task of fascism lies not only in destroying the Communist vanguard but in holding the entire class in a state of forced disunity. To this end the physical annihilation of the most revolutionary section of the workers does not suffice. It is also necessary to smash all independent and voluntary organizations, to demolish all the defensive bulwarks of the proletariat, and to uproot whatever has been achieved during three-quarters of a century by the Social Democracy and the trade unions.[2]

Yet the major lesson we should draw from the history of the fascist states of the 1930s is that, even in a 'highly civilized' country, as long as capitalism continues to exist, there is always a possibility of it adopting a barbaric political regime. This lesson has been reinforced in a different way by the atrocities committed in Chile since 1973. Chilean parliamentary democracy was replaced not by fascism, but by a military junta. The Chilean upheaval demonstrates that even in a country with well-entrenched democratic traditions and institutions a military coup can occur if capitalism feels its hold threatened. It is this possibility that we turn to in the next chapter.

8
Military Intervention in Politics

The year 1974 was the culmination of a period of increasing industrial unrest. At the start of the year, the miners' strike brought down the Tory government, and there followed a mushrooming of 'citizen's armies' dedicated to help in any showdown with the trade unions. But fascism was not the only spectre which raised its head. This was also the year in which troops first appeared at the airports and in the streets of Britain, and some people began to wonder aloud whether the Army might not provide the 'strong leadership' needed to deal with the nation's political and economic turmoils. In January, the right-wing American commentator William Buckley asked whether the Army might take over because of the 'impotence' of an election.[1] Speculation along these lines continued to grow. In August, Lord Chalfont, former Labour minister, wrote an article entitled 'Could Britain be Heading for a Military Takeover?'[2] which was taken up eagerly in the columns of *The Times*.

Such speculations are certainly alarmist, but they are not exactly misplaced. They are alarmist because in a society such as Britain there are compelling reasons against a military coup even being attempted. They are nevertheless relevant because the Army is already deeply involved in politics, and will become more so. The intervention is not overt but largely hidden, and all the more effective for that.

The armed forces possess a virtual monopoly of all effective weapons, a highly disciplined organization and an intensely cultivated sentiment of solidarity. This inevitably makes them a major locus of power within the state apparatus. So 'instead of asking why the military engage in politics, we ought surely to ask why they ever do otherwise'.[3]

With the sole exception of the French army coup over 'Algérie Française' in 1958, there has not been a successful military coup in any major advanced capitalist country. So the standard reaction is that 'it can't happen here'. But, as we shall see, the arguments used to try and explain why Britain should be immune from military takeover are quite shaky, and certainly don't support the view that the military will 'stay out of politics'.

One of the arguments used to deny the possibility of military intervention in politics is the 'professionalization' of the Army. The officer is now immersed in the technical expertise of his own craft and adopts the professional's limited view of his role and responsibilities. The state is the customer who defines when the expertise is to be unleashed. The Army, on this argument, will refrain from meddling in political affairs, which is the job of politicians. But this argument really will not stand up. In fact, it is easier to turn it on its head. To the upper echelons of the Army, politicians often seem incompetent at managing affairs of state, especially where military matters are concerned. The 'mismanagement' of government results in the Army being presented with unwanted tasks, or being subject to unwelcome 'political constraints' in the execution of its tasks. The more the government comes to lean on the support of the Army, for example at times of severe economic and political crisis, the more likely is the Army to consider itself better able to carry out the technical business of running the country.

Against this it is commonly argued that the Army is so deeply 'apolitical' that it would never see itself as a political force – in fact, that it is just not interested in politics. But this argument takes a probably transient phase in the history of the Army as an eternal verity. The Army is an integral part of the state apparatus, and is no more 'neutral' than is the state itself. Indeed the Army is the last resort of those in whose service the state is administered. So long as the government is able and willing to pursue those interests the Army may well be 'apolitical'. But this apparent disinterest cannot survive any serious threat. It is salutary to recall that, only two years before the Army coup in Chile, President Allende, maintaining that the

Army was a neutral force, told a meeting of Chilean peasants: 'the Armed Forces and the Carabineers have a professional conscience. They respect the law and the Constitution, which is not the case in the majority of Latin American countries, and this constitutes an exception in this and even in other countries.'[4]

Another argument which is advanced against military intervention is that the Army is deeply inculcated with the notion of the 'national interest'. But this would hold the Army back only if the government and the nation were completely identified in the mind of officers. And there is plenty of evidence from many countries in Europe of cases where the officer corps has decided that the government is betraying the national interest. The 1920 Kapp putsch in Germany (discussed below) is just one example. The widely reported unwillingness of the British military to take any offensive action against their 'kith and kin' in secessionist Rhodesia in the mid-1960s is another. Any British government which gives in to threats of strike action or terrorist campaigns may well find itself having to deal with an Army which appoints itself as the ultimate arbiter of the national interest.

More forcefully than these theoretical arguments, the British Army's record in the Northern Ireland campaign shows clearly that it is fully capable of playing an influential role in the political arena. The Irish campaign has forced a greater political awareness on the officer corps. Through the co-ordinated civil–military–police operations described in Part One, the Army has gained experience for the first time of running a province of an advanced capitalist country at grass roots level. As one major put it, 'now we have very much closer insight into the working of the political mind'; and generals too have become involved in intimate political relationships and are learning how to wheel and deal.[5]

Much of this could have been anticipated from the French Army's counter-insurgency experience in Algeria, of which an American historian wrote: 'Quite early in the war the Army had already taken over the essential functions of the state. French officers had perforce become psychologists, sociologists, agronomists ... the social territory had become the primary concern of the generals.'[6] Protracted counter-revolutionary warfare has a profound effect upon military consciousness. The French theorist Duverger was remembering both Indochina and Algeria when he said: 'An army prepared for subversive war ... cannot stay isolated in the nation, it cannot stay out of politics. Psychological war implies political activity, a quasi-permanent intervention in the life of the nation.'[7] He could have been talking about Northern Ireland.

The Northern Ireland campaign has already thrown up a number of issues on which the Army has taken an independent line, at variance with government policies. Just one example is the way in which, since the IRA has been identified as the enemy, the IRA's enemies (principally the Protestant UDA) have at times been treated by the Army as allies. In any case, the UDA's 'nationalist' sentiments must evoke a sympathetic response within the Army. There has for years been a steady flow of information from the Army to Protestant organizations[8] – one highly confidential Army intelligence document landed up in the hands of the Reverend Ian Paisley.

So the conventional reasons given for why 'it can't happen here' are paper-thin. In fact military intervention in conventional political life is already taking place. A military coup is indeed quite unlikely – though for a quite different reason. This is that parliamentary democracy provides a highly sophisticated instrument for the purpose of the British ruling class. It would have a great deal to lose from the crudities of direct military rule. Tanks on the streets and officers in the factories would shatter the fragile balance between the ruling and working classes.

Parliamentary democracy is the strongest and most stable form of political order in the advanced capitalist countries precisely because it is the form which most effectively obscures where the real centres of power lie. Except in revolutionary periods it is implicitly accepted as legitimate by the masses. Every adult is given a vote and therefore theoretically has a share in the decision-making. The working class has its representatives in Parliament who claim to defend its political interests, and it tends for that reason to confine its struggles to the economic sphere. Yet the working class could never be persuaded to look to the military, or to a government installed by the Army, to solve its economic problems or to safeguard its political interests. And once parliamentary democracy has been destroyed or undermined by military intervention, it would be very difficult to restore it.

The Army may dispose of sufficient force to overwhelm any opposition, but it cannot compel obedience. Only if the authority of a government is seen as 'legitimate' can such obedience be won. Democratic institutions may be under heavy criticism, but they still retain the implicit allegiance of the mass of the population. There is little chance that a military government could clothe itself in respectable legitimacy; it lacks the advantage of either an extreme nationalist sentiment or a military ethos in the population at large. But without such legitimacy, even if the regime were able to establish itself in power, it would need to exert a continuing repression which would only compound its difficulties.

A military coup would face a range of problems, from the short term to the long term. In the short run, the coup itself can be defeated by the united action of the working class. This is what happened to the Kapp putsch in Germany in 1920. Germany was then in the throes of the economic and social turmoil which followed the First World War. The Army had been badly defeated, and was suffering drastic cuts in manpower under the terms of the peace agreement. Nationalist feeling was offended by the Allied demands for the prosecution of war criminals, and monarchist feeling was alarmed at the strong working-class resistance to the restoration of the monarchy. The German revolution had failed only two years previously. A section of the Army marched into Berlin on 13 March and installed Wolfgang Kapp, an ex-civil servant and leader of the extreme nationalist Fatherland Party, in the Chancellory (an attempt to clothe the coup in civilian legitimacy). There was no military opposition – General Von Seeckt, effective Chief of Staff, declared 'Reichswehr shall not fire on Reichswehr'. The government fled to Dresden.

No victory could have seemed more complete. Yet in four days the coup collapsed, and Kapp himself fled to Finland. The coup received no support, even from business or finance capital. The higher civil servants refused to collaborate with the rebels. And, most importantly, a general strike called by the government-in-exile was devastatingly effective. Attempts by the rebel troops to force workers back to work led only to some futile casualties. The German Army learnt its lesson – that a military dictatorship without a mass base could not be maintained. Thereafter the Army remained well hidden behind the scenes – indeed it was only after the Kapp putsch failed that 'the true reign of the Reichswehr began'.[9]

Legitimacy was also crucial in 1958 when the last of a line of weak French governments was faced with an armed uprising in Algeria. On this occasion, the generals took the precaution of first approaching De Gaulle, a charismatic figure because of his wartime leadership. Seemingly unconnected with the revolt, he could command enormous popular support, if called upon to become President. Even so, a demonstration called by the Communists and Socialists mobilized over half-a-million protesters.

Another possible short-term effect, more serious for capitalism even than the possible failure of a coup, is that the resulting polarization of the working class may not stop short at a return to the *status quo ante*. Indeed, following the Kapp putsch the Communists in the Ruhr attempted (though unsuccessfully) to turn defensive action against the putsch into an offensive action against the capitalist state. A mobilized working class may realize both the extent of its own exploitation and the potential of its own united strength, and press home its advantage. In Britain a general strike to defeat a coup might mark the beginnings of mass opposition which could eventually lead to an attempt to seize state power.

Even if a military coup were to succeed, the medium-term difficulties confronting the new regime would be formidable. Unless an appearance of legitimacy could be achieved – a virtually impossible task in Britain today – the economy could be crippled by strikes and sabotage. The British Army, only about

170,000 strong, could not think of running Britain by itself. (With that number of people, as a general pointed out, you couldn't run a large-sized industrial concern.[10]) It is neither large enough nor skilled enough even to administer vital services and sources of essential supplies during any extensive period of unrest following a coup, and certainly it could not do so on a permanent basis. It could provide only a 'broken-backed' attempt to operate the power stations (according to the *Investors Chronicle*[11]), and would be unable to work the railways – still the two most vulnerable points in a modern economy.

Under the 'legitimation' of liberal democracy it is possible to maintain the co-operation of the labour force, and so preserve production in the interests of capital. In the face of united opposition of the working class the only solution for the Army would be to try and break the strike through fear. Yet the 30,000 dead necessary to subdue the relatively tiny Chilean working class has left the Chilean economy in a disastrous condition despite copious outside aid. Government by bayonet does not generate the social peace necessary for high productivity. Unlike a fascist party, the Army, because of its isolation from civil life, would have no means of mobilizing support inside the factories. The opportunities for sabotage (the working class's residual weapon) are immense.

For the ruling class, the long-term problem of a military regime is that it is difficult to end. Once the crisis which provoked the coup has been repressed, the interests of capital would be best served by a peaceful return to the more sophisticated and stable format of parliamentary democracy. But the military, once in the saddle, may not readily hand over the reins of power. More seriously, once the hold of liberal democracy has been broken it may not be easy to restore its once unchallenged legitimacy. The working class, having seen the façade of democracy shattered in a rival class interest, may not so easily be persuaded of the inevitability of pursuing its own interests only through democratic institutions. Spain, Portugal and Argentina all in their different ways bear witness to this.

For all these reasons, an Army attempting direct military

intervention would be unlikely to get backing from any significant section of British society. In particular, those who control business and financial interests would probably be opposed to any such move unless it were the only way to prevent an imminent socialist revolution. And it is their views which the British officer caste reflects. They would fear the immediate effects on the working class, the medium-term effects on the economy and the long-term effects of the overthrow of parliamentary democracy, with all the advantages this system brings for the ruling class.

However, military intervention in politics is not limited to military coups. There is a whole spectrum of levels of intervention. At the lowest level is influence over the government, which operates continuously so long as there is an army. There is pressure or blackmail, where the Army presses some policy on the government, with threats of resignation or disobedience as the lever. There is displacement of one civilian government in order that another, more favoured by the military, may come to power. All these stop short of outright military takeover. Many of them operate behind a dense cloak of secrecy.

These events do not occur only in the torrid capitals of countries sadly deprived of our British sense of fair play. For example, Field-Marshal Montgomery recalls in his memoirs how he assembled the military members of the Army Council and got them to agree to resign in a body if the Labour Cabinet decided on anything less than eighteen months' National Service. As recently as April 1975 the GOC Northern Ireland, Sir Frank King, publicly criticized the government's attempt to phase out internment. And in July of that year, the Northern Ireland Secretary Merlyn Rees made it clear in the House of Commons how difficult it was for the Labour government, though it found internment distasteful, to overrule such pressure.

The strike called against the Sunningdale agreement on power-sharing between Protestants and Catholics in Northern Ireland by the (Protestant) Ulster Workers' Council in May 1974 seems to have been a watershed as far as the British Army's intervention in politics is concerned. Up to that time, although the Army was operating in a highly political role at grass roots level it was not involved, for example, in the development of the political strategy which led to the Sunningdale agreement. In the eyes of the government there was a division between military and political strategy: the military's job was to establish a secure military situation as a precondition for a political solution. However the UWC strike changed all that, as it became clear how closely military and political strategy were linked. At a critical moment of the strike, the UWC were threatening to close down the power stations and bring Northern Ireland to a standstill. At this point, the salvaging of British government policy in Northern Ireland depended on the willingness of the Army to run the power stations if the UWC carried out their threat. Discussions were held at top civil–military level to determine whether the Army was capable of running them; it was reported that the general feeling was that the military were reluctant not so much because they felt incapable of handling the power stations, but more because they were afraid that this would lead to the necessity of their running other essential services. Nevertheless, after forty-eight hours of deliberation, Rees announced that the troops would go in to run the petrol stations. As expected the UWC responded by calling all workers out of the power stations, and began the threatened shut-down of the Province.

In spite of lengthy discussions, the Army never moved in to run the power stations. On the morning of the shut-down, Prime Minister Wilson arranged a major broadcast for that evening. Everyone expected him to take a hard line against the strikers and announce that he was sending in troops to break the strike. He did indeed take a hard line – but he announced no action on the part of the Army. The Minister of Defence, Roy Mason, had issued a 'profound warning' to him that the Army could not possibly break the strike successfully. Wilson gave way, even though he was sceptical about the Army's claim of the danger of Protestant violence. The power-sharing Northern Ireland government collapsed, and the Sunningdale agreement was a dead letter.

The Army's reluctance to run the power stations was typical of its approach to the strike. Earlier, when barricades had been set up all over Belfast in support of the strike, it made no attempt to dismantle them or to stop the hijacking of vehicles. The Army claimed that no request for assistance had been received from the police, and they were therefore not empowered to intervene. As Fisk points out, no such scruples had ever restrained them from activity in Catholic areas.[12]

After the strike, the *Sunday Times* carried an article giving details of the discussions between the Army and Rees. And they were not just about the logistics of running power stations. From the start of the strike, it said, the Army was convinced that Britain could not hope to impose law and order on the strikers. The Army told Rees that it was trained to fight terrorists, not to break strikes. Further, it claimed that it was badly positioned to deal with insurgence in Protestant areas since most of the troops were concentrated in Catholic districts. It refused to move them even though there was virtually no IRA activity during the strike.

In our view there is another reason why the Army ensured that it did not have to try to break the Loyalist strike. The Army has, since 1970 at least, regarded its job in Northern Ireland as the defeat of the IRA, and certainly not the suppression of the Protestants. We have already commented on the friendly relations between the Army and the UDA. A junior officer serving in Northern Ireland at the time, writing in the Monday Club journal under the pseudonym of 'Andrew Sefton', said that in 1972 the Army 'chose quite deliberately to give the UDA tacit support, and allowed it practically to run East and North Belfast. There is also much evidence that the Army fraternized with the strikers, even giving them cigarettes on the barricades.

It is natural that both government and the Army establishment should want to keep what happened between them over the UWC strike out of the public gaze. For the Army was in Northern Ireland as Military Aid to the Civil Power. In deciding which orders it found convenient or judicious to obey, it was relegating the government to the position of Civilian Aid to the Military Power. As 'Andrew Sefton' claimed, 'For the first time the Army decided that it was right and it knew best and the politicians had better toe the line.'

The political lessons which the Army has been learning in Northern Ireland – the possibility of a grass-roots penetration of civil life, and its power over a government which depends on it over crucial issues of policy – will not be forgotten as the Army crosses the water back to Britain. And the Army's increasing role in what have traditionally been regarded as civilian affairs is already clear: security exercises at Heathrow Airport and elsewhere (see Chapter 12) are one example, clearing rubbish in the Glasgow dustmen's strike in April 1975 is another.

If the Army is called in to perform these functions, particularly in a period of increasing domestic strife, it will inevitably demand a voice in the political decision-making process, after its experience in Northern Ireland. If Kitson's advice is followed, triumvirates of the civil, military and police powers will be set up at all levels to ensure full consultation. But once the principle of consultation over military strategy has been established, it is a short step to consultation on other political issues. Decisions made by the government in the attempt to restore political and economic stability do, after all, inevitably have a bearing on the military situation.

It might seem at this stage that there will be no problems unless the military and the government disagree on how to handle the crisis. But the very fact that the military has been called in may well create tensions, because it will be an admission of the government's failure to deal with the situation by other means. Even if it has no other military role to play, the Army is not likely to be enthusiastic about clearing dustbins and running power stations. It is possible that it would insist on harsh measures to restore the *status quo*. And the pressures of the Army would be difficult to resist once the government was in a position of reliance upon it. Without any overt signs of change, the Army could come to play an increasingly important role in British political life. Yet this role would fit perfectly the future development of liberal democracy – an empty political shell, with the real decisions controlled by forces hidden from political view. It would be another big step on the road to the Strong State.

9
Steps to the Strong State

Fascism and military dictatorships are types of 'Strong State'. The power relations in the society are clear to all. Under these regimes, every attempt is made to prevent opposition and alternative political ideas developing. The media are heavily censored or totally controlled by the government. The family must be a bastion of moral values. The education system must faithfully echo the national ideology. All political activities other than those sponsored by the state are prevented as far as possible by blanket surveillance – most effectively by a secret police. Should open opposition occur, it is suppressed with massive and brutal force.

Capitalism can and does operate within this type of political set-up. Nazi Germany, fascist Italy, Franco's Spain, present-day Chile and Brazil are just some of the many examples of highly repressive capitalist states. In liberal democracies, by contrast, the power relations are veiled. The major role of the police appears to most people to be that of controlling non-political crime; of the Army, that of fighting external enemies. In general the state machinery appears to exist in order to carry out the will of Parliament. The state is viewed as legitimate by the vast majority of citizens. Capitalism continues to operate by general tacit consent, because the real relations between people and institutions are masked.

Even within parliamentary democracies, though, legitimacy can break down. The use of the police or Army on an increasing scale against the working class can make the real nature of the state emerge more clearly. At times of crisis there may be no party or coalition of parties available which can produce a stable political regime under which the economy can function, so emergency rule becomes necessary. Such political crises are

Steps to the Strong State 69

not, of course, autonomous. They normally arise from an inability to cope with an economic crisis, and its consequent political and social effects. The Indian experience in 1975, when Mrs Gandhi introduced the imprisoning of political opponents, press censorship, the banning of political meetings and open surveillance of post and telephones demonstrates that a liberal democracy can become a Strong State perfectly constitutionally.

Strong States, therefore, somewhat paradoxically, arise in countries which are politically weak – countries where no government that could maintain the existing economic relations would be accepted as legitimate by large sections of the population. This is not just a phenomenon of capitalism. For instance, the bureaucracies that control the Soviet Union and the Eastern European states lack even the legitimacy of Western capitalist governments. The official ideology of socialism – of control by the masses – conflicts sharply with the existing social structure in which a bureaucracy has usurped all political power. And the bureaucrat is much better off than the worker or the peasant. In Russia there is a saying that the bureaucrat has his or her 'place at the trough'. So the bureaucracy is saddled with an ideology which teaches the non-legitimacy of its own existence. The result is that power relations are very apparent. A worker cannot even move to another city without permission. It is not at all surprising that these regimes have been strongly challenged four times since 1950 – in East Germany in 1953, in Hungary and Poland in 1956 and, in a more indirect way, in Czechoslovakia in 1968. As in any other Strong State, if the continuous blanket surveillance, total control of the media and elimination of political opposition fails to suppress dissent, open opposition is massively and brutally suppressed.

It is often alleged by apologists for capitalism that a Strong State necessarily results from a socialist revolution. The argument conveniently neglects the fact that no socialist revolution has yet occurred in an advanced country. So all have been faced by almost impossible problems. The young Russian revolution, for instance – itself almost bloodless – was almost immediately beset by invading armies from other countries (Britain included) and then by foreign-supported Tsarist armies. The savage wars and famines that followed left three million dead and the underdeveloped economy in ruins. Drastic emergency organization was vital for the development of the totally isolated Soviet economy. This led to the indiscriminate recruitment of a large number of administrators. The working class was unable to prevent this army of bureaucrats gradually usurping political power. But its failure lay not in any inherent consequence of revolution but in the Russian working class's small size, exhaustion and relative political backwardness.

After a successful military coup, the power relations change very suddenly and clearly. A state becomes fascist in an equally obvious transformation. In advanced capitalist countries today, as we discussed earlier, such dramatic transformations have many drawbacks. The rapid imposition of a Strong State can meet massive resistance in the form of general strikes. Even if these can be suppressed, subsequent passive resistance can lead to a deteriorating economic position.

However, a Strong State need not necessarily come about through one sudden catastrophe. The repressive capacity of a state can increase gradually over a long period in ways which may not be at all apparent to its citizens. The changes can be made in small steps. They can be changes in the mode of operation of the security forces to shape them for countering internal dissent; in the harshness of the law toward working-class actions; in state control over the media; in academic freedom and the freedom to organize politically; and in the adoption of the technology of political control.

Some of the moves are not made public. New contingency plans for countering internal dissent provide an obvious example. Others are part of seemingly rational processes, such as the re-structuring of the security forces. Yet others may be justified as legitimate responses by the state to particular events. So the 'draconian' Prevention of Terrorism Act, 1974 was accepted – and even welcomed – by most people after the Birmingham bombing of that year. Such measures are liable to be reversed only through mass political action, or after a long period of economic stability.

Steps to the Strong State 71

Many such small steps are recorded elsewhere in these pages, particularly those concerning the new mode of operation of the security forces and changes in the law – the major changes that have been occurring in Britain. But it would be easy to ignore just how many different ways have been used to strengthen the state. A drastic reduction in academic freedom has occurred, for instance, in Germany, where over 300 left-wing teachers have been prevented from teaching as a result of a law passed in 1974. Attempts to control the media are already occurring in Britain. There were threats to prosecute the BBC for showing an Open Door film made by the NCCL which included material on the Incitement to Disaffection Act. It is believed there is 'a document in existence in Whitehall drawn up by civil servants which suggests the kinds of measures that might be taken in a national emergency to curb the ability of BBC radio and television to broadcast statements by leaders of a politically inspired strike'.[1] In France in 1974 the government attempted to curtail political activity by outlawing the Ligue Communiste, the largest Trotskyist group. This ploy failed when the group successfully defied the ban.

The increasing involvement of the state machine in the reproduction of an educated and reasonably healthy work-force offers many opportunities for increased social control. A state which provides welfare benefits also has the power to withdraw them. The Bad Debt Act, the response of Stormont in 1971 to the rent and rates strike is a classic example. In Britain itself there has been increasing pressure on the government to cut off state benefits from strikers and from students disciplined for political activities. (In addition the Welfare State has necessitated the collection of a vast amount of information about people, which is clearly of great potential value to the security forces.)

The ease with which such changes can be introduced depends very much upon the traditions of a particular country, the political situation there and the detailed structure of its state. For instance, relatively tight control over the press would be much more difficult to achieve in America than in Britain. In America, freedom of the press is specifically protected by the

Constitution. In Britain it is already enfeebled by the libel laws, the Official Secrets Act and *sub judice* contempt laws.

The introduction, operation and legitimation of such changes depend primarily upon decisions by what may loosely be called the 'state élite'. The 'state élite' are those who are concerned in the direction of the important non-economic areas of a modern state. It might seem obscure why they should act in the interests of capitalism. But, as Miliband clearly shows, they act that way because of their frequent family connections, selective recruitment (applicants for 'sensitive' civil-service posts undergo 'positive vetting'), possible future employment, the social milieu in which they move and the whole mode of functioning of their jobs, since they tend to be intimately linked with business.[2] Even the social democrats among the 'state élite' accept the desirability of capitalism surviving and prospering, at least in the medium term.

They perceive economic militancy as a short-sighted threat to general economic well-being, and revolutionary political views as crazy but dangerous delusions, which must be combated. They will therefore participate entirely willingly in the individual steps which they see as necessary – if 'regrettable' – to reduce a grave short-term economic or political danger to the existing social system or to increase its general efficacy. Very few are consciously committed to the introduction of a Strong State. Yet if the decay of capitalism continues it will force them to take more and more 'small steps'. The end product would be a Strong State.

The role of the leadership of social-democratic parties such as the Labour Party, when in power, does not differ greatly in this respect from that of governments of other parties. Even those dedicated in principle to the introduction of socialist policies become dominated when in office by the need to maintain capitalism in operation. The logic of their position forces them, whatever their reluctance, to co-operate with the rest of the state élite in taking 'small steps'.

One of the most lurid examples, and one with great relevance today, occurred in the very first Labour government of 1923. A secret organization was set up in the early 1920s to operate against a future General Strike. Its architect was a close confidante of Baldwin's in the Tory Cabinet, J. T. C. Davidson. In his memoirs, Davidson recalls that when the 1923 Labour government took over, he wrote to his successor as Chancellor of the Duchy of Lancaster, Josiah Wedgwood. 'I told him that, whoever was in power, it was his duty to protect the Constitution against a Bolshevik-inspired general strike ... I begged him not to destroy all I had done and not to tell the Cabinet of it ... He promised not to interfere with the work we had done.'[3] Wedgwood was true to his word!

More recently, Labour governments have called in the Army to break strikes, and have used the Special Branch to monitor militancy. It was a Labour Home Secretary who, in 1965, set up the Special Patrol Group, the section of the police specializing in riot control. And it was another Labour Home Secretary who introduced the Prevention of Terrorism Act.

The reason why advanced capitalist states are confronted with the 'need' to take such steps towards more authoritarian rule is that they are all faced with the economic and political consequences of the end of the post-war boom. They all face in addition a working class used to an increasing standard of living, and which in some cases is very militant. But there are a number of other factors which reinforce the tendency or make it easier to achieve. They are especially relevant to us, as they facilitate the introduction of the technology of political control.

The first factor is the enormous post-war growth in expenditure on the security forces. This has had political and economic causes. Politically, it has helped to fulfil two major requirements of Western policy – to try to maintain economic control over the Third World and to head off dissent internally. At the same time it has had important economic functions – military spending has been perhaps the most useful part of the state sector for stimulating the economy.[4] For instance, profits of US military industries averaged 17.5 per cent on capital invested, compared with 10.5 per cent in the civilian sector during the mid-1960s.

Military spending has also spawned a large number of new technologies which can be readily adapted for controlling internal dissent. One of the legacies of the war was that the military learned to rely on science. Whereas before it had put higher priority on the horse than on the tank, afterwards it became highly technology-conscious. Through the Vietnam war this technological approach found a new area of application – counter-insurgency warfare. Nor have the applications been limited to Vietnam. Quite a number of technical developments stemming from the Vietnam war – in sensors, in helicopters, in night-vision devices – have been adapted for counter-insurgency uses in the USA – the process of reverse Vietnamization. The Pentagon is now deeply involved in the technology of the 'home front'.[5] Many of these devices are now being adopted in Britain.

The second major factor which facilitates the creeping control of internal dissent is that the administrative part of the state machine has over a long period of time being gradually gaining influence over decision-making at the expense of the legislature. The massive involvement of the state in the economy will accelerate this trend. 'Small steps' are most easily taken when hidden from public view, so as they increasingly become the province of the state bureaucracy, rather than the legislature, they become easier to execute.

The growth of the state apparatus has also facilitated the growth of technocracy. This is the process by which the 'state élite' increasingly justifies its actions by appeal to technical experts, who appear to base their recommendations on objective, scientific forms of knowledge. The opportunity to do this is offered by the growth of a myriad of management and policy 'sciences' – fragmented specialisms concerned with the difficulties of running large bureaucratic organizations (particularly industrial ones) with alienated labour, and with the problems of co-ordinating social policy so as to provide a stable environment within which capitalist industry can operate. While many of these specialisms do contain a nub of genuine content, this is often dressed up in a whole panoply of 'scientific'-seeming accoutrements. The methods of the natural sciences are aped, with the result that the ultimate objects of all this attention – people – end up being analysed and treated as if they were inanimate objects.

Steps to the Strong State 75

This tendency has a number of useful effects for the managers of the state. First, the approach is heavily quantitative, and so necessitates the collection of large amounts of information, which may well be useful for the control purposes of the state. Second, the approach appears to legitimate any steps taken to reduce still further the effective power of the mass of the population to control public policies. Problems defined as technical are made to seem the province of experts. Thirdly, it legitimates the philosophy of the technological fix – the construction of an over-simple definition of a complex social problem, so that purely technical 'solutions' can be applied. And, finally, the often repressive nature of these 'solutions' can be largely hidden from the general view by the adoption of neutral scientific-seeming language. As Roszak[6] points out, to bomb more hell out of a tiny Asian country in one year than out of Europe in the whole Second World War becomes 'escalation'. A concentration camp becomes a 'strategic hamlet'.

These tendencies are quite evident in the development of the technology of political control. As an example of the effects of this trend in the area of internal defence, there is the report of the Commission on Law Enforcement and the Administration of Justice set up by President Johnson in 1965 to stem the rise in 'crime on the streets' after the Watts riots. It castigated the American criminal justice system as inefficient, untrained and 'technologically backward' and recommended that it should be reorganized to become a 'sophisticated, technologically advanced system'.

The result was the setting-up in 1968 of the Law Enforcement Assistance Administration. The LEAA now allocates grants for local police departments to modernize by buying equipment such as computers, and for developing special groups such as riot-control units. Like the Pentagon, they also fund police training in universities and contract out research into new police weapons. Their first report indicates their basic philosophy. Attacking the fractionated and isolated, tradition-bound police and legal systems, the report argued that 'statistical analysis, operations research, management studies and role analysis must be brought to many of these age-old problems'. Which are the age-old problems that are going to succumb to the onward march of science? In its second year of operations the control of riots and civil disorders received 19.7 per cent of its budget – the largest single sub-division. By contrast organized crime received 4.4 per cent and community relations 4.3 per cent.

The third special factor is that the growth of monopoly capitalism has both necessitated and facilitated a growth in anti-dissent mechanisms on an international scale. The role of the United States as a self-appointed global policeman is by now well known. Vietnam is the prime example. But it has also gained valuable if vicarious counter-insurgency experience through the activities of puppet police forces and armies throughout Latin America, and in other parts of the world. The US Army and the CIA complement each other in this role. Even in Europe the hands of NATO and the CIA can be seen, in events such as the 1967 military coup in Greece. And the CIA has also been involved in boosting the right wing of European social-democratic parties and trade unions in order to attract support away from left-wing alternatives.

Further international opportunities for the intensification of anti-dissent activities could arise from the development of supranational political institutions in the EEC. Theoretically, for the EEC to work effectively for European capitalism it needs to take on the functions at present performed by nation states. Whether this is politically feasible remains to be seen. If it could be achieved it would produce a massive growth of the power of the bureaucracy; and the European centralization of security forces would lead to a rapid increase in their effectiveness in controlling dissent. A portent for the future may be the novel addition to the annual EEC summit meeting in Rome in December 1975. At the instigation of the Home Office, co-operation of the respective police forces 'notably in the fight against terrorism' was discussed.

Finally, internationalization has led to the growing together of security-force methods all over the capitalist world. For instance, the 1974 command course attended by twenty-four United Kingdom Superintendents and Chief Superintendents involved study visits to police establishments in six European countries to study public order, traffic and training. International electronic crime counter-measures conferences are held, dealing with such matters as command and control systems, night-vision devices, sensors and other useful law-enforcement techniques. There are also numerous international information-sharing agreements, such as the Quadripartite Agreement, by which the USA, Canada, Britain and Australia have exchanged information on such matters as riot-control equipment.

These factors – the high level of spending in the security forces, the increased size and changed mode of operation of the state bureaucracies and the internationalization of capitalist control mechanisms – have had major effects on the greater competence of the security forces in dealing with internal dissent. They are all factors which magnify the tendency of the state to react to political or economic crisis by 'small-steps' measures, by making them technically easier to achieve. But it is the basic cause, the deteriorating capitalist economy, which makes this assistance so welcome to those who govern the strengthening states. A fully-fledged Strong State could only come about after a process of this kind lasting many years. When, later in this book, we refer to the 'Strong State', we mean this end result rather than the current situation with its conflicting but suggestive tendencies.

10
'Small Steps' in the Law

It might seem alarmist to suggest that Britain, the archetypal liberal democracy, could ever become a Strong State. It is obviously still far from it. Yet the bulk of economic and political forces is moving it in that direction. And it is already altering fast. The changes in the security forces and their developing technology demonstrate this clearly. But changes in another area – the law – deserve some attention. Over the past five years there has been an increasing tendency for the state to employ legal sanctions against groups or individuals involved in political or industrial action. This is in part a response to the growth, since the early sixties, of protest movements which use 'direct action' as a method of political expression. It is also a response to the increase in grass-roots industrial activity characterized by new forms of industrial action such as 'flying pickets' and factory occupations.

The British legal system has always been inherently inequitable. Its major function is to protect property in a society where most individuals own no property of economic significance. However, a system of 'class justice' is not necessarily always an instrument of direct political repression; there are times when laws are enacted which defend the right of political expression, albeit under pressure from various groups. In a situation of economic and social crisis, however, there is much less room for manoeuvre by the government and judiciary. They may then seek to restrict certain civil liberties which give scope for industrial or other forms of political action.

The effectiveness of the law as a means of political control stems from three major factors. Firstly, it is extremely flexible. If the introduction or re-interpretation of a law provokes mass protest, it can always be repealed or softened, or simply not used. The history of the Industrial Relations Act, 1971 provides several examples of this, notably the occasion in 1972 when five dockers were imprisoned by the National Industrial Relations Court for contempt. The Law Lords ruled that the union was responsible for ensuring its members' obedience to the law, and so were able to order the release of the men just in time to avert a threatened general strike. British law is particularly flexible. Its emphasis on common law and precedent permits considerable changes without any parliamentary discussion whatever.

Secondly, if the law is used cleverly it is less likely to provoke an adverse reaction than the use of more overt repression by the security forces. The ideology of respect for law is very deeply rooted in British society. People are extremely reluctant to break the law, even if they consider that it threatens their freedom of political expression. The press launched a vicious campaign against the Clay Cross councillors who refused to implement the 1972 Housing Finance Act because they believed it would lower the living standards of many people they represented. But it is often forgotten that there were many councils which had declared their opposition to the Act, but stopped short of breaking the law once it became clear that the Tory government was determined to implement it.

Finally, the law is a highly complex and technical subject. Most people probably do not even know their rights if they are stopped in the street or arrested by the police. They certainly do not recognize the full significance of new legislation passed by Parliament, or understand the implications of particular rulings by judges. This widespread ignorance lays the basis for the subtle application of legal means to suppress movements which threaten social passivity.

An excellent example of the operation of these three principles is the case of the Shrewsbury building workers who were convicted in 1973 of 'conspiracy to intimidate'; three of them were subsequently imprisoned for periods of up to three years. The power of the 1875 Conspiracy Act lies precisely in its vagueness. 'Conspiracy', despite its lurid overtones, is difficult to define and therefore admits of wide interpretation.* And, convictions on conspiracy charges can carry much longer sentences than those for most other criminal charges. A conviction for intimidation carries a maximum sentence of three months; yet Des Warren, one of the Shrewsbury pickets convicted of conspiracy to intimidate, received a sentence twelve times as heavy. In fact, conspiracy charges can carry a maximum sentence of life imprisonment. The prosecution of the Shrewsbury pickets was a direct attack on the right of trade-unionists to organize 'flying pickets' in support of industrial action.

No arrests were made on the day the picket took place at Shrewsbury, nor even immediately afterwards. It was only one month later, after a speech by the Home Secretary urging the police to prosecute in such cases ('The law as it stands ... makes it clear that such numbers attending can of itself constitute intimidation'[2]), that the police began the investigation which led to the conspiracy charges. The men were arrested, not on the picket line in full view of their colleagues, but in the privacy of their homes. The original twenty-four defendants were charged, not only with conspiracy, but with unlawful affray and assembly, although the latter charges were subsequently dropped owing to lack of sufficient evidence. When their defence counsel complained to the jury that 'some of these men met for the first time on these sites,' the judge interrupted, 'you know very well that it can be a conspiracy when they never met or knew each other.'[3] The mere fact of being in the same place at the same time as large numbers of people determined to end the lump system in the building industry was enough to convict the Shrewsbury pickets. A leading textbook on English criminal law states that: 'The crime of conspiracy affords support for any who advance the proposition that the criminal law is an instrument of government.' †

Despite the flimsiness of the charge and the serious implications of the verdict for future industrial action involving large

*The judge in the 'Angry Brigade' trial told the jury that 'a nod and a wink can amount to conspiracy'.[1]

† An excellent account is given in G. Robertson, *Whose Conspiracy?* NCCL, 1974.

numbers of pickets, the trade-union leadership made no attempt to confront the working of the law. Had they done so, the law could have been made unworkable – just as organized resistance defeated the Industrial Relations Act.

The conspiracy charge shows the state's use of the law at its most subtle. Its increasing use is just one of the ways in which the law is being developed as a repressive tool. Other examples are the changes in picketing laws, the use of the Incitement to Disaffection Act, and the removal of the right to challenge the occupations of jurors. But the clearest example of a law which provides a foretaste of what is in store for us if Britain became a Strong State is the 1974 Prevention of Terrorism (Temporary Provisions) Act.

In November 1974, twenty people died as a result of two bomb explosions in Birmingham pubs. The bombings were immediately attributed to the IRA, and in the outcry which followed demands were made for the reintroduction of hanging for terrorist offences and the banning of the IRA. In this atmosphere of hysteria, the Prevention of Terrorism Act* was passed in a single night by both Houses of Parliament. Based in part on the Northern Ireland (Emergency Provisions) Act of 1973, it appears that the government was waiting for an opportunity to introduce it; a draft had been prepared well before the Birmingham bombing.

The three sections of the Act dealt with, firstly, a ban on the IRA; secondly, a new power for the Home Secretary to exclude from Britain any person suspected of terrorism; and thirdly, power for the police to hold suspects for up to forty-eight hours on their own authority and for a further five days with permission from the Home Secretary. The Act was to last, in the first instance, for six months, after which time it could be renewed, in whole or in part.

As soon as the Bill was published, the NCCL and other organizations opposed it on the grounds that it gave dangerous powers to the police which could extend far beyond the immediate situation of an anti-terrorist campaign, and could not be

*See the NCCL Report on the first four months' operation of the Act, on which much of our account is based.

challenged in the courts. The Home Secretary himself described the Bill as 'draconian legislation' and 'unprecedented in peacetime'. However, in the aftermath of the Birmingham bombings, opposition arguments went virtually unheard.

After four months of the Act, the NCCL produced a report substantiating their earlier fears about the way such legislation would be used.[4] They found that the second and third parts of the Act had been used most. Under the second part, which gave the Home Secretary power to exclude suspects, forty-five exclusion orders had been made, of which thirty-eight had been served by 9 April 1975. Only eleven people had made representations against the Act, because many of those served with orders believed that they had no chance of successful representation, or that they could fight the order once they had been deported. Of these eleven, five were able to get the order revoked, mostly owing to the actions of local trade-unionists and MPs. The Home Secretary had refused police requests to sign exclusion orders on only twelve occasions. As with internment, the suspect has no right of appeal in an open court. The NCCL pointed out that in most cases there was no evidence to suggest that those excluded were involved in terrorist activity. This is borne out by the fact that the majority of those deported were not actually detained on arrival in Northern Ireland.

The third part of the Act – which gives powers of search and detention to the police – has been most widely used. By 9 April, 489 people had been detained, of whom only twenty were subsequently charged with offences in Great Britain, and one in the Republic of Ireland. Three people charged with murder were detained for over two months before the charges against them were dropped; in the vast majority of cases, no charges were preferred at all. The police appear to have used their new powers for widespread information-gathering and harassment of the Irish in Great Britain. Legal access, or contact with the family of the detainee, has been denied in some cases. Part of the process of harassment has been to question people for the first three or four days and then to leave them in the cells until the seven days are up, even though no charges have subsequently been preferred.

More recent figures present a similar picture. By November 1975, 1,174 people had been held under the Act. Only sixty-one of them were ever charged with any offence – and many of those were charged for offences totally unconnected with terrorism, such as tax evasion, burglary and 'wasting police time'. Of the thirty-six people deported to Northern Ireland, not one was charged with any offence, although nine were arrested on arrival and made to undergo further interrogation.[5]

The NCCL report demonstrated that the operation of the Act has not produced results which, even on pragmatic grounds, could be used to justify its continued existence. Nevertheless, in May 1975 the House of Commons extended the legislation for a further six months. Only ten MPs voted against. In November 1975, the Home Secretary, Jenkins, announced the government's intention to make the legislation permanent. And the fears which had previously been expressed about the potential application of the Act were justified in late 1975 by the arrest of Pat Arrowsmith, a well-known pacifist, for handing out a leaflet explaining the role of troops. Shortly afterwards, forty-two people were detained for seven days under the Act in connection with an arms find in Southampton. The police put out a statement saying that they intended to clear some of the detainees to avoid holding people 'who have accidentally come into the net'.

The remarkable history of these 'temporary provisions' is by no means unique. The most crucial clauses of the Official Secrets Act were somewhat similarly rushed through the Commons one afternoon in 1911 to deal with a German spy scare. Again, there was virtually no debate. The Act is based on the theory that all official information belongs to the Crown and may not be divulged without authority. It is reinforced by the D-notice system* which advises editors that 'an item of news may well be protected by the Official Secrets Act and ... the act of publication is considered to be contrary to the national interest'. It led Cecil King, then chairman of the *Mirror* group, to remark: 'In an arbitrary and indeterminate way the British press is very effectively censored.'[6]

*Since 1967 replaced by *ad hoc* agreements similar to it.

The Prevention of Terrorism Act gives wide powers to the police to investigate and detain suspects. But it only allows for detention of up to seven days on application to the Home Secretary. In order to introduce preventive detention for a longer period in Britain, the government would have to bring in a new statute by the usual procedure through both Houses of Parliament. In a situation regarded as an emergency, this legislation could however be passed very quickly, as we saw in the case of the anti-terrorist law.

The Northern Ireland Act, 1972 and the Commonwealth Immigration Act, 1968 are both examples of legislation which provides for preventive detention. Other precedents, the Emergency Powers (Defence) Acts, 1939-40, are worth mentioning. The 1939 Act authorized the making of regulations for the detention of persons on security grounds and for the amendment of *any* prior Act of Parliament. The 1940 Act authorized the making of regulations for the trial of civilians by special courts *if the military situation so required.*

In Northern Ireland, there is a wealth of legislation which represents threats to freedom in some form or another, including the 1920 Special Powers Act and the Northern Ireland (Emergency Provisions) Act, 1973, renewed in 1974. For those arrested under the Act, bail and trial by jury have virtually been abolished, and a person on trial has no right to know who is giving evidence against him or her, and sometimes is not even told the nature of the offence.[7]

The change in the mode of operation of the security forces, and the increased likelihood that the Army may operate in some capacity in a period of industrial and political unrest in Britain, makes it worthwhile considering the laws which govern the introduction of the military for purposes of internal security or maintenance of essential services.

The *Manual of Military Law* is extremely vague about the limits on the legal right of the civil power to call on the Army for assistance. All that can be said is that there must be a 'genuine disturbance' necessitating the use of troops; and that the civil power must be satisfied that the police cannot adequately handle the situation. The manual gives examples of five such situations, but does not make it clear whether these are the only times the troops can be called in. They are: a national emergency under the Emergency Powers Act, 1920; the intimidation of workers under the Conspiracy and Protection of Property Act, 1875 (the Act under which the Shrewsbury pickets were convicted); unlawful assembly; riot; and insurrection. Should the government be unable or unwilling to summon the troops, there is another route by which the military can intervene in such crises: the Crown has a prerogative power to direct the use of troops.

Technically a government decision to bring in troops can be challenged in court, but the court cannot prevent their introduction since it can only adjudicate the case after the event. The legislation in the *Manual of Military Law* thus gives extremely wide powers to the government in respect of bringing the military into Britain.*

The military themselves are certainly aware of the uses of the law in intensifying repression – we have already pointed out that the Army has put pressure on the government to retain the powers of internment in Northern Ireland. In *Low Intensity Operations*, Kitson outlines two possible uses for the law in the 'preparatory period of subversion'. This is the period when the government uses legal sanctions rather than more overt repression to quell protest. Kitson's first alternative is the use of the law as 'just another weapon in the government's arsenal, in which case it becomes little more than a propaganda cover for the disposal of unwanted members of the public'. The antiterrorist law is a good example of this. When it was introduced, *The Times*, almost echoing Kitson, wrote that this law and the power of internment in Northern Ireland serve the same purpose – 'to put out of the way people suspected of terrorist activity against whom convictions in court are unlikely to be secured'.[8]

Kitson's second alternative is that the law 'should remain impartial' and should be administered 'without any direction from the government'. He says that this is not only 'morally right' but

*We are grateful to the NCCL for the use of unpublished material by Bill Birtles on emergency and military legislation.

also 'expedient' because 'it is more compatible with the government's aim of maintaining the allegiance of the population'.[9] Here Kitson is simply distinguishing between subtle and blatant uses of the law in repressing dissent. The mere fact of his discussion of alternative approaches implies a view of the law as an instrument to be manipulated to meet the needs of the political situation. If the law really were impartial, then it would not be at the discretion of the government to determine how it should be used.

Kitson's proposals and the examples we have considered give us some insight into the use of the law in circumstances where a violent response from the state would be counter-productive. However, legal sanctions can be effective only as long as the majority of the population continue to respect the law. Once that stage has passed, other methods would have to be employed. The law thus has a limited application in any situation of open conflict, but it can play a very important role in attempts by the state to prevent that type of situation arising.

Part Three
The Strong Arm of the Strong State

11
From Counter-Insurgency to Internal Defence

In the previous section we argued that, as long as British capitalism continues its steady decline, the security forces are likely to be involved increasingly in countering dissent within Britain itself. In the next chapter we describe the changes which have already occurred in the security forces and which make them much more suited for this purpose. Precisely how these forces may be used, and in what circumstances, can only be a matter for speculation, given the complexities and uncertainties of our economic and political situation. But there are some who have speculated – a small but growing group of military theorists and strategists of domestic counter-insurgency warfare. Their speculations may tell us little directly about the future of Britain, but they can tell us a lot about the nature of the police–military machine which is being refashioned for a more political role.

Since 1945, the role of the Army has been changing with the decline in conventional warfare between states. The growth in nuclear weaponry and the formation of trans-national power blocs at one time led to speculation that the Army would have no future role. But the decline in conventional warfare has been accompanied by a massive increase in revolutionary wars: in the first two post-war decades the NATO powers between them killed over four million people (mainly peasants) in counter-revolutionary actions.[1] Now that Britain is rapidly running out of colonies to 'defend', the future of the Army has once again become problematical. So in recent years a new breed of military theorist has emerged – those who are concerned to show that the Army can have an important role to play in countering internal dissent and maintaining internal stability. The theorists and strategists we consider include a number of high-ranking serving officers and others working for bodies such as the Royal United Services Institute (RUSI) and the Institute of Conflict Studies (ICS), as well as other civilian commentators on defence matters. The analysis of all these commentators leads them to the conclusion that internal dissent is likely to be a prevalent feature of future political life. We have also made use of the Army's counter-insurgency manual – the *Army Land Operations Manual, Volume III: Counter-Revolutionary Operations* (henceforth referred to as *ALOM*).*

The writings and speeches of the new military theorists serve several purposes. Firstly, and most obviously, they provide technical information on how to fight counter-insurgency campaigns. Secondly they serve to influence Army Command, the government and the ruling class as a whole towards a position of support for the renewed † role of the Army in countering internal dissent. The Army is a very traditionalist organization, and there are still important sections of the leadership which believe that the Army's primary role is defence against the proverbial 'Soviet threat'.[2] British governments – particularly Labour ones – are constantly under pressure to cut defence spending; military theorists are an obvious counter-balance to this pressure. Thirdly, the writings of these theorists and strategists help to prepare the ranks of the Army – and indirectly, via the media, the population as a whole – for the possibility of military intervention in Britain. However, if the Army is to be used against any significant section of the population, we would hardly expect to find this discussed *openly* by any of the theorists. We can therefore expect omissions or distortions in their writings, which must consequently be analysed in some detail.

---

*The *ALOM* is classified as 'Restricted' under the Official Secrets Act. Volume III was written in 1969, and revised in 1971 and 1973 in the light of experience in Northern Ireland.

† The Army was, of course, widely used in this role in the early nineteenth century and before, as E. P. Thompson shows in *The Making of the English Working Class*.

Background to the Developments

Brigadier R. G. S. Bidwell, editor of the influential *RUSI Journal*, has outlined four historically determined roles for the Army which we can take as the starting point for our analysis.[3] In order of priority they are: to secure the lawful government from overthrow by force; to defend the state against external aggression; to pursue external goals by military force (this is in line with Clausewitz's classic dictum that war is a continuation of diplomacy by other means); and to provide Military Aid to the Civil Power (MACP*) – which includes such functions as disaster relief and the maintenance of essential services during strikes.

In the post-war period the public has been led to believe that the purpose of the Army is primarily defence against the 'Soviet threat' – which falls under Bidwell's second category – and NATO has been presented as the main vehicle for this. However, a critical evaluation of the development of NATO leads to a very different conclusion.[4,5] There are many factors which suggest that when NATO was set up it was an aggressive rather than as a defensive force.[6] Even the then American Secretary of State, John Foster Dulles, admitted at the time, 'I do not know any responsible official, military or civilian, in this government or in any government who believes that the Soviet government now plans conquest by open military aggression.'[7]

The threat which *was* uppermost in the thoughts of these people was that of post-war revolutionary activity in such countries as France, Belgium, Italy and Greece, as well as in a number of colonial countries. In the Truman Doctrine of 1947, President Truman had branded the Soviet Union as the instigator of internal dissent. By this careful blurring of the distinction between Soviet expansion and internal revolution, he was able to justify the need for military intervention to prevent countries going communist. Thus the statement cited above was not intended to imply that the Soviet Union did not pose any threat to the West, merely that the threat was expressed in a different

---

*The actual term MACP – pronounced 'MacPee' in military circles – did not come into use until fairly recently.

form from overt military aggression. The Truman Doctrine – which declares support for any nation in its resistance to communism – was justified as a legitimate response to this.

It is clear that many military activities which appear to belong to Bidwell's second role, defence of the country, are really a part of the third, the pursuit of external goals through military force. The sheer scope of this third role may be judged from the fact that, between the end of the Second World War and 1969, Britain has been involved in *no fewer than fifty-three* small wars. *ALOM* describes all but two of these (Korea and Suez) as 'counter-revolutionary-type operations'. With the fading of Britain as an imperialist power there has been a decline in this role. But the Army's experience of fighting these wars has had a crucial influence on its theory of counter-revolutionary warfare.

The Army's fourth role, according to Bidwell, that of providing military aid to the civil power, is of minor importance in times of stability, though it does provide valuable propaganda for the 'benevolence' of the Army.

With a move towards a Strong State, Bidwell's first role, securing the government from overthrow by force, gains steadily in importance. For the government must prepare to maintain itself increasingly by the selected and sophisticated application of force. The first line of defence is the police. But the Army must be ready in case the police should be unable to control internal dissent. The Army theorists have not been slow to take up discussion of this new role. One of the RUSI annual essay topics clearly shows the importance the Army now attaches to 'internal security' operations as a guarantee of its own future:

Operations in Northern Ireland over the past 3½ years have created for the Army many difficulties, problems, and much personal hardship ... However, there have been some parochial military advantages, not least in providing the Army with a sense of purpose stemming from a real operational setting. Such a sense of purpose is not always achieved within the limitations of our peacetime role in Europe. It has been sustained in the past twenty-seven years by our many and varied small wars further afield. Looking to the future after Northern Ireland discuss the difficulties of maintaining a strong sense of purpose in a peacetime Army.

From Counter-Insurgency to Internal Defence 93

Since the prospect of direct intervention by the Army in Britain poses considerable ideological problems, even among its own ranks, the military theorists have provided at least two arguments linking internal dissent with the cold war. One line of argument is that internal dissent weakens the ability of the Army to conduct a satisfactory defence against any external threat. Horst Mendershausen of the Rand Corporation expressed this view in *Nato News*: 'Domestic disorder is turning peoples' concern with security away from protection against foreign adversaries ... A protective alliance [such as] NATO cannot for long survive this replacement of awareness of an external threat ... [with] internal threats to the nation.'

Other theorists have developed the International Civil War Theory, the origins of which lie in the Truman Doctrine. According to this approach, militant internal dissent is nothing but a new form of international warfare between communism and the 'free world'. Thus Brigadier Calvert, speaking on the role of armed forces in peace-keeping in the 1970s,[8] gives a graphic description of the way in which 'Britain has been chosen by our enemies to be the main target of subversion'. According to him, subversives are being trained at schools of political warfare in Russia and China, and they 'will be activated as soon as the situation demands it'. The idea that communists 'infiltrate' while 'moderates' somehow belong in industry and the trade unions is a direct reflection of this approach.

In addition to linking internal dissent with the 'Soviet threat', the military writers have often grossly distorted the aims and methods of political opponents. Clutterbuck,* for instance, claims that: 'Revolutionary techniques are seldom used except by minorities because no one else needs them.'[9] And again: 'The dilemma will be to break the few dozen guerrillas without eroding the liberties of millions of innocent people.'[10] This is a highly ideological picture of liberal democracy. And the author totally ignores the history and possibility of mass revolutionary struggles in which the working class plays a leading role. Deane-

---

*Ex-Major-General Richard Clutterbuck, PH.D., O.B.E., described on the flyleaf to his book, *Protest and the Urban Guerrilla*, as 'one of the world's leading authorities on revolutionary warfare'.

Drummond (former Assistant-Commandant of Sandhurst), along with a number of other propaganda-oriented writers, claims that the 'aim' of political leaders is to force the security forces to over-react. Consider his comments on rioters and demonstrators: 'Modern rioting techniques,' he states (citing no evidence to show that they are any different from the old type), 'are specifically designed' to make soldiers 'lose their cool' and 'go berserk'.[11] So state repression is justified by this supposed neo-witchcraft aimed against the troops. This in turn provides 'ready-made propaganda to be exploited by the ruthless leaders of the riots': 'Staged martyrs with bleeding heads will provoke the soldiers so that pictures may be taken of arrests.'[12]

Who do the theorists think these revolutionaries are? Clutterbuck, in particular, has conducted a 'know your enemy' survey of the major revolutionary groups in Britain[13] which might be thought to use such tactics. Crozier has catalogued some of the 'aims' of the various groups in the event of their coming to power. For example, under Communist Party leadership he claims that 'a secret police with sweeping and arbitrary powers would be established ... the usual liberties would be abolished'. The Trotskyists 'in the unlikely event of their finding themselves exclusively in power ... would do all the things the communists would do, possibly with greater speed and brutality'.[14] Such propaganda is hardly new; but no doubt it still has the same effectiveness in propagating the idea that the aim of revolutionary groups is to gain power for themselves rather than to build mass movements which will seize power for the whole working class.

In one of his more bizarre passages Crozier speculates on whether rebellion might be 'a matter of chromosomes'.[15] Deane-Drummond, too, attempts to explain away the perplexing problem of why so many people are attracted to such barbaric ideologies. He describes in detail the way Marxist 'indoctrination' produces a 'Frankenstein [sic] motivated only by hate and doomed to destroy or be destroyed'.[16] Another approach has been to speculate that political dissidents are mentally unbalanced. Thus guerrilla warfare expert Michael Calvert concludes that guerrillas often suffer from hyperactivity, which 'can be caused by lead poisoning' and which causes people to be 'unable to settle down'.[17] Another example of this attitude is a long article in the *Sunday Times* of 19 August 1973, 'The Mind of a Terrorist', in which the reporters raise the question of whether 'mentally unstable individuals are attracted to terrorism, motivated purely by violence, with only the thinnest of political veneers'. They go on to imply that other revolutionaries, too, are not quite 'normal'. 'In Britain, more than one member of extremist organizations (not all on the left) has been convicted of offences involving sexual abnormality.' This approach will be discussed further in the chapter on prisoner control.

An important defect in the writings of many of the military theorists which makes their strategic evaluations very dubious is the way in which they attempt to blur the distinction between different types of action. They use the widespread horror that terrorist actions such as bombings provoke, in an attempt to tar *all* potential struggles against the state as acts of violent minorities. One remarkable example of this approach was given in a secret civil–military seminar in 1974. A Lieut-Colonel in the Lancastrian Volunteers said: 'We have just seen the trade unions bring down the elected government of the country. Where does the industrial guerrilla fit in?' He added that the main concern of the Army was the 'industrial guerrilla'.[18]

The military theorists have written extensively on the problems posed by guerrilla warfare – for obvious reasons. In recent years guerrilla groups throughout the world have been able to demonstrate the vulnerability of certain strategic installations – and, even more, of public places and individuals. The British Army has had considerable experience of guerrilla wars in the past three decades, and Northern Ireland has clearly shown that this type of warfare can come much nearer home. A number of theorists have suggested that guerrilla warfare may arise in Britain along the lines pursued by the Provisional IRA. However, there is a crucial difference between Northern Ireland and Britain which belies this simple comparison. In Northern Ireland, the Provisionals have a wide base of popular support from an oppressed caste. In 1971 even the British Army was forced to concede that as many as a quarter of Northern Irish Catholics were actively helping the IRA, and approximately half were broadly in sympathy with them.[19] In Britain the only possible basis of mass support for a guerrilla movement would be the working class, which is more likely to turn to alternative forms of direct action.

A revolution requires active mass involvement. Guerrilla activity by its nature must rely on fairly small and clandestine groups. Moreover terrorist tactics have often only served to alienate the vast majority of people from the terrorists' cause. Nor do guerrilla actions use the potential strength of the most powerful sector of industrialized society – the working class, with its ability to organize in mass and to contest the control of production. Unlike the peasantry, among whom the most successful revolutionary guerrilla groups have operated, the working class is already organized on a mass basis. As a result, it both understands and moves into mass actions such as strikes and factory occupations. It is this ability that gives it on occasion the power to challenge the very existence of the state. Indeed both the Russian Revolutions of 1917 and the German Revolution of 1918 were initiated not by terrorist actions but by massive waves of political strikes. So, while we cannot exclude the possibility of guerrilla warfare, action based on mass activity by the working class is much the most realistic scenario for revolution in Britain – and the one accepted by most revolutionary groups.

Why then has this possibility not been discussed publicly by the military theorists? Partly, perhaps, because of the British Army's own lack of experience in dealing with this type of movement. But also because guerrilla groups are an acceptable focus for public debate. Few people are prepared to argue about measures taken to defend against terrorist attacks. The reaction would be very different if the government declared openly that preparations were necessary to protect the state against a potentially revolutionary working-class movement. Deane-Drummond is one of the few writers who do discuss working-class mass activity as part of a revolutionary process.

But his scenario develops into scenes of individual acts of violence including snipers and (specially trained) 'fire-raisers' and 'explosives experts', all of course attempting to make the security forces 'overreact'.[20]

Though the military theorists have not seriously discussed the possibility of revolutionary activity based on mass activity of the working class, they have cited Marxist theoreticians in order to explain the reasons why guerrilla warfare in the West is unlikely to succeed. For instance Robert Moss of the *Economist*, in *Urban Guerrillas*,[21] emphasizes that the major reason why such campaigns have failed has been the guerrillas' inability to organize active mass support. 'Today,' he writes, 'it makes more sense to read Lenin or the Communist theorists of the 1920s in order to understand the likely pattern of urban guerrilla operations than to read Mao Tse-tung, General Giap, or even Che Guevara.' Reflecting on the events in France in 1968, Moss says: 'What made revolution in France in 1968 impossible was ... the lack of a class basis for revolt, and above all the absence of a "vanguard party".' Significantly, as the possibility of working-class revolt becomes increasingly apparent, Moss ignores the class nature of society in his more recent writings, and refers solely to the threat of terrorism; he recommends a number of repressive measures and supports demands for the introduction of identity cards.[22] It need hardly be pointed out that these measures would also prove extremely useful to the state against a revolutionary working-class movement.

There is general agreement among the theorists that widespread internal dissent – of an imprecisely defined nature – is likely to arise in response to a deteriorating economic situation. Thus Deane-Drummond, in *Riot Control*, states that 'increasing inflation and rising unemployment provide precisely the conditions in which disorder and dissension can flourish': And in a much-quoted passage from the first chapter of *Low Intensity Operations*, Kitson states.[23]

If a significant and serious grievance arose such as might result from a significant drop in the standard of living, all those who now dissipate their protest over a wide variety of causes might concentrate their efforts and produce a situation which was beyond the power of the police to handle. Should this happen, the Army would be required to restore peace rapidly. Fumbling at this juncture might have grave consequences, even to the extent of undermining confidence in the whole system of government.

Charles Douglas-Home has been more explicit on the form this protest might take. In a *Times* article, denying the possibility of a military coup, he suggested that the Army would be more likely to be brought in to 'protect the community from the more violent consequences of hyperinflation – food riots, looting, and major demonstrations'.* [24] This last statement also illustrates another idea which is common to the writings of the more propaganda-oriented theorists: that military intervention will be necessary to protect the '*community*'. The assumption seems to be that the 'community' will starve peacefully in the grateful knowledge that the security forces are dealing with those who choose to protest instead.

In a situation of widespread mass protest, the dilemma for the security forces is how to overcome the 'insurgents' without overreacting to the extent that the rebels may win more support for their cause. (In military parlance, this is known as the 'principle of minimum force'.) In general most of the theorists hold out little prospect for the dissidents obtaining very widespread support. 'Attempts at revolutions,' writes Clutterbuck, 'are less often rewarded with success than with a backlash.'[25] This may take the form of increased repression by the state, or, according to Clutterbuck, of an outburst from the 'silent majority': 'The danger of overreaction by the government, however, is not the only danger, nor even the worst danger. Should the government seem unable or unwilling to maintain law and order, a segment of the population may take the law into its own hands, and this can be far worse than government repression.' He also discusses the possible effects of a high rate of in-

---

* In Los Angeles, too, the police are being specially trained to deal with food riots. In January 1974, Police Commander Frank Brittel explained the need for such training: 'Food riots,' he said, 'might be more difficult to handle, because of the emotions involved.'

flation. He concludes that working-class militancy could result in 'the kind of desperation which leads to violence and backlash. The worst inflation of this century threw up its most evil and destructive leader – Adolph Hitler.' He seems to imply that a strong fascist movement could arise in Britain. As we have seen, this is a woefully inadequate account of the roots of fascism, but the parallel with Hitler has been widely touted. Should the incidence of terrorism decline to the extent that it is no longer a plausible 'threat', it may be that the 'threat of fascism' argument could be used to 'justify' the need for military intervention.

Counter-Revolutionary Strategy

The most coherent publicly available account of military strategy for dealing with internal unrest is Kitson's *Low Intensity Operations*.[26] The author is a former head of the School of Infantry at Warminster in Wiltshire, and has been promoted to the position of Major-General since the publication of his book. In January 1976, he took over the position of GOC, 2 Div., BAOR. *Low Intensity Operations* is primarily an account of counter-revolutionary strategy in a rural setting. But the author's reference to Britain which we quoted above makes it clear that his aims in writing the book extend far beyond simply providing the Army with a manual for war in distant colonies.

An important aim of the book was almost certainly that of promoting the Army's 'new role' in dealing with internal dissent, as well as to initiate an open debate which would accustom the public to the idea that the Army might be used at home. The nature of the support which the book received indicated that it was not merely an expression of one person's views, but represented widespread Army opinion. The foreword was written by General Sir Michael Carver, then Chief of the General Staff. The book was defended in the House of Commons by the Tory Minister of State for Defence, Lord Balniel, who maintained: 'This book is written by a most experienced officer in counter-insurgency, and it is regarded as being of valuable assistance to troops who will have to operate in the field.'[27] A further measure of its importance may be seen from the way in which Kitson's ideas correspond closely with those put forward in the *Army Land Operations Manual*.

Kitson draws heavily on his experiences in a number of counter-insurgency campaigns – in Malaya, Cyprus and in Kenya (where fewer than one hundred whites were killed, in contrast to the slaughter of over 10,000 Kikuyu insurgents).[28] Our discussion here deals only with those parts more relevant to potential Army operations in Britain, and will be supplemented by examples from *ALOM*, and from other theorists.

Kitson distinguishes three stages in the counter-insurgency campaign: the Preparatory Period, the Non-Violent Phase, and Open Insurgency. Many types of operation are not limited to any one phase; we examine them here in the context of the stage in which they could first be used. It should also be noted that the phases cannot be rigidly distinguished from each other and that a campaign may not necessarily progress through them in strictly linear fashion.

The Preparatory Period

As its name implies, this is the period during which both sides make initial preparations for the outbreak of expected dissent. As far as the state is concerned, the security forces are strengthened and the law is used as the primary means of suppressing political and industrial activists. This is also the period when 'the process of tying civil and military measures together into a single effective policy' must begin.[29] Kitson believes that success against a unified revolutionary movement can be achieved only if the forces which are fighting it and the civil administration are themselves unified. At the national level, he advises the setting-up of a supreme body consisting of 'the head of the government together with the individuals controlling the most important departments of state such as Finance, Home Affairs and Defence'. He says that representatives of the armed forces should participate in preparations for counter-insurgency by the government. 'There is no danger of political repercussions to this course of action, because consultation can be carried out in the strictest secrecy.'[30] If there are no political constraints, command machinery should also be set up at the lower levels.

This stress on the integration of civil and military decision-making is one of the keynotes of *Low Intensity Operations*. (As we have seen, Kitson actually put this into effect at the lower levels in Northern Ireland.) Joint civil–military committees from the highest to the lowest level are only one aspect of this. There are many other ways in which future co-operation between Army, police and civil service can be facilitated by activities during the preparatory period. Take, for example, the civil–military seminars organized by such bodies as the Royal United Services Institute. These bring together influential members of the armed forces, the police, the Ministry of Defence, prominent right-wing politicians, academics and defence correspondents of national newspapers. A typical RUSI seminar held in 1971 was chaired by an Air Vice-Marshal. The panel consisted of Mr Geoffrey Johnson-Smith, then Under-Secretary of State for Defence; Jeffrey Vowles, a defence researcher; Enoch Powell (who, as the Chairman said, 'needs no introduction'); Professor Foot, Professor of Modern History at Manchester University; Sir John Waldron, then Commissioner of the Metropolitan Police; and Brigadier Thompson, Defence Correspondent of the *Daily Telegraph*. The topic under discussion: civil–military relations.

Another of the many seminars was held in secret in 1974 at Lancaster University. This time the subject was revolutionary warfare. The intention was 'to promote discussion between academic thinkers and serving officers on the practical problems in understanding revolutionary warfare'. The list of people who attended it reads like a north-western Army and police *Who's Who*, plus military experts in academia and journalism and the right wing of the Tory Party. The Army delegation was led by GOC, North-Western District. The police contingent included three Chief Constables and four Assistant Chief Constables; there were seven university professors, and the Tory Party was represented by William Deedes, a member of the Monday Club and editor of the *Daily Telegraph*. Also present was Robert Moss, correspondent on counter-insurgency for the

Economist. The topics discussed included the Clay Cross councillors, urban guerrillas, the SAS (Special Air Services) and the necessity for a 'third force'.[31]

Such seminars are undoubtedly valuable in ensuring that key sections of the security forces and of civil society develop a common understanding of their purpose and tactics, before the situation escalates out of the preparatory period. On an operational level, too, it is vital that the police and Army learn to work together.

A second of Kitson's main recommendations is the establishment of an effective system of intelligence designed to obtain a large volume of 'low-grade' information. Again, it is clear that this recommendation has been adopted in Northern Ireland.

Thirdly, Kitson stresses the need for a department of 'psychological operations' ('psyops'). Drawing on the works of Mao and other guerrilla writers, military theorists have long recognized that the crucial battle in any counter-revolutionary campaign is for the 'hearts and minds' of the people. *ALOM* recognizes that 'the communists* have evolved a technique of revolutionary warfare which relies mainly on popular support for its success'. According to the military theorists the Army must therefore attempt to turn support away from the guerrillas towards the government and armed forces – a strategy which has been referred to as 'Mao minus Marx'.[32] The most obvious way in which this can be achieved is by 'putting the government's point of view' at every opportunity. 'Extremists' in the unions are denounced, communists feature as the 'bad guys' in radio plays, and the government explains how 'humane' CS gas will avoid the use of guns.

Fourthly, the Army must be prepared psychologically and tactically for the possibility of intervention in Britain. Attempts must be made to 'foster a sympathetic attitude on the part of the troops towards the government',[33] a process which is achieved in part through the sort of propaganda outlined above. In addition, training in the preparatory period lays a heavy

ALOM uses 'communists' as a generic term for any kind of anti-government movement.

stress on the responsibility which needs to be given to individual soldiers if they are to adopt a policing role. As *ALOM* states, 'it is essential to train junior leaders of all arms [of the security forces] to make sound decisions and to act on their own'. It also recommends the 'training of all ranks in the art of deception and general security measures'.

The Non-Violent Phase

The name given by Kitson to this phase is somewhat misleading, since it is taken to include 'limited acts of violence' even extending to guerrilla war. *ALOM* divides this period up into two stages, the first being termed 'Active Resistance (Terrorism)' – which is taken to cover civil disobedience, disturbances, riots, strikes and lawlessness, as well as its more conventional meaning. (This would clearly cover a situation similar to the 1926 General Strike.) The second stage, the 'Insurgency Phase', is characterized by guerrilla warfare.

As already indicated, it is highly unlikely that mass actions in Britain would be led by guerrilla forces. Major strikes and political demonstrations are more likely to prevail here. Nevertheless, many of the measures which the theorists propose are equally applicable to any type of active dissent.

The aim of the government in this period is essentially to separate off the leaders from their base of support, either by psychological or physical means. The first may be achieved by the 'judicious promise of concessions'.[34] However, economic concessions may be difficult to grant in a period of economic crisis, and political concessions, too, may be difficult, as the government has found to its cost in Northern Ireland. Alternatively, in specific instances it may be thought tactically wrong to allow demonstrators or strikers to achieve their immediate goal. In any of these cases, the government will have to apply more direct methods to quell the protest. If at this stage the police are unable to cope, it will be necessary to bring in the Army, in the role of Military Aid to the Civil Power (MACP).

Many of the activities carried out by the security forces in the preparatory period will be continued in the non-violent stage, although it will be possible to conduct them in a much more open manner. Covert methods of information-gathering will continue, but in addition the security forces would probably be empowered to act more overtly, to stop people in the streets or detain them for interrogation, and to conduct house-to-house searches. Deane-Drummond blandly recommends that patrols must include 'movement across back gardens as well as roads and alleys'[35] – a standard procedure in Northern Ireland. *ALOM* recommends the introduction of curfews following 'serious incidents'. These will prevent movement while the searches are being carried out, as well as ensuring that further disturbances do not arise.

'Psyops' will also be stepped up, since the government will need to convince the population – and also the troops – that its actions are justified. In addition, the impression must be given that the government is firmly in control. According to *ALOM* the Army should hold displays and participate in local sporting and civic events. In addition, individual troops should be encouraged to perform 'spontaneous' acts of kindness. Thus *ALOM* recommends that the troops should exercise courtesy on the roads, give simple aid to individuals ('helping a fisherman with a damaged net') and show kindness to old people and children, and respect for religious leaders. This of course has the added advantage of encouraging the individual soldier to believe that he is fighting on the side of benevolence. In Northern Ireland the Army (under the direction of Kitson) initiated a system of community liaison officers – 'Mr Fixit' – to improve relations with the community.

On the other hand, 'psyops' will be directed against the enemy. One example of this is the black propaganda put out on the IRA. This has included forgeries of Provisional literature admitting that the army was winning the war, and posters which showed a defeatist approach. One cleverly designed copy of a Provisional poster which originally carried a silhouette of a gunman and the legend 'Victory '74' bore the additional words 'but not through the barrel of a gun' in the Army version. Another example of 'psyops' was the cut-price laundry service run by Army undercover agents. This not only gave the agents the ability to move in Catholic areas without suspicion, but also enabled them to carry out forensic tests on the clothing to see whether the owner had been handling firearms.

There have been a number of other incidents which cannot easily be explained away. One of particular importance is the explosion of two car bombs in Dublin in December 1972. This took place at a time when the Irish government was trying to push through new legislation extending police powers of arrest and detention – a Bill unpopular both with the opposition parties and with dissidents in the ruling party. The bombs resulted in two deaths and numerous injuries. The Bill was passed amid outraged cries of 'mad IRA bombers'. It was later discovered that the cars used for the bombings had been hired in the North by a man with a British accent. And only a few hours before the explosions an Englishman took a taxi from Dublin over one hundred miles to Enniskillen in the North. On arrival, he refused to pay, pulled a gun and ordered the driver to return to Dublin. Eight months later the taxi driver spotted his passenger at the Dundalk races. When the police were called, documents in his possession showed the man to be a Major Thompson of the British Army.[36] The evidence, while not conclusive, points strongly in the direction of Army involvement in the bombings.

Other, less direct forms of 'psyops' have been suggested by Deane-Drummond. He recommends that 'true stories can be put about on the methods and motives of the terrorists'. Presumably 'true stories' here encompasses the propaganda-oriented descriptions of revolutionaries cited above. *ALOM*, less concerned with propaganda, recommends that 'rumours can be spread by local agents', but warns that they may 'misfire' if used without caution.

After each of three major bombings in Britain, stories appeared in the press in which various Trotskyist groups were reported to have claimed responsibility. When people have eventually been brought to trial on each of these charges, none of the accused has ever had any connection with any Trotskyist organization. The source of the allegations is not known, but what is certain is that someone was keen to associate left-wing groups in Britain with the bombing campaign – and that their allegations were credible enough to be taken seriously by the national press and by radio and television authorities.

As we can see from this last episode, the media can be a very useful vehicle for 'psyops'. *ALOM* recognizes that 'the press properly handled is one of the government's strongest weapons'. Strict censorship is considered to be counter-productive, although in times of emergency, as *ALOM* points out, 'the government obviously cannot allow the publication of subversive propaganda'. Similarly, Crozier states: 'most people will normally accept the need for some restrictions in the interests of security'.[37] Deane-Drummond recognizes that 'the press generally give the police their backing'. This is hardly surprising since, as Robert Fisk of *The Times* found in Northern Ireland, if journalists don't play ball, the Army can make life very difficult. Fisk was followed by military intelligence, and his Army contacts were warned not to give him information. Deane-Drummond also recommends that, when necessary, 'information can then be selectively released to tell the people what is happening and help the security forces in their efforts in this situation. Some call this propaganda and a degree of censorship on the bad news is implied.'[38] Indeed, it seems that the BBC has already drawn up new plans to help ensure that its broadcasts do not conflict with 'The National Interest'.[39]

Media 'psyops', according to *ALOM*, include 'speeches by leading personalities, news commentaries, interviews and even ... such things as drama, musical or religious programmes'. Ever ready with useful advice, Deane-Drummond recommends that in order to give 'a much more rounded view of events' articulate spokespeople from all ranks of the Army should be allowed to give a personal view of events – providing of course that a 'certain amount of selectivity' is used in choosing the person concerned.[40] If these recommendations by the theorists are accepted, 'psyops' will be widely used in the 'non-violent' period. They are in essence only an extension of the 'government's point of view' on 'extremists' which is put over in the preparatory period.

When dealing with mass actions, the security forces must attempt to avoid reacting too harshly, since this may only increase popular support for the dissidents – a constant theme running through the writings of all the military theorists. However, the smaller the number of security force personnel, the greater will be the level of minimum force necessary. If disturbances are widespread Army and police resources may be stretched to such a degree that only a limited number of personnel would be available. Kitson calmly calculates that 'three or four times as many troops might be needed if they were restricted to using batons and gas as would be required if they were allowed to use small arms'.[41] The new riot-control technologies described later are a highly significant aspect of the armoury of the security forces precisely because they enable a relatively small number of forces to deal effectively with disturbances. In addition, the development of 'command and control' systems (also discussed in Part Four) achieves economy of resources by enabling the security forces to concentrate quickly at the scene of any disturbance, with the additional advantage that they may be in time to disperse it before it develops and becomes much more difficult to control.

The Phase of Open Insurgency – Armed Insurrection

The aim of activities in the first two stages is to prevent dissent escalating to the third stage, when, according to *ALOM*, 'the revolutionary movement assumes the form of a people's war against the government'. How this could ever arise in a country where the state's forces are 'protecting the interests' of the vast, silent majority is not of course explained.

According to Kitson, the main task at this stage is simply to find the enemy and to eliminate it. The careful attempts to retain the allegiance of the population having failed, the security forces may resort to direct harassment of the community as well as its leaders. (This aspect has featured prominently in the Army's strategy in Northern Ireland.) But in the event of the British state itself being threatened, it is unlikely that the military would have much difficulty finding the enemy; it will most likely be present in the form of a mass working-class movement. If the 'battle for hearts and minds' has been lost by the state to the revolutionaries, the government may well be faced with a mass workers' militia, including many of its own former troops. If the government still retains any degree of control, counter-guerrilla strategies and the type of technologies described in this book would on the whole be succeeded by conventional weaponry.

However, it should be noted that a number of armed workers' insurrections, if badly planned, can occur in succession without the situation being resolved in either victory or total political defeat. This is what happened in Germany between January 1919 and October 1923, when there were four such uprisings. In such cases there can be a rapid reversion to the previous stage.[42]

Military Theorists after Kitson

In *Low Intensity Operations*, Kitson assigned a central role to the Army in dealing with internal dissent. This was understandable for a number of reasons. Firstly, he had a sectional interest to defend. He was concerned to show that the Army had a coherent strategy for dealing with internal dissent. Secondly, in 1971 the Army actually *was* the only force equipped to deal with internal unrest. The police at the time were organized into 122 separate forces, with liaison between them dependent to a large extent on 'good-neighbour' relations. And they had no contingency plans even for dealing with large demonstrations. The then Metropolitan Commissioner of Police, Sir John Waldron, had distinctly antiquated views about the role of the military, which he expressed at one of the RUSI seminars: 'There is nothing I hate to see more than policemen wearing steel helmets and protective clothing rushing forward with sticks and tear gas ... if conditions became so bad that the marchers started to throw bombs at us, which is possible, I would have to call out the military; I would call them out for one purpose only, and that would be to kill.'[43] Thus the debate at that time was centred round the question of whether a situation which it was beyond the power of conventional police forces to cope with *could* ever arise. Those who thought it could tended to agree with Kitson that the Army would lead the moves to restore law and order, as it had done in Northern

Ireland. Among those who apparently supported Kitson's view was Brigadier Thompson, defence correspondent of the *Daily Telegraph*. At the same RUSI seminar in 1971 he maintained: 'I do not believe that we can say that we will not have situations arising which are beyond the control of the police in this country, and this must be thought out beforehand with the chairmen of the local security councils.'[44]

Before long the focus of the debate shifted; the rapidly deteriorating economic situation made widespread unrest seem an increasingly likely possibility, and the discussion now came to centre round the question of *which* of the security forces should be used to contain it. Sir Robert Thompson, one of the world's most influential counter-insurgency experts, had always strongly maintained that as far as possible the police should be equipped to take on a counter-insurgency role.[45] By 1973, Brigadier Thompson had also come round to this way of thinking. In another of the RUSI seminars[46] he said: 'the military may have to intervene and must be prepared to intervene, but God help us if they have to; this eventuality must be kept as far away as possible by having the right police forces.' The government evidently reached the same conclusions.

When Waldron retired in 1972, he was replaced as Metropolitan Commissioner of Police by Sir Robert Mark. Since then, as part of the reorganization of local government the police have been drastically regrouped into a smaller number of forces. But Mark himself has also had a profound effect upon the police force and he has adopted a much more political role than his predecessor. His attitude to political demonstrations is well known. In March 1975, for instance, he claimed that the police had shown 'excessive tolerance' in dealing with demonstrators. In future, if necessary, they must be prepared to 'meet force with force'.[47] Since Mark took over, a number of special squads have been set up and equipped to deal with militant industrial action and major demonstrations. In fact, as we shall see in the next chapter, the police are gradually developing the ability to perform many of the functions which were previously the sole province of the Army. Before examining the reasons for this policy, we shall look briefly at the alternative forces which could be called on by the government: private armies, a 'third force', and the Army and police reserves.

During the summer of 1974, a good deal of publicity was given to the attempts by Colonel David Stirling and General Sir Walter Walker (among others) to set up 'citizens' armies'. These would 'provide on a volunteer basis the minimum manpower necessary to cope with the immediate crisis following a general strike or a near general strike in the knowledge that the government of the day must welcome our initiative'. However, far from welcoming these groups, the public reaction of both the government and police was mainly one of scorn. After all, the middle-class strike-breakers in the 1926 General Strike achieved little except to provide publicity for the government. With the increasingly skilled nature of jobs in the essential services and prospects of even fewer blacklegs prepared to do the work, the role outlined by Stirling above looks ridiculously ambitious. As one commentator put it: 'How many volunteers would one trust in the control room of a modern power station? It is not nowadays a question of willing hands to the stokehold. How many volunteers could even find their way to the lavatory in a crossbar telephone exchange – or even a strowger one come to that?'[48]

However, there was a much more important reason behind the government's antagonism. In a tense situation any attempt to introduce a group of middle-class strike-breakers would be much more likely to escalate the dispute than to cause demoralization and a return to work. More Machiavellian interpretations of the Stirling and Walker initiatives are possible – for example that the real purpose of these organizations was to push the *government* into making more preparations. Certainly their existence could be indirectly useful to the authorities. We referred earlier to the way in which the threat of reaction could come to replace the 'threat of terrorism' as the new demon of the ruling class. The mere existence of 'citizens' armies' could be used in future to justify this 'threat'.

Britain is the only major country in Europe which does not have a third force (an independent body between the conventional police and the Army, such as the CRS in France and the

Carabinieri in Italy) dealing specifically with riots and big demonstrations. Clutterbuck has examined the question of a third force in some detail.[49] The arguments which he cites in favour of such a force are, firstly, that it relieves the police of their 'most abrasive task', so enabling them to retain their relatively good public image. Secondly, since a third force is free of other routine duties it can be more readily mobilized than the regular police. And, finally, the existence of a third force reduces the likelihood that the Army would have to be called in. However, as we show in Chapter 12, the police themselves have been reorganized to include groups which fulfil all except the first of these conditions. Thus the 'grey area between the police and the military' no longer exists. This adaptation of the police force as an alternative to setting up a third force is supported by Clutterbuck. It has two major advantages. It avoids public debate which might rebound on the government; also, if serious disturbances made it necessary for the security services to work together, the absence of a third distinct chain of command would avoid many difficult problems of co-ordination.

The Territorial and Army Volunteer Reserve (TAVR) and the Special Constables could undoubtedly be used in a situation of conflict, but given their inevitably limited training they would be more likely to provide back-up services than to be used in the front line. *ALOM* also describes a role for the Specials of 'offensive patrolling against insurgents ... [and] static defence of vital utility installations against sabotage'. One important feature of these reserve forces is their ideological commitment. Together with a fairly high level of discipline this makes them a very reliable auxiliary arm of the security forces.

However, the main agents of state power will inevitably remain the police and the Army. In view of the difficulties involved in obtaining volunteers, the notion of reintroducing conscription has been mooted. But those who do advocate conscription are out on a limb – most Army officers and politicians would probably agree with the remark made by Lieut-Colonel Baynes: 'Anyone who could advocate conscription in Britain in 1970 other than as a devious step to provoke anarchy can hardly have considered the difficulties, and is certainly no friend of the armed forces.'[50] Following widespread unrest among conscripts in the French and Belgian armies in 1973-5, an editorial in *The Times* also questioned the reliability of conscripts: 'if they insist on holding demonstrations, writing pamphlets and forming trade unions, can they be trusted to fight or carry out military duties when ordered to do so? The question becomes especially pertinent if the Army is called upon to undertake tasks related to internal security.'[51] Conscription is very unlikely to feature as one of the elements of a 'National Plan' for internal defence.

Traditionally the Army and the police have been organized in radically different ways as a result of their contrasting objectives of military victory and 'the penetration and continual presence of central political authority through daily life'.[52] But the distinction between soldiers and the police is less sharp than it used to be. The Army's experience in Northern Ireland and other campaigns has given soldiers some experience in the role of 'armed policeman'. And the military-based high technology with which the police are now being equipped is simultaneously achieving their rapid militarization.

Why then has the government, with virtually no public debate, chosen to develop the police force rather than to rely on the Army in the way advocated by Kitson? To some extent the decision simply reflects an attempt to increase the total strength of all the security forces. But there are other, less immediately obvious reasons. Firstly, the Army has undeniably failed to control the situation in Northern Ireland, and there is an increased realization that the failure to build up the RUC has been a major error of the campaign. The troops are demoralized and there is a high incidence of desertion. In addition, there are signs that Army Command is dissatisfied with the government's handling of the situation (discussed in Chapter 8). The increasing politicization of Army officers could lead to a major rift between the government – particularly a Labour government – and the Army, especially if the Army were in overall charge of the security forces. Secondly, the introduction of the Army in a strike-breaking role – or, even more so, if they were called in to deal with pickets or demonstrators – could be highly provocative – a factor discussed in more detail in Chapter 8.

Finally, there is the danger that the troops themselves might mutiny and change sides in large numbers – as they did in Russia in 1917 and Germany in 1918. There are a number of factors which make the police more likely than troops to remain loyal to the government. The authority of police officers is 'original and not delegated'. This means that, as individuals, they are responsible for a large number of policy decisions, and bear a personal responsibility for ensuring that the law is upheld. Because of this they absorb ruling-class ideology in a very direct way. Soldiers, by contrast, are disciplined primarily to obey commands. In order to throw off the ideological basis which directs their actions they only have one link to break – to refuse to obey the commands of a superior.

The profound class divisions which exist in the Army would become even more apparent if troops were required to take action against the working class. In an interview with a *Sunday Times* reporter one Army colonel spelt out the dangers of this; 'We're wholly dependent on the trust between officers and men and it is inconceivable that we could maintain it if we were asked to do internal security duty during, say, strikes. The soldiers are sons of working-class fathers, most of whom are trade-unionists themselves.'[53] And the situation in France in 1968 provided a striking example of the dilemma facing governments. De Gaulle was forced to travel to Germany to General Massu (his old enemy), to be sure of finding enough men who could be relied upon to deal with demonstrators should the Army be needed. The French Army is largely conscripted, hence the severity of its problems. Nevertheless, *ALOM* clearly recognizes the danger of such a revolt. 'When a mutiny has taken place,' it states, 'it must be suppressed in the shortest possible time in order to prevent it spreading like a contagious disease.'

The police version of the new government policy is contained in a *Sunday Times* report in July 1975.[54] The report of course made no mention of the likelihood of mutiny by the troops, nor of the increasing politicization of the Army Command, nor of the political polarization which could be brought about by the use of troops to break mass pickets. The justification given for the policy of using police rather than troops was simply that the police had 'insisted that it was their job'. The report stated:

> Measures to involve the Army's élite Special Air Service in the alert against terrorism have been worked out behind the scenes in Whitehall. So have contingency plans for using troops to provide essential services during prolonged strikes in England and Northern Ireland. But an idea floated after the miners' strike three years ago, that the Army might in extreme circumstances help the police to deal with disorders such as violent picketing, has been firmly squashed. It was resisted strongly by police chiefs who insisted that it was their job. They argued successfully that they only needed troops in the more spectacular cases of terrorist activity. And they are increasing their independence of the Army for other terrorist threats by training more police sharpshooters with superior weapons ... more sophisticated troops are available to the police in the more serious terrorist attacks – so called Stage II operations *
> ... the new plans reinforce the primacy of the police in acting against civil disorder.

These new plans, of course, do not mean that the Army will not be used in countering working-class activity – merely that the police will be trained and equipped to deal with most of the early stages of a revolutionary upsurge. The 'police versus Army' debate among the military theorists has therefore been resolved in practice.

*The 'Active Resistance' phase referred to above.

12
Low-Intensity Operations in Britain

What happened at Aldershot, what happened at the Old Bailey, reminds us that what happens in Londonderry is very relevant to what can happen in London, and if we lose in Belfast we may have to fight in Brixton or Birmingham. Just as Spain in the thirties was a rehearsal for a wider European conflict, so perhaps what is happening in Northern Ireland is a rehearsal for urban guerrilla war more widely in Europe, and particularly in Great Britain.[1]

The author of these remarks is a Conservative MP and member of the right-wing Monday Club. He was introducing a discussion, not in political or business circles (although many such discussions take place in those milieux), but at a seminar of the Royal United Services Institute in 1973 attended by a bevy of brigadiers. His views, as we have seen in the previous chapter, are not by any means unique. Along with Kitson and the other theorists, he is recommending that the security forces in Britain prepare for new tasks. In this chapter we shall describe in greater detail the nature of these forces and the way they are adapting to the new political situation.* We shall also look at some of the 'rehearsals' they have been taking part in, using urban streets as their backdrop.

The Army
Many individual Army officers, politicians and businessmen certainly hold views similar to that quoted above. But in any situation short of military takeover or martial law, it is not up to them to decide whether or not to send troops on to the streets of Britain. It is the government which has ultimate responsi-

---
*The History and Practice of the Political Police in Britain, by Tony Bunyan (Julian Friedmann, 1976), covers in detail various areas to which we have referred only briefly.

bility for determining when and how the Army is used. At the pinnacle of the political and command structure of the armed forces stands the Prime Minister. Below him or her is the Cabinet and the Secretary and Minister of State for Defence. Below them is the Defence Council, comprising the Secretary and Minister of State for Defence, Parliamentary Under-Secretaries for the three forces, the Chief of the Defence Staff, four service chiefs and three civilian advisers. This body directly oversees the Ministry of Defence. The Army Board of the Defence Council keeps an eye on all British land forces: in Northern Ireland, in the UK, on the Rhine and elsewhere overseas.

The winding-down of military commitments overseas and the reassessment of the 'Soviet threat' has made the Army increasingly vulnerable. In recent years it has been forced to fight to maintain its position in the economic pecking order. In December 1974 (when its numbers dipped below 170,000), there were about 40,000 troops stationed in the United Kingdom (including Northern Ireland); about one-third of the total were stationed in West Germany, with the majority in the British Army of the Rhine (BAOR) and about 3,000 in West Berlin; and a total of about 17,000 serving in Hong Kong, the Far East and the Mediterranean. In addition, there were about 54,000 members of the Territorial and Army Volunteer Reserve (TAVR), about 8,000 members of the Ulster Defence Regiment (UDR) and 356,000 regular reserve forces.[2]

In September 1974, Lord Chalfont, that well-known champion of the armed forces, warned darkly that 'any decision to reduce the number of troops available at home is bound to have considerable implications, especially in the light of the current controversy about a possible breakdown of law and order'.[3] His voice was one of a chorus attempting to ward off the day when the Labour government would put into operation its manifesto pledge to cut defence spending. In 1975, claiming to honour that pledge, the government White Paper proposed a 38,000 cut in the armed forces by 1979, and cuts of more than 30,000 civilian jobs.[4] Most of the savings were to be made by further reduction in overseas commitments. It is possible that the government heeded Lord Chalfont and his like, because redundancies in the Army were to number only about 6,000, and these mostly among older officers. The Tribune group of MPs denounced the cuts as 'phoney' – and in this had the unlikely support of the *Economist*: 'The "cuts" are not reductions at all, even measured in constant 1974 pounds, but actual *increases*.'[5]

These cuts can be seen as a rationalization of the armed forces, so that they are better able to fulfil their new role. The cuts in overseas commitments would seem to bear this out. So does a brief examination of which forces are not affected by proposed cuts. In particular, the TAVR is to remain unchanged, 'with an enhanced operational role. It will be more closely integrated for training with the regular Army.'[6] Mr Mason, the Secretary of Defence, explained that 'with a smaller regular Army it would be an even more important and effective partner for the regular Army than before'.[7] Indeed, the Territorials are now considered important enough to advertise for members on television.

What is the reason for this sudden emphasis on the TAVR? In the first place, of course, Territorials are cheaper than regular soldiers. More important, they are a mobile reserve force which can be called up at any time. Proposed reorganization includes the formation of three new battalions in the North of England, which will not be earmarked for assignment to NATO, and will therefore be available to deal with internal disorder.

Some military experts have strong views on the importance of the TAVR. Brigadier Calvert thinks that 'possibly the best answer for the internal defence of Great Britain would be the true revival of the Territorial Army' (the predecessor of the TAVR).[8] In 1974, 600 TAVR members took part in stiff tests of their capacity for rapid mobilization. A senior warrant officer on the exercise told *The Times* that he would be 'quite happy' to take the men to Northern Ireland.[9] It is hardly likely that they will be asked to go. But it is more probable that the TAVR would play an important role in maintaining essential services inside Britain in the event of an emergency.

Although the establishment of the regular Army has been

reduced, it will still continue to have manpower problems for both officers and other ranks. It is likely that economic conscription will raise the level of rank-and-file recruitment, although it is unlikely to bring it up to establishment.* The problem of recruitment is increased by the refusal of some local Labour-controlled councils to allow it to take place in schools. In 1972–3, the Army spent £2.9 million on a massive recruiting campaign.

But at the officer level the Army has even greater problems. There is no better indication of the relative decline of the Army than the fact that it is no longer considered to be a desirable career for an ambitious young man. Rewards are much greater in industry, where the hierarchy is relatively less entrenched. The bright young lad from grammar school is forced to battle in the Army for promotion against the sons of the élite who have controlled it internally for generations. Of the Army's eight Field-Marshals, for example, seven have fathers or fathers-in-law who held top ranks in the armed forces.

In order to attract officer material, the Army has adopted a new approach. Full-page advertisements in the quality press throw down the gauntlet: 'ARE YOU A PATRIOT? ... Are you prepared to fight if necessary to prevent people taking control of this country by force or other unconstitutional means?' It has also enlisted the help of those who have most to gain from a strong Army. Eleven heads of big business each made a personal statement to the effect that 'three years as an Army Officer can equal three years at University'. The Army used it to sell the idea of Short Service Commissions.

A small professional Army, beset by recruiting problems and threatened by the economic axe, must find as many sources of support as possible from civil society. Links with big business through Short Service Commissions are one aspect of this. Discussing areas of mutual interest is another. In 1974, a columnist

---

*The connection between recruitment and unemployment rates was shown in *Labour Research*, December 1974; in 1974, the area of greatest Army recruitment was Liverpool and Manchester, which had a rate of unemployment of 7·3 per cent compared with a national average of 3·9 per cent.

of the *Investors Review* toured Army officers' messes in the North of England. The topic under discussion: 'What would the British armed forces do if faced with a stalemate political situation ... with the extreme left pushing for power?'[10] And the director-general of the Economic League (a group formed to counter 'subversives' in industry) spoke at a number of courses at Ministry of Defence establishments in 1973.[11]

Another area of civil society which the Army is keen to penetrate is the universities. They reap a number of benefits from close links with the academic establishment. In the first place, they can farm out research to distinguished scientists who would not wish to be employed by the Army on a full-time basis. Zoe Fairbairns has listed sixty-five British colleges and universities which receive funds from military sources (including the Ministry of Defence, the US Department of Defense and NATO) amounting to over £2 million per year.[12] Secondly, through various civil/military committees, they can stimulate interest in the Army with a view to recruitment. Thirdly, they can accustom students to accept the role of the Army through 'War Studies' or special courses – and, of course, forge useful links with the academic community.

In this and many other ways, the Army is trying to secure a place for itself in British society after a long period when its activities have been conducted in faraway places and it has lost contact with the population. Clearly this will be an advantage if it is to be used in operations inside Britain.

The Police

Like the Army, the British police force has been changing very rapidly over the last years. It has been reorganized to create larger, more centralized forces with a closer relationship to local government structures. It has increased in size. It has become a more mobile, more highly trained force with special units to deal with particular industrial and political problems. It has seen the rapid introduction of new technological aids to law enforcement. And its major spokesmen have come to play an increasingly important role in the political arena. In short, the police force is moving towards a situation in which it will be able to combat industrial and political action without calling in the Army to help.

One of the major events in the history of the British police force occurred in 1974 – the restructuring which took place as a result of local government reorganization. It affected nearly every force outside the Metropolitan area. The police in Birmingham, for example, were merged into a 7,000-strong force covering the West Midlands. And the Scottish police force was reorganized into eight Scottish districts. Outside London, each force is run by a Police Authority comprising local councillors and magistrates. Subject to the approval of the Home Secretary, it is responsible, among other things, for appointing a Chief Constable and his deputy, fixing the establishment of the force, and approving collaboration with other forces. In the Metropolitan area, the Police Authority is the Home Secretary, who appoints the Chief Officer, the Commissioner. The area is divided into twenty-two land divisions and one covering part of the Thames. Control is exercised through the four branches: 'A' Department, for administration and operations; 'B' Department for traffic and transport; 'C' Department for criminal investigation; and 'D' Department for organization and training.[13]

The size of the police force can be measured in two different ways. The first is establishment – the number of police that are considered necessary by local Police Authorities and the Home Secretary at any time. The second is strength – the number of officers serving at any time. Whichever way you look at it, the numbers have increased rapidly in the last ten years. In the period 1963/74, the police establishment rose by one-third. In the same period, the number of regular police in Britain rose from 90,000 to 112,400, a rise of almost 25 per cent. By December 1974, the total uniformed strength of the Metropolitan Police was 21,024,[14] and the strength of police outside the Metropolitan area in England and Wales was 75,941.[15]

The police force also employs civilians; in 1974, there were 9,028 working for the regular police.[16] But the police want to limit the number of civilians in the force – at the annual conference of the Police Federation (the house 'union' of the force) in 1974, a motion was passed calling for a limit to the number of civilians employed by a police authority because as the *Daily Telegraph* put it: 'The efficiency of the police service could be badly impaired if the civilian staff they employ decided to take industrial action such as a strike.'[17] One delegate claimed that an officer of the National and Local Government Officers' Association had threatened to 'black' the police if they scabbed during a union dispute.

The regular police are also assisted by volunteer Special Constables – Specials – who perform back-up tasks to free them from routine duties. In 1973, following a decrease in their number, a recruiting campaign was authorized by the Home Secretary. Between 1973 and 1974, the number of Specials in the Metropolitan area rose by over a quarter to more than 2,000.

By the end of 1974, the total number of Specials in England and Wales stood at 24,168,[18] though they were still very much under establishment. This renewed government interest in the Specials has largely developed in the period following the 1972 miners' strike and has been further stimulated by the growth of do-it-yourself private armies. Clearly the government would rather have the 'law-and-order' merchants where they will be subject to the discipline of the police force and so less likely to provoke independent confrontations with strikers. And of course, because they are volunteers, it is much cheaper to raise the establishment of the Specials than that of the regular police. (The Police Federation argued in 1974 that Specials were filling gaps in the professional ranks so that they could be used instead of the recruitment of regular officers, which would necessitate offering higher pay.[19]) But it is not likely that Specials will play a front-line role in countering internal unrest, although they have the same powers and duties as ordinary policemen. Their lack of training for this specialized task means that they will probably carry out support duties.

The growth in numbers of regular police and Specials is not the only indication that the police force is being strengthened. There has also been a considerable growth in public expenditure on the police. Between 1969/70 and 1973/4 this rose from £342 million to £588 million, an increase of 72 per cent.[20] Even more dramatic was the rise in expenditure on research and development: in the three years ending in 1972/3 the Home Office Police Scientific Development Branch increased its spending by 50 per cent and it was estimated that it should increase by 100 per cent by the end of 1973/4.[21] Despite this increase, the police still spend only a tiny proportion of their budget (about 0.25 per cent) on research, in comparison with the Army (which spends about 10 per cent). One of the reasons why this figure is so low is that the police can often obtain joint funding for projects with local authorities. The Metropolitan Police Central Integrated Traffic Control experiment (CITRAC – see Chapter 14) is one example of this: it is run jointly by the police and the Greater London Council.

Police expenditure on technological aids is likely to increase very rapidly over the next few years. In December 1974, the Home Secretary told Parliament: 'Chief constables had been urgently reviewing their requirements for equipment with the help of officers from the police scientific development department ... the equipment included metal detectors, devices for detecting explosives of various sorts, low-dosage X-ray equipment and other devices, the details of which it would not be in the public interest to reveal.'[22] The Chief Inspector of Constabulary listed many more projects in his 1974 Report, including 'development, testing and evaluation of equipment and techniques' for areas such as intruder alarms, night vision, optical aids, weapons lethal and non-lethal, and explosives and drugs detection.[23] And in October 1975 Scotland Yard provided two technicians and 'certain technical equipment' – apparently bugging apparatus and night-vision or low-light cameras – to the Irish police at the Dr Herrema siege. In the Metropolitan area, work is going ahead on a command and control system embracing one section of the force, and involving vehicle identification and control. We discuss some of these new technological developments in more detail in Part Four.

Another development which will enable the police to conduct counter-insurgency operations more effectively is the increasing centralization of police forces. The reorganization referred to above is only one aspect of this. The power of local police authorities has declined and the Home Office now exerts a powerful influence over local police forces. It pays 50 per cent of their costs, can enforce amalgamations of forces and its approval must be given before a Chief Constable is appointed.[24] And special centralized groups and squads are being set up which will reduce the decision-making powers of local forces still further. Those relevant to internal defence operations in Britain will be discussed later. Others include the Regional Crime Squad, which consists of nine forces covering the country under a national co-ordinator. It works in conjunction with local forces and consists of 'a highly mobile specialist force designed to deal with modern and well-organized mobile lawbreakers'.[25]

In the field of intelligence, too, there is a move toward centralization with the setting-up of the Police National Computer (see Chapter 13) and the collater system in local police stations by which all intelligence information is made easily accessible to other forces and to Scotland Yard. In fact, the logic of this trend is toward a national police force under the direct control of the Home Secretary. This could only be realized at a time of emergency, since it would be strongly resisted by many sections of the population. A typical view was expressed by one prospective Liberal parliamentary candidate: 'The question of who controls the police is basic to the civil liberties of the British. If central government gains control of the police forces and should some tyrannical party gain control of central government then the future would indeed be grim.'[26] Political expediency forces the government to retain the present structure of the police, at least for the near future. Nothing prevents it from strengthening the police force invisibly but inexorably.

The ability of the police to combat insurgency is going to depend to a large extent on the effectiveness of its intelligence forces. Each force has a criminal investigation department, which deals with ordinary crime. But for political offenders, a political police is needed – the Special Branch.

The Special Branch

'The Special Branch is the best organization to be responsible for all internal security' because it is part of 'a state organization reaching out into every corner of the country and will have had long experience of close contact with the population'. This is the view of Sir Robert Thompson, the counter-insurgency expert. He could also have added other powerful arguments in favour of the Special Branch. For instance, it is very difficult to find out what it is up to. Its budget is secret. The Home Secretary, Henry Brooke, once gave this Catch-22 answer to questions in Parliament about the Special Branch: 'The Security Service is, after all, a secret service. That is part of its essence. Its cost is borne on the secret vote and one must therefore bear in mind that the number of parliamentary questions which could be put to me with any hope of an answer being properly given is very limited.'[27] And of course good intelligence saves on vital manpower, which is especially important when the police is under strength. In October 1974, after bomb attacks on MPs, Scotland Yard issued a statement saying that it did not have sufficient manpower to provide each MP with bodyguards. 'Instead ... we have decided to increase our squads assigned to infiltrating these various terrorist groups.'[28]

In combating the IRA campaign in Britain in the 1970s, the Special Branch has in a sense come full circle. It was set up in 1884 as an offshoot of the CID to deal with the Irish republican bombing campaign of 1883–5, which culminated in an explosion in the crypt of the House of Commons. It was then known as the Special Irish Branch. When this campaign ended, the Branch turned its attention to the European anarchist movement, but it was not until the end of the First World War that its name was changed to Special Branch. Today it is still nominally under the control of the CID, but it is operationally under the control of the Department of Intelligence (Home Office).

There are Special Branch officers attached to almost every police force in Britain – the Metropolitan area has the largest division, numbering about 300. They carry out three basic duties: protecting leading political figures, visiting heads of state and so on (this is the responsibility of a sub-section called the Special Branch Personal Protection Squad); gathering information on 'subversive' or terrorist organizations and investigating offences against the security of the state; and keeping watch on sea and airports for criminals, making inquiries into illegal immigrants and so on. Officially, Special Branch officers have the same powers as other police officers, and are recruited after serving three to four years in the uniformed branch. All members of the branch are trained marksmen, and receive regular practice at a remote range in Essex. They must also speak at least one foreign language.[29] The Branch is divided into specialist sections concentrating on the major political issues of the day, such as the Middle East, illegal immigration, and Ireland (the Irish Squad was reported in 1974 to have about seventy members). A Portuguese expatriate in London has told us that he received frequent visits from the Special Branch, who were clearly collaborating with the Portuguese Secret Police (PIDE) before the demonstrations protesting at the visit to London of the Portuguese dictator Caetano in 1973. Similar arrangements are known to exist with the South African BOSS and presumably with the secret police of other 'friendly' countries.

The major activity of the Special Branch is intelligence-gathering. Its methods range from the traditional, such as the use of informers and infiltrators, to the most sophisticated applications of communications interception. In 1975, *The Times* published a picture of a bugging device 'believed to be used by the Special Branch'. It was smaller than a twopenny piece. Not unexpectedly, *The Times* reported: 'Although no figures are issued by the government, it is widely understood that there has been a big increase in recent years in the amount of surveillance by the Special Branch.'[30] As well as installing and monitoring bugging devices, the Special Branch frequently taps phones and opens mail. The Home Office refuses to substantiate or deny any estimates of the extent of these practices.

Once the information obtained by these and other methods is collated, it is stored on files at regional Criminal Records Offices or at New Scotland Yard. The NCCL and other sources have estimated that the Special Branch maintains at least two million files – which could easily include the membership of every extra-parliamentary political group of the left and right.

The Special Branch also makes extensive use of cameras to obtain information. An ex-member of the Essex force told the NCCL that 'photographers are present at all demos, and photographs are kept and compared, hence the identification of the so-called "flying squads" of demonstrators'. They seem to be rather indiscriminate about whom they catch in the surveillance net. Tom Litterick, MP for Selly Oak, complained to the West Midlands police force about being photographed on a demonstration. If the Special Branch spend their time photographing MPs and other such subversives, then the estimate of 2 million files is probably on the conservative side.

The activities of the Special Branch are not confined merely to surveillance of members of political groups. The recent growth in trade-union militancy has been matched by a growth in its involvement in industrial disputes. In June 1974, questions were asked in the Commons about the presence of Special Branch photographers at a nurses' demonstration against low pay. In reply, the Home Secretary implied that the officers had been remarkably restrained – they had indeed been present at the demonstration with cameras, but no photographs had been taken![31] In April 1974, the Special Branch were involved in a strike at Strachan's factory in Hampshire. The management passed information to them about certain workers who were 'sitting in'. In return, detectives told the manager that the strike was 'politically motivated' and controlled by 'outside forces'. They identified three ring-leaders and three 'sleepers' who could be 'activated' at any time.[32] 'Special Branch sources' in London told the *Daily Telegraph* that 'such investigations throughout the country were not unusual. They constituted an important part of detectives' work.'[33]

This sort of activity is clearly not in line with the statement that same year by the Home Secretary that 'the Special Branch has no interest or power to intervene in trade disputes as such'.[34] By the end of the year, so many MPs had tabled questions on the subject that the Under-Secretary of State at the Home Office was obliged to clear up some of the 'misconceptions' about the Special Branch: 'It is fully recognized [she said] in the police service that Special Branch officers should concern themselves in industrial disputes no more than is necessary for the maintenance of law and order and for the acquisition of any necessary intelligence on any subversive background to disputes.'[35] We can only assume that taking photographs of nurses on a demonstration is part of 'the acquisition of any necessary intelligence on any subversive background to disputes'.

The use of political police in industrial disputes is not by any means new. The Attlee administration in 1945–51 established a separate squad of the Special Branch to investigate communists in the trade unions and to report on unofficial strikes. Indeed, Labour administrations seem to have made extensive use of the political police to keep watch on the very people whose interests they claim to represent! Take Harold Wilson, for example, in the 1966 seamen's strike. He records in his memoirs of that period that the Special Branch kept close watch on the movements of the seamen's leaders, and informed him that they were visited by members of the Communist Party.[36]

As the economic crisis deepens and the level of trade-union militancy rises, we can expect that the Special Branch will step up its activities inside the trade-union movement. They are likely to pay particular attention to those political groups which are building an industrial base. And when it comes to giving information to the press blaming industrial militancy on 'politically motivated infiltrators', the secrecy of the Special Branch is not so carefully preserved. This newspaper report on the Strachan's dispute is typical: 'The political group identified by the police were the International Socialists. The IS has a local branch in Portsmouth which has been distributing literature to the men sitting-in on how to claim maximum social security benefits'.[37] And of course, the police don't have to reveal their sources: any information they give to the press must by definition be reliable!

Compared with internal security organizations of most other countries, the Special Branch is very small and has relatively few resources. But there are plenty of private organizations which are only too eager to give information to the political police. One of these is the Economic League, which was founded in 1950 as a limited company. The main donors in 1972 included British Leyland, GKN, Slater Walker and the Midland and National Westminster Banks.[38] It acts as a clearing-house for industrial troubles with workers, and publishes information sheets giving names of the more prominent militants and their political affiliations. Other organizations which maintain blacklists on 'subversives' or circulate information sheets on suspected militants include Industrial Research and Information Services, Common Cause Ltd and Management Information Service.

One of the major targets of the Special Branch in recent years has been the Irish community in Britain. Organizations and individuals (many of them opposed to guerrilla tactics) have been under heavy surveillance amounting sometimes to continual harassment. By July 1974, the NCCL had received so many complaints about this that they printed special forms for complainants to fill in. Sinn Fein has also amassed its own files; records typically describe this sort of incident: 'Raids take place early in the morning or very late at night. Doors and furniture are damaged. The number of raiders is usually far out of proportion to the number of people being raided. Uniformed officers are often posted outside the premises being raided, so that an entire neighbourhood knows what is going on.'[39]

There is one remarkable case which reveals clearly the extent of Special Branch operations against the Irish community in Britain: the Lennon Affair. Kenneth Lennon was an Irishman living in Luton who worked for the Special Branch as a paid informer, passing on information about the activities and membership of the local Sinn Fein Branch. There are two conflicting versions of the Lennon story. One is contained in a statement given to the NCCL by Lennon himself, three days before he was murdered. The other is a report on Special Branch involvement in the case, written by Deputy Commissioner Starritt. Both throw new light on the methods used by the Special Branch.

Lennon claimed in his statement to the NCCL that he was blackmailed by the Special Branch into infiltrating the Luton Sinn Fein and that threats were made against members of his family in Ireland. Starritt wrote that, on the contrary, Lennon had approached the Special Branch and offered to become an informer because he desperately needed money. (His wife was seriously ill in hospital.) The real facts will probably never be known. But if Lennon was in it for the money he certainly made a bad deal. Until his death he received a total of £128 from the Metropolitan Police Branch Information Fund. And it is now known that the Special Branch *were* in possession of the information that Lennon claims was used to blackmail him at the time he started work for them.[40]

The Special Branch has never denied that it uses infiltrators to obtain information on political groups. To Lord Widgery, in his appeal court judgement on the case of Lennon's accomplices, who claimed that he had trapped them into an armed robbery, this type of activity is the very stuff of which British justice is made: 'We think it right in these days of terrorism that the police should be entitled to use the effective weapon of infiltration. It must be accepted today that it is a perfectly lawful police weapon in proper circumstances.'[41] He did not elaborate on what those 'proper circumstances' might be. But he was in no doubt that the Special Branch had acted correctly in this case.

There is also strong evidence to suggest that Lennon was not simply an informer and infiltrator, but acted as an agent provocateur – with the full knowledge of the Special Branch. He claimed to have 'set up' an armed robbery involving three other members of Sinn Fein. The Luton Three, who were convicted of the robbery (and whose appeal was dismissed by Lord Widgery) maintained that Lennon had supplied the guns. They said that he had taunted them with being 'Glory boys afraid to form a military unit'.[42] (The Sinn Fein is the political wing of the Provisional IRA and does not usually get involved in military action.)

After the imprisonment of the Luton Three, Lennon was a prime mover in a plot involving Sinn Fein to get them out of

Winson Green Jail. While reconnoitring the jail, Lennon and another Sinn Fein member were picked up by the Birmingham police and charged with conspiracy to 'effect the escape of person or persons unknown'. A series of manoeuvres by the Special Branch followed. They highlight the relationship between the British political police and the legal establishment. After consultation with the Deputy Director of Public Prosecutions, the Special Branch decided that it would look too suspicious if the case against Lennon were simply dropped. Starritt reported that the representatives of the Director of Public Prosecutions 'expressed a complete understanding of the situation'. They were confident that, with the 'help' of the senior prosecuting counsel, a jury verdict of 'not guilty' would be returned on Lennon. And so it was: 'In fact, cross-examination of the police witness was minimal and the account of the interviews with the two defendants were virtually unchallenged ... The jury returned verdicts of guilty against Mr O'Brien and not guilty against Mr Lennon.'[43]

The Special Branch 'protection' of Lennon in this case — although covert — nevertheless made him a target for the IRA, who would naturally be suspicious of the outcome of the case. Realizing this, he fled to London, where the Special Branch gave him some money, but did not offer him protection — despite the fact that he expressed to them his fears about returning to Luton. The Special Branch maintain that the last contact they had with Lennon was on 9 April 1974. The next day he made the statement to the NCCL. His parting words to NCCL legal adviser, Larry Grant were: 'I would not be surprised if the Special Branch tried to do me in and make it look like an IRA job.' Three days later his body was found in a Surrey ditch. There were two bullet holes in the back of his head.

At the inquest on Lennon's death, the coroner refused a request by the lawyer acting for Lennon's family that the two Special Branch officers who had directed Lennon should be called to give evidence. The jury returned a verdict of 'murder by person or persons unknown'. Nor surprisingly, Starritt found that 'the suggestion that Special Branch were directly or indirectly responsible for his death has not, in my opinion, any basis in fact'.[44]

The Starritt report was the first public investigation into the Special Branch in its ninety-year history. It shows that we cannot rely on the police, the law or the government to lift the veil of secrecy which covers its activities.

The secrecy surrounding the other British intelligence services is even more impenetrable. MI5 (Military Intelligence 5), now renamed DI5 (D for Defence), and officially known as the 'Security Service', is responsible for internal security and counter-espionage. Arrests for MI5 are made by the Special Branch. MI6 (or DI6), the Secret Service, is responsible for foreign intelligence. The third major branch of British intelligence is the military wing, headed by the Director General of Intelligence. Until recently, the Director General and the heads of MI5 and MI6 were the coequal chiefs of British intelligence, co-ordinated by the Joint Intelligence Committee. But it was reported in mid-1975 that the services were to be reorganized and placed under a single head, Sir Maurice Oldfield, who would be directly responsible to the Prime Minister.[45] No official information is publicly available on funding for these services.

With changes taking place in the structure and method of operation of the security forces, the question of intelligence-gathering has, according to the *Sunday Times*, become a matter of debate.* The debate revolves around whether Britain needs a National Security Agency to co-ordinate the Special Branch, DI5 and DI6. Army chiefs, on the one hand, appear very much in favour of an integrated intelligence service to provide 'high-grade warnings and briefings to ministers and the civil contingencies committee'. Police and other security experts, on the other hand, say that such a merger would not work because of the different roles and modus operandi of the respective forces. With the stress on integration and convergence between the police and Army, it seems not too unlikely that the Army view,

*This information appeared only in the (earlier) Manchester edition of the *Sunday Times* of 13 July 1975. The London edition, for some reason, omitted any mention of it.

if correctly reported by the *Sunday Times*, will eventually win.

Internal Defence in Practice

'The whole period of the miners' strike has made us realize that the present size of the police force is too small. It is based on the fundamental philosophy that we are a law-abiding country. But things have now got to the state where there are not enough resources to deal with the increasing numbers who are not prepared to respect the law.'[46] This was the opinion of Brigadier Brian Watkins of the Army General Staff, after the 1972 miners' strike. This period was a turning-point for internal defence planning in Britain. After the strike, Prime Minister Heath set up a Cabinet Committee under Lord Jellicoe to make a full inquiry into threats to public order. Following the massacre of Israeli athletes at the Munich Olympics later in the year, the terms of reference of the Committee were extended to cover every possible threat to public safety. In the three years which followed, the security forces, the Home Office and the Ministry of Defence re-examined their plans for dealing with internal disturbance, from strikes to urban guerrillas.

The main outcome of these discussions has been to encourage a convergence of Army and police roles. The Army would be trained in internal operations where superior fire-power was needed, for instance in a hi-jack, or bomb attack. The police, meanwhile, would increase their independence of the Army by training more men in weapons handling with superior weapons. They would get more practice in guarding 'vulnerable points'. And they would learn to work together with the Army if necessary.

The result of this new approach is that the government has greatly increased its capacity for a 'flexible response' if there is any threat to the state. There are three major routes by which this has been achieved. Firstly, plans have been made for the use of existing specialist Army squads, and new police specialist squads have been set up. Secondly, there is now a much greater degree of co-operation between the Army and police in training and joint investigation. Thirdly, the Army and police have actually conducted joint exercises, and troop units have practised in urban areas inside Britain. We shall discuss each of these new developments in turn.

In 1975, it was reported that there is now a special desk in the Ministry of Defence Operations Room where 'panic buttons' can summon the Special Air Services (SAS) at Hereford or any other specialist unit.[47] The SAS is effectively the 'dirty tricks' unit of the British Army. Its functions, according to the *Army Land Operations Manual*, include the setting-up of 'assassination parties' and liaising with 'friendly guerrilla forces' operating against 'the common enemy'. It is notorious for its activities in Northern Ireland, where it is widely believed to have been involved in several assassinations.* Another Army unit which might be called in is the Bomb Disposal Squad. Most of the other specialist squads are drawn from the police. In Britain, the nearest equivalent to the continental 'third force' is the Metropolitan Police Special Patrol Group (SPG). This was set up in 1965 by a Labour Home Secretary to provide 'a highly mobile force ... which can be ordered at short notice to give saturation coverage to an area'.[48] It is equipped to reinforce any police force in the country, supposedly to look for stolen property or missing persons; but, because it is readily available and mobile, public order work, especially crowd control, forms a large part of its duties. All members of the Special Patrol Group receive weapons training.

Since the appointment of Sir Robert Mark as Commissioner of the Metropolitan Police in April 1972, the Special Patrol Group has played an increasingly important role. From mid-October until the end of that year, units of the SPG patrolled central London 'in anticipation of possible terrorist activities'. One unit of the SPG was constantly armed for protection duties, providing a twenty-four-hour back-up to the armed police who permanently guard embassies. (This function is likely to be taken over by the new Diplomatic Protection Group.) It was this unit of the SPG which took part in the

*The presence of the SAS in Northern Ireland was belatedly 'announced' by the British Government in January 1976, as a propaganda response to right-wing demands for tougher action.

India House incident in 1973, when two young Pakistanis armed with toy guns staging a protest against Indian treatment of prisoners-of-war were shot and killed.

By 1974 the number of SPG men had doubled since 1965 to 200, forty of whom were permanently armed. They stopped 13,001 people in the street in 1974, a decrease of 9 per cent from 1973; but the number of vehicles stopped and searched rose by 40 per cent, to 28,303.[49] In September 1975, the SPG provided much of the manpower for the occupation of the Workers Revolutionary Party Education Centre in Derbyshire – the biggest political raid since the war. But their best-known action was at the June 1974 Red Lion Square demonstration in London, which resulted in the first death at a demonstration in Britain for over fifty-four years. The inquiry into the demonstration, headed by Lord Justice Scarman, brought to light many aspects of SPG activity.

The order to send the SPG into the demonstration was given by Deputy Assistant Commissioner John Gerrard – a ubiquitous fellow of whom we shall have more to say later. One SPG officer told the court that his unit cut through the demonstrators 'like a knife through butter' (a simile to catch the imagination, unless you happen to be the butter). Other witnesses described how the SPG pursued a group of demonstrators down a side-street and attacked them without warning. Under cross-examination, one of Mark's deputies, the Chief of 'A' Department, which is known to liaise with both the SPG and the Special Branch, admitted that the SPG took part in joint exercises with the Army. He said that they had been taking place more regularly over the past year.

Forces similar in structure and function to the SPG have also been set up in other parts of England. Essex police have set up a 'Support Unit', which was described as a full-time armed unit of hand-picked men with over four or five years service in the police force. They carry .38 Smith and Wesson pistols, and can give 'professional service to any division in Essex, from a drugs raid to a bomb scare. They are also skilled in crowd control and marksmanship.' Their duties include drug raids, assistance at demonstrations and industrial disputes.[50]

In October 1974, it was disclosed that 300 men, mainly under the age of thirty-five and single, were being recruited from the Greater Manchester Police Force to handle 'political and industrial unrest'. These men can be called off the beat at any time to provide a 'mutual support unit' in response to calls for help from surrounding areas. Although the Home Office refused to discuss how many such units there were in England, the Greater Manchester police have said that the scheme is 'in common with all other police forces throughout the country as part of a mutual aid arrangement'.[51]

Concern about the handling of the 1972 miners' strike centred on the inability of the police to handle the mass picket at Saltley coke depot. Should such an incident occur again, the police have made sure that they will be in a better position to handle it. In September 1972, in the wake of the Saltley, Shrewsbury picket and Pentonville Five incidents, Sir Robert Carr, then Home Secretary, announced that he would be discussing with local Chief Constables how to combat 'violence and intimidation' in industrial disputes. As a result of these consultations, a national police intelligence unit was set up in November 1973, to co-ordinate the handling of strikes. Its official title is the 'Anti-Picket Squad'; its function is to arrange for local forces to co-operate in providing picket squads so that reinforcements can be sent at short notice. 'Scotland Yard maintains a central picket control branch under a Deputy Assistant Commissioner where two sergeants collect and co-ordinate information on disputes, militant trades-unionists, flying pickets, etc. and send this out to local forces.'[52]

The head of the Anti-Picket Squad is Deputy Assistant Commissioner John Gerrard. He had had special training in police–Army operations and anti-picket tactics: in 1971 he attended the US Police National Academy in Atlanta, Georgia, where the CIA send secret police to be trained for operations in Latin America. The local anti-picket squads consist of regular policemen who have received special training in riot control and 'toe and wedge' tactics 'based on the Army's experience in Ulster'.[53]

Government concern about militant picketing, already considerable after the 1972 miners' strike, rose to new heights during the run-up to the 1974 miners' strike. Between December 1973 and February 1974 the Tory government's military and para-military preparations for a possible showdown became widespread. It is worth listing just a few of these to show how far the government was able to take this process, even in a period without open conflict, without the media taking much notice:

(1) In Yorkshire alone there was a squad of 800 police on permanent stand-by throughout the strike. 'A special unit kept watch on known extremists in such areas as Stainforth, near the Hatfield Main colliery, and Cadeby, near Mexborough. Gregory [the Chief Constable] says that he has identified possible trouble areas and a plan of action has been worked out.'[54] The plan apparently included equipping the West Yorkshire police with 'riot kits'. And London police are reported to have been issued with extensive riot-control equipment after the confrontation started in December.

(2) The moribund local-government 'Home Defence and Emergency Planning Committees' were drastically expanded. The Greater London Council's Committee, formerly one man and a secretary, had its complement expanded to a team of thirty-six. These are the committees which are supposed to improve local-government preparedness for a war emergency. They also co-ordinate plans for peace-time emergencies.

(3) Helmets Ltd of Wheathampstead (Herts.) was given special exemption from the three-day-week restrictions. Their product – 500 riot helmets a week, for the Army.

(4) In late 1973 a special appeal was made for railway workers to join the Territorial Army Volunteer Reserve, so that they could assist in a 'national emergency'. Just before Christmas, soldiers going on leave were warned that all heavy army goods vehicle drivers might be recalled for duty during their leave period.

(5) Midlands Electricity Board devised a computer-updated identity card (based on pay slips) which 'could prove useful to the board in industrial disputes when the right of pickets

and others to enter premises are in question'. (A crucial weapon of the miners in the 1972 strike had been the picketing of power stations.) The occasion of the blowing-up of an Army bus was used by Ian Gilmour, then Secretary of Defence, to fly a kite for the issue of identity cards throughout Britain.

Gerrard co-ordinated all the anti-picket activity from his specially equipped operations room at Scotland Yard, where he was kept in touch with Chief Constables. The Home Office also had a Telex hotline to the Chief Constables to pass on policy advice. It was a model military-style operation.*

Training for Internal Defence

The Army, as we have seen, has had plenty of experience in counter-insurgency campaigns since the Second World War. As long ago as 1971, Kitson claims that over 50 per cent of students at Sandhurst chose the course option of 'guerrilla and revolutionary warfare' rather than the four other available options. The Army's most recent and continuing campaign in Northern Ireland has added knowledge of how to fight against urban guerrillas. Every regiment of the British Army has now had tours of duty there. Before each tour a military unit has two months' internal security training. This consists of specialist training – in search, intelligence, and photographic and sniping techniques – as well as non-specialist training in crowd control, riot drills and ambushing and patrol drills.

The 'warm-up' culminates in two weeks of concentrated training at centres with special facilities, such as the new urban warfare school in Hythe. This 'urban tactical training' includes

* In the *Sunday Times* (22 February 1976) it was revealed that in December 1973 Heath alerted the alternative government that can take over in Britain in an extreme national emergency. The secret bunkers which house the regional seats of government were prepared and regional commissioners (see p. 147) were put on standby. It was also pointed out that the detailed planning initiated after the miners' strike of 1972 had included the setting-up of the 'Civil Contingencies Unit', a group of very high-level civil servants headed first by Lord Jellicoe and then by Jim Prior, Leader of the House. Its task was to plan the reduction of the potential economic and social impact of a strike by a limited but crucial group of workers such as the miners, power workers or water workers.

a series of simulated peaceful demonstrations, full-blooded riots and 'fire-fights'. The last of these involves the 'Close-Quarter Battle (Urban)', which takes place in a network of streets, complete with houses, shops, cars, anti-Army slogans, etc. (Such mock villages have been claimed to exist at Dungeness,* at Imber in Wiltshire, and at Larzac in France.) Instructors, using remote-control consoles, can subject the patrol to a barrage of crowd noises, flashing headlights, bomb blasts and pop-up sniper targets. Thought is being given to the development of a laser fire simulator, for even greater realism.[55]

In the past, the Army has had considerable experience in performing at least one function as assistance to the civil power: strike-breaking. In 1910, troops were sent in to Tonypandy to protect imported scab labour during the miners' strike; in 1911 practically the whole Army was used in the railway strike; in the General Strike of 1926, although police and special constables were used to protect scabs, troops were standing by.

Whereas before the Second World War troops were used mainly to protect blacklegs, after the war they were used repeatedly as blacklegs themselves. 'During the period of the Attlee government (1945-50) the Army was used on no less than nine separate occasions for this purpose.'[56] This pattern has continued right up to the present day. During the 1972 dock strike, the Army was used to clear rotting fish; it was used in the Glasgow firemen's strike in 1973; and again in Glasgow in the dustmen's strike of 1975.

When it comes to public order, however, the Army has less British experience. The last time it was called out in a public-order capacity was in 1919 during the police strike in Liverpool. Two people were killed by Army fire on that occasion. But public order is not likely to be a task for the Army, at least in the early stages of an internal defence campaign. Current Army and police theory seems to indicate that it would be the responsibility of the police. And they are already preparing for such a task. The police are rapidly incorporating new types of training so that they will be able to handle internal disturbances both independently and, if necessary, in co-operation with the Army.

*Presumably associated with the urban warfare school at Hythe.

Low-Intensity Operations in Britain   139

In 1968, the Chief Inspector of Constabulary reported that for the first time arrangements had been made for a police officer to attend a six months' course at the joint services staff college. Since then, senior police officers have attended Army colleges every year. In return Ministry of Defence police attend detective courses run by the police; the number attending such courses rose from twelve in 1973 to twenty-two in 1974.[57] In addition, almost every British Chief Constable has had a short training stint in Northern Ireland.

The police also run numerous training courses both centrally and on a local level. The 1974 Report of the Chief Inspector of Constabulary gave a detailed breakdown of the numbers attending such courses as Drugs and Computers. It was more reticent when it came to those more relevant to our subject: 'a number of local courses on such subjects as the handling of firearms ... were held.' There was a sharp increase in the number of courses on crowd control.[58] Police tactics for crowd control are looked at in detail in Chapter 15. Here we shall concentrate on police training for firearms handling. It provides us with dramatic evidence for our thesis of the convergence of the police and Army.

It is a common boast of the British that, in contrast with other less law-abiding nations, they do not require an armed police force. The reality is fast becoming far removed from this conventional truth. Some police officers, including many members of the Special Branch and the other specialist squads described earlier, are permanently armed. It has been estimated that at least 200 policemen in London (including some at Heathrow Airport) carry guns all the time. In all, an estimated 10,000 policemen – a tenth of the regular force – are qualified to shoot.[59]

The police are issued with .38 Webley hand pistols which fire standard (Smith and Wesson) .38 bullets. But there are moves afoot by some forces to use more powerful ammunition. In 1973, the Home Office working party on 'Police Firearms for Use in Peace-time' suggested that the police should buy hollow-point bullets for their .38 pistols. The bullets are a version of the notorious 'dum-dum' bullet, a form of expanding ammunition banned by the Hague Convention. At least three forces had tested the bullet, but not used it in action, before the Home Secretary in January 1975 stepped in and asked them not to use it. But *The Times* reported that the hollow-point bullet fulfilled the requirements for a 'man-stopper' which some police firearms experts felt they should have.[60]

The police are now buying up rifles to add to their range of shotguns and handguns. Six forces, including Thames Valley, West Yorkshire and West Midlands, have bought the Parker-Hale .22 rifle. It has good credentials: it is similar to the one used by the New York police. But at least one force (on the South Coast) has decided that it needs something stronger. It is reputed to have bought a version of the Sterling sub-machine gun.[61]

Apart from those guns permanently carried by policemen, weapons are kept under lock and key at the local station and issued only on the authority of a senior police officer. Another Home Office working party is considering whether this procedure should be changed. Some senior officers argue that it slows down the ability of the police to respond quickly and effectively. Ronald Gregory, Chief Constable of the 5,000-strong West Yorkshire police force, has said that he is 'seriously contemplating' whether or not men under his command should carry arms in 'certain cars'.[62] The West Yorkshire Police Federation immediately issued a statement supporting the Chief Constable.

There is now a greater emphasis on training police in expert marksmanship. At least one force in the Home Counties has adopted a three-part training procedure. The first course is in conventional marksmanship with stationary and moving targets to develop accuracy. The second is a running battle, in the street or from house to house, in which gunmen are engaged. Several Army techniques 'based on experience in Northern Ireland' have been adapted by the police for inclusion in training courses. The third and most arduous part of the course is a full-scale day and night exercise which involves stalking gunmen hiding in thick woodland. Those who pass the course are known popularly inside the force as 'legalized assassins'.[63]

When it comes to crack shooting, the police obviously turn to the Army for help in training. In 1973, a Birmingham journalist discovered that the police were being trained at the Army barracks at Sutton Coldfield in the use of Walther PP handguns. He later found that firearms manufacturers had given lessons to joint Army–police groups in the use of light automatic weapons as well as handguns. Police and Army spokesmen claimed that the presence of police at Army barracks was 'an isolated incident'.[64]

By August 1974, the incident was no longer isolated. Nurses at the Royal Devon and Exeter Hospital complained that gunfire from a nearby barracks was disturbing their sleep. A senior police officer from the Devon and Cornwall force told the *Western Daily Mail* that handpicked uniformed and CID officers from all divisions were being trained to use .303 sniper rifles and .38 revolvers by the Army.[65] And of course it was admitted at the Scarman Tribunal on the Red Lion Square demonstration that the SPG train at Army ranges.

Is it possible any longer for the British to boast that their 'civilized' police force has no use for guns? The convergence between the roles and training of the British Army and police is directed towards a single end – the development of a force which will permit a flexible response to situations of internal subversion. If possible, the government would like to keep the Army out of the proceedings. The police may not always be able to cope, and then the Army will have to be brought in. At that time, it is vital that the Army and police should be able to work together as a single force. The next set of developments we shall consider are designed to achieve this.

Army–Police Co-operation

In January 1974 the Metropolitan Police and the Army staged the first major combined security operation at a British airport. For over a week the national newspapers carried front-page articles on the 'ring of steel' surrounding London's Heathrow Airport, together with pictures of soldiers armed with rifles standing by while policemen searched vehicles. The reason given for this dramatic activity was that Arab terrorists armed with SAM-7 missiles might shoot at an incoming aircraft. The official line was later changed to become the threat of an American Redeye anti-aircraft missile in the hands of an unnamed terrorist group. Neither the terrorists nor the missiles ever materialized, but the troops and police remained at the airport for a further three weeks as part of a 'continuing exercise'.

No evidence has since been advanced to confirm the story of the terrorist threat. Indeed, there are a number of factors which suggest that it was wholly apocryphal. Other European airports were put on terrorist alert on Boxing Day 1973. Heathrow was put on alert only on 5 January 1974, fully ten days later. If fear of terrorists really had been the reason for the alert, surely the British would have embarked on safety measures at all other airports and would have done so at the same time as neighbouring countries? The delay was certainly not due to lack of preparation. At least one source alleged that contingency plans for Heathrow-type operations had been in existence for over a year.[66] There had even been a rehearsal the year before at Stanstead Airport, in April 1973, when an SAS group 'hi-jacked' an RAF VC10 and was met by the SAS counter-terrorist unit – all under the watchful eyes of senior ministers and defence experts.[67]

There is a second major flaw in the official story of the terrorist threat. SAM-7 and Redeye missiles are reputed to have a height range of 3,000 feet and a radius of three miles.[68] As one commentator has pointed out, incoming and outgoing aircraft frequently pass over central London at heights lower than 3,000 feet, and almost certainly fly over West London at less than 2,500 feet. 'An Arab terrorist armed with a shoulder-fired missile needs only to sit on his patio in Richmond and listen to Air Traffic Control on his VHF Radio in order to pick off, say, the El Al flight coming from Tel Aviv.'[69] Yet the troops and police set up checkpoints only within a one-mile radius of Heathrow, with patrols further out to the east and west.

There has been no satisfactory justification for the first deployment of troops and police at Heathrow Airport. But it certainly came at a convenient time as far as internal defence planning was concerned. Military theorists had long been advocating such exercises as practice for the police and Army in fighting insurgency. The pressure on the authorities responsible for internal security to prepare contingency plans and test them in action had been mounting in the period prior to the Heathrow exercises. Just one example is the Bow Group's 1972 pamphlet 'Peace Has Its Price', which urged: 'Co-operation between the Ministry of Defence and the police needs to be strengthened considerably ... to prepare contingency plans for dealing with unrest in Britain ... arranging joint exercises between police and Army units.'[70]

The *Army Land Operations Manual*, drawing from the experience of the British Army's post-war counter-insurgency campaigns, stresses that 'the military forces and the police must be considered as one security force operating jointly to a *previously rehearsed* deployment plan' (our italics). After the airport manoeuvres, Major-General Clutterbuck confirmed that 'Heathrow was such a "joint exercise", the "colonial experience" imported back to Britain'.[71] More recently, Deane-Drummond pointed out that 'it is useless to rely on emergency measures designed *ad hoc* after an emergency has developed'.[72]

This barrage of advice from various quarters stressing the need for rehearsals cannot have escaped the notice of those at the highest level of the civil–military–police machine who are responsible for internal security. Robert Mark, the Commissioner of Metropolitan Police, who issued the request for troops to participate in the Heathrow operation, actually accompanied Deane-Drummond on a tour of several countries to examine their riot-control and counter-insurgency techniques in 1970. The threat of terrorists and hi-jackers should thus be seen as only one dimension of joint Army–police operations at British airports.

However, it is one thing for committees involved in contingency planning to recognize the need for joint police–military operations. It is quite another to put them into operation without provoking fear and alarm in a population unaccustomed to seeing Saracen armoured vehicles rolling past their front doors and fully armed soldiers on the public highway. Hence the need

144 The Strong Arm of the Strong State

for an official story about a threat from terrorists which would justify such a 'ring of steel' operation.

The Heathrow manoeuvre thus not only provided an opportunity for practice – it was also geared towards public relations. Michael Elliot-Bateman, a lecturer in military studies, has been quoted as saying: 'I think this represents very definitely the pattern of the future for the Army. I would see it as an exercise partly to get army and police officers ... to work together, and partly as a public relations exercise.'[73]

The press certainly played their part in the field of public relations: the newspapers gave extensive coverage, and, from the detailed nature of the reports, appear to have received ample co-operation from the Army and police. They reported that 200 members of the Metropolitan Police, together with the same number of soldiers from the 2nd Battalion (infantry) Grenadier Guards and armoured units of the Household Cavalry, were present at Heathrow. The troops were accompanied by the new Scorpion reconnaissance vehicles, equipped with turreted and co-axial machine guns. These were withdrawn after three days because, according to one source, they posed 'something of a public relations problem'. Their use in Belfast had transformed television newsreels into 'scenes reminiscent of Budapest and Prague'.[74] The soldiers were equipped with live ammunition and were believed to have been issued with instructions on opening fire similar to those given to troops in Northern Ireland. Armed Special Branch officers were also present.

Throughout the operation, the Ministry of Defence and the Home Office emphasized that, although it was a joint operation, the police were in overall control. The question of 'control' is, of course, a technical one, since the Army are far superior both in experience and firepower. The importance of insisting that the police are in charge is that it reassures the public.

The Heathrow operation was undoubtedly a great success, both in terms of military–police co-operation and public response. On 24 January, answering questions in the Commons, the Home Secretary refused point-blank to give an undertaking that troops and police would not be used together to break strikes.[75] This was, of course, the period just before the long-awaited miners' strike. And it was reported that: 'It is believed that the people involved have been pleasantly surprised at the lack of public protest and shock, and the public seems to have accepted that the measures were necessary to counter a threat which existed.'[76]

In June 1974, troops and police again ringed Heathrow, this time in response to a 'threat of terrorism' against the Israeli delegation to the Socialist International conference. About 500 troops and police were involved. The whole Special Patrol Group took part in the operation.[77] There were also more than twenty Saracen tanks and an Army helicopter. The operation was again a success: Miles Copeland (an ex-CIA agent living in London, who remains sympathetic to the CIA) described it as 'one of the most impressive of its kind I have ever seen'.[78]

The operations continued throughout the rest of the year and even spread to other airports, such as Gatwick and Manchester Ringway. In August the *Guardian* diarist commented that 'troops on the streets are now commonplace – which may well have been the object of the whole exercise'.[79] By November, the presence of troops at Heathrow had declined in news value to such an extent that it warranted only seven lines in *The Times*.[80] There was no mention of terrorists: the Scotland Yard press release simply stated that it was part of a 'continuing exercise'. By October 1975, it was possible for the police to refer to yet another Army occupation of the Heathrow area as 'all part of the normal security screen'.[81]

In January 1975, the first real-life operation involving troops took place at Stansted Airport. The SAS was deployed when a British Airways jet was hi-jacked from Manchester to London. In the end, the hi-jacker gave himself up after negotiations. There is no evidence that Scorpion tanks would have proved more persuasive.

There is one final point of interest about the airport manoeuvres. The man responsible for overseeing operations at Heathrow was Deputy Assistant Commissioner of Metropolitan Police, John Gerrard. Gerrard is also head of the Anti-Picket unit at New Scotland Yard. Will he be able to make use of his experience in commanding troop–police operations in other situations – for example, if the police are not adequate to deal with industrial disputes? After all, the sight of troops accompanied by tanks in major cities of England would have seemed bizarre not so very long ago.

There have been other incidents in which police and troops have moved into urban areas. But, by contrast with the public relations coverage around the Heathrow exercises, these have been kept very quiet indeed. For they have no 'terrorist threat' to justify them. Some have only come to light when local residents have complained to the Ministry of Defence. Routine exercises conducted by troops are normally carried out in remote areas, and, despite the fact that people in Britain are accustomed to seeing newsreels of soldiers on the streets of Belfast, they are shocked when it happens on their own doorsteps.

The lack of public response to the Heathrow operations has obviously encouraged the Army, and reports of troops on the streets of Britain have been more common since January 1975. In February of that year, a unit of the Territorial Army staged an operation at lunchtime on a Sunday in a quiet residential area of Hull in Yorkshire. The detachment of about thirty to forty men made an assault on the only derelict house in the street. Eyewitnesses reported that at least one of the soldiers was carrying riot gas equipment. The operation had been given no prior publicity, and took place at a time when only minimum staff were present at national and local newsdesks. When protests were made to the Ministry of Defence, an Army spokesman claimed that this type of exercise is an accepted part of infantry training, and that the local police had been informed. The Hull Chief of Police, however, denied any knowledge of the operation.[82]

Less than a month later, again without warning, residents of Corby New Town in Northamptonshire spotted troops in midnight exercises. The soldiers were members of the signals platoon of the Fifth Royal Anglian Regiment, wearing combat jackets and accompanied by military vehicles. This was a much more ambitious operation than the one in Hull. According to the *Workers' Press*, it was part of a war game devised by the

Low-Intensity Operations in Britain 147

Ministry of Defence, in which Corby was the capital of a mythical country populated by 'North European immigrants'. The task of the soldiers was to defend the government against two rival factions, the Brickies and the Sparkies, who each held separate parts of the town.* As the operation was going on there were imaginary reports of parcel bombs, crowds gathering and demonstrations. The Anglians were referred to during the exercise as coming to the aid of the civil power.[83]

There are many examples of other, less dramatic operations in urban surroundings conducted by the military. In January 1974, Army scout cars shadowed a Workers' Revolutionary Party demonstration in London. And soldiers of the 31st Signals Regiment of the Territorials were spotted training at midnight on Wimbledon Common. The press office of the London Area Army headquarters told *Time Out* that the ground on which the exercise occurred was a 'military training area' (in a suburb of London?).[84]

One of the results of all this activity by the Army and police was revealed in the *Sunday Times* in July 1975. Contingency plans have now been laid to facilitate rapid action by the state forces in the event of an emergency. They involve the coordination of police, military and civil administration at both regional and national levels. The plans cover not only major limited strikes (for example, one involving both the coal and the electricity industries) and general strikes but also insurrections involving considerable parts of the country.† In some of these the SAS are likely to play a major role.

In the event of a strike which poses a threat to the maintenance of essential services, there is now a Civil Contingencies

---

* The similarities with Northern Ireland are marked: for example, the Official IRA are known in local parlance as the 'Stickies'.

† Tony Bunyan's *The Political Police in Britain* (pp. 278–9) gives more details of this National Security Plan. He points out that each police station is linked into the emergency communication system to Strike Command, the Army having their own secure communication system linking every regional district H.Q., regional centre, air-force base and naval base. At the regional level, effective power would be exercised by a government-appointed Regional Commissioner, the Chief Constable and the District's GOC.

Committee which would consider requests for troops to be brought in. It is also responsible for stockpiles of food and other essential supplies. And the circumstances under which the Army may be called in by the government have been redefined. One category is basically disaster relief. Another, called Military Aid to Civil Ministries (MACM), is technically 'maintenance of essential services'. In reality, it is nothing less than strike-breaking – soldiers taking the place of workers on strike.

If they are required (as in the General Strike of 1926) to protect strike-breakers rather than do the job themselves, troops will be called in as Military Aid to the Civil Power (MACP). This is a public order role, but also includes incidents involving armed terrorists and other threats to the state. If the police cannot handle a situation like this, a unit of the SAS can be called out from Hereford, and other specialized Army units are on call.

These would seem to be impressive plans. But they are far from foolproof. The government, the Ministry of Defence and the Chiefs of Police are only too aware that they are not sufficient to deal with a general strike or widespread mass demonstrations. Major-General Clutterbuck has said that the greatest strength of our police force lies in its 'social contract with the public'.[85] The same obviously applies to the use of the Army when intervening in domestic affairs. If the working class breaks its side of the contract, then the best-laid contingency plans may well go astray.

Part Four
The Technology of Political Control

13
Watching and Waiting

In the remainder of this book, we shall describe the more significant aspects of the technology of political control. We do not consider every technology which can be used to control or suppress political dissent. Instead, we have concentrated on new developments (mostly dating from the Vietnam war) or new variations on old themes. We have tried to give a general survey of the field rather than a detailed examination of each device or technique. Where feasible, we have indicated possible counter-measures which may be taken.

For convenience, both for ourselves and for our readers, we have divided the discussion into Kitson's three phases of subversion, which were discussed in detail in Part Three (pp. 100–108). As Kitson himself points out, these phases do not occur in strict time sequence, but may overlap or regress, depending on the particular political circumstances. The technologies are considered in the context of the phase in which we expect them to be first employed; they may continue to be used in later phases, or even be employed in particular situations earlier on.

Finally, the examples we use draw heavily on the experience of the United States. There are two reasons for this: firstly, the USA leads the world in almost every field of technological development. It is therefore not surprising that it leads also in the development of the technology of political control. Secondly, political dissidents in the United States were the first victims of the colonial experience imported to the 'home front'. We in Britain can draw valuable lessons from this experience.

Of course, it would be a mistake to assume that every such development within the United States will automatically be adopted by other Western states. As we have stressed before, specific national political, economic and social factors are all constraints on this process – or render it unnecessary. In particular, the police force in Britain, highly centralized and relatively poorly funded as it is, does not allow for direct comparison with the United States, where the relative local autonomy of police forces and the existence of bodies such as the LEAA are powerful spurs to the development of new law-enforcement technology. Nevertheless, the existence of information-sharing agreements, the role of the United States as 'global policeman' and the increasing trend towards internationalization in this field make it vital to consider the most advanced developments.

The technology of political control needs no further introduction. So let us begin at the beginning, the preparatory period.

Information-Gathering

Once trouble of any kind has broken out, the state has an army of weapons and techniques for quietening it down again. But half the battle is lost already if a group has been able to demonstrate the possibility of effective action. So the organization of dissident groups is to be disrupted, and the planning of public manifestations is to be aborted. For this, the authorities need information. And before you can use information, you have to collect it.

In fact, there are a number of reasons why the security forces need different types of information. The main distinction is between political (or general) intelligence and operational intelligence. *Political intelligence* is not collected to obtain foreknowledge of particular events, but to achieve a general understanding of the strengths and weaknesses of dissident groups. *Operational intelligence* is needed for planning government counter-actions to opposition moves, or pre-emptive strikes to stop them from happening. Operational intelligence will, according to Kitson, require a larger number of relatively low-grade sources of information than will political intelligence. Political intelligence is gathered by the state at all times, though efforts will be increased as the non-violent phase is entered.

Naturally, if a particularly juicy piece of information is turned up in the course of political intelligence collection, it may be used for operational purposes. Or political intelligence information may usefully form the basis of conspiracy charges – as has commonly happened in the United States. The trouble from the security forces' point of view is that this may blow the cover of infiltrators and so endanger the future supply of information.

What happens to the information once it is collected? More and more frequently, it will go into the computer (although there are limitations to this, as we shall see later); or it may be stored on microfilm (increasingly being used by the police departments in the USA). Or it may be added to a manual file, or just be kept in the head of a member of the intelligence service.

Either political or operational intelligence may be gathered by any available means: by undercover agents or informers, by mail covers, by phone taps or room bugs. Philip Agee, an ex-agent, tells us that much of the information gathered by the CIA came from overt sources, such as publications from the groups under surveillance themselves. Of the more technical methods, telephone tapping is probably the most popular and productive. But despite all the technological advances, the inside agent or informer is still the most productive source. This was confirmed at the Chicago Seven conspiracy trial, in which no fewer than thirty of about forty substantive prosecution witnesses were police agents or infiltrators. It is an easy step from spy to *agent provocateur*, encouraging acts of violence to encourage arrests. Many such provocations were attempted against anti-war groups in the United States. The cases of Kenneth Lennon and the Littlejohns demonstrate the willingness of the British security forces to use similar techniques. In the United States, radical groups in the 1960s developed elaborate procedures for 'checking-out' the identities and backgrounds of new recruits, as a precaution against infiltration.[1]

Harassment of political groups, using all the resources of the state, is another technique brought to perfection in the United States. The FBI's COINTELPRO programme, directed against a variety of black activist, radical and socialist groups during the 1960s and 1970s, was designed to 'expose, disrupt and otherwise neutralize the groups' and to 'frustrate every effort of these groups and individuals to consolidate their forces or to receive new youthful adherents'. Even this was only an intensification of accepted practice. A law suit by the US Socialist Workers' Party forced disclosures of a mass of documentation on the FBI's interference with the SWP over thirty-one years. No idea was too trivial or fatuous to be tried. Writing scurrilous letters to the press about the sex life of candidates standing for election, or tipping off a state liquor control board to raid a SWP vacation camp for serving liquor without a licence – all these were grist to the mill. The SWP is a perfectly legal Trotskyist group. Over the past thirty years it has never been charged with any offence.

Who gets the information? In Britain, the normal 'non-political' police may use many of these methods in bona-fide criminal investigations. And there is a great deal of industrial espionage using advanced methods. But for political cases the information will go to one of an array of intelligence agencies, some of which are described earlier in this book. Up to at least 1957, almost all official interception of communications was carried out by the Metropolitan Police, the Board of Customs and Excise, and the Security Service.[2] In the United States, the system is far more widespread. As many as twenty-two Federal agencies have publicly *admitted* to the use of 'electronic surveillance' methods – otherwise known as bugging and tapping.[3] And electronic snooping is by no means limited to the government. Firms bug their competitors, and their unions. Even the private citizen can get in on the act.

It was the 1968 Omnibus Crime Control and Safe Streets Act which explicitly made it illegal in the United States to manufacture, sell, purchase, possess or use electronic eavesdropping equipment. But this Act did not apply to 'national security', and the use of electronic surveillance by law-enforcement bodies (by court order) was explicitly legalized for the first time. The need for a court order proved to be no obstacle: in the first six years of the Act, only five or six of the total of more than 3,500 applications have been turned down.[4] Despite the laxity of the courts, law-enforcement agencies practise 'substantial wildcatting' – that is, set surreptitious taps without court orders.[5] The

Watergate scandal revealed such wildcatting at the very highest levels.

In Britain, the official position is that no phone-tapping can be done without the permission of the Home Secretary. (In theory, this will be given only if the person under surveillance is suspected of a crime which could carry a prison sentence of three or more years.) However, this is the only form of electronic surveillance subject to restriction. And the paranoid secrecy of the establishment on such matters is extreme. Since 1957, no statistics have been given on the number of official warrants for telephone-taps, and it is official policy not to provide information on this subject. Before 1957, the number of warrants issued to all agencies averaged 150 a year. But unofficial estimates of 600 warrants in 1970 and 1,200 warrants in 1972 have been made. There has even been an allegation (in the House of Commons) of *twelve thousand* taps in 1966.[6] We know nothing about the duration of even these officially sanctioned telephone-taps. In the United States we do know that a 'national security' wire-tap lasts on average between seventy-one and 200 days and somewhere between 5,000 and 15,000 conversations are overheard.[7, 8] One mammoth tap went on for twenty-five years. 'People grew up and died and had babies and this wire-tap continued all this time.'[9]

Just as in the United States, there is a great deal of electronic surveillance apart from that officially sanctioned. The police need ask nobody's permission to use bugging (as opposed to tapping) devices. And there is plenty of private enterprise activity. Industrial espionage is a growth area. An example is the case of Betta Steel Co. Their phone was tapped via the telephone junction box on the roof of the offices. A wire ran 150 yards to an outbuilding where there was an off/on switching device and a tape recorder. Phone-taps like this can be rigged up without the Post Office knowing that it is going on. In another reported case, an ex-policeman turned private detective set up a Post Office telephone junction box at a street corner, with a specially installed monitoring unit. He taped every call to and from the phone of a woman involved in a divorce suit.[10] And in October 1974 the notorious private investigator Barry ('bug-and-be-damned') Quartermain pleaded guilty to a charge under the Wireless and Telegraphy Act for a similar offence.

There are also known cases of political bugging. A bug which, to judge by its design, was ten to twelve years old, was discovered in the offices of the Communist Party in London in early 1975. And Mr Ralph Matthews, an ex-Military Intelligence man turned 'security adviser', claimed that telephones in the Labour Party headquarters in Transport House were tapped for long periods in 1972.[11] Until 1964, the government carried out tapping of MPs' phones, and may do so again, should circumstances change. In France, a member of the staff of the satirical weekly *Le Canard Enchaîné* surprised counter-espionage 'plumbers' in the office one night in December 1973. The officers – members of the French security forces – had entered the building on a number of occasions, pretending to be interior decorators.

One of the facts which emerges from a study of this murky area is that many of the people involved, either in illicit electronic espionage or counter-measures, learnt their trade in the security forces. There is thus some reason to suppose that what they now practise as private agents they also practised in government service. This would imply that there is a good deal of 'unofficial' tapping and bugging being carried out by the British police and military intelligence. Indeed, with the evidence we have of how similar bodies behave in other countries, it would be foolish to come to any other conclusion.

Does this mean that the era of Big Brother has arrived? Do unseen eyes and ears observe us in our most private moments? Many people think so. Justice Brandeis foresaw this possibility as long ago as 1928, when he wrote that technology now made it possible for the government, 'by means far more effective than stretching on the rack, to obtain disclosure in court of what is whispered in the closet'. Another US judge warned in 1963 that if such devices continue to proliferate, we would end up with a society where the only safe course is 'to keep one's mouth shut on all occasions'.[12]

It is certainly true that the technology to make this grim picture come true exists. Some of it is relatively undeveloped, but time and the attentions of military and police research and development may soon see to that. But there are still several reasons why mass electronic surveillance is not practicable in the immediate future. Firstly, in Western liberal democracies the point has not yet been reached where mass surveillance would repay the effort involved. Secondly, counter-measures are possible, as we shall describe later. Thirdly, mass surveillance may be technically feasible, but it is not so socially and economically. Tapping and bugging are not, in fact, a lazy person's way of conducting an investigation. Apart from the time spent reconnoitring, planting and servicing the device, extensive work is involved both before and after the event. You have to find out who is likely to be worth watching and listening. You have the labour-intensive job of monitoring the equipment; and even if that can be handled automatically, there is still the task of identifying overheard voices and names mentioned in conversation. Unless there has been an extensive preliminary investigation, this may prove impossible.[13] And if the electronic surveillance is for operational intelligence, it will often lead on to physical surveillance – 'tailing'. Here the labour requirements and costs sky-rocket. In the United States in 1973, the cost of a normal four-man team was in the range of 50 to 100 dollars per hour.[14]

Research and development teams are working on ways of making surveillance less labour-intensive. There have been reports of devices under development to monitor large numbers of telephone lines simultaneously and automatically. Two 'speech-recognition' programmes could potentially greatly help such monitoring. One is the development of speaker-recognition techniques – the 'voice-print'. The other is the development of a programme for detecting 'key words' such as 'demonstration', 'strike', or the names of political organizations. Only conversations involving 'critical people' or using key words would then be recorded. The importance that such techniques might have in the future is shown by the Pentagon's admission in 1973 that it was spending up to $7 million on speech-recognition research.[15]

As yet, voice-printing programmes are capable of high accuracy (greater than 95 per cent) only if the voice to be identified is one of a very limited set of about twenty to thirty. This, by itself, could produce a very big saving in listening time in certain situations, such as when a line used by a number of people is being tapped. But it seems likely that many of these experimental programmes are very easily tricked by changes in voice or stress, or by voice disguise. More serious still, many of the projects are impracticable, since they require the person whose voice is to be identified to speak a sample test.

'Key word' detection is a still more remote prospect. This is because voices differ greatly in the way they pronounce the same word. The ultimate in automation – the machine semantically decoding the unknown message – is complete science fiction at the moment. Intensive theoretical work in this area over the last twenty years had made relatively little progress. The British and American governments are probably no nearer to solving the problem of voice identification than Stalin's prisoners were in Solzhenitsyn's *The First Circle*. The era of practicable mass surveillance is still many years off.

There is no reason to feel complacent about this. Undoubtedly *selective* political surveillance does go on. And so does deliberate action by the security and secret services to induce paranoia. There is evidence to suggest that some of the clumsy 'slip-ups' of police phone-tapping or mail coverage are not mistakes at all, but deliberate attempts to disrupt radical groups. One FBI internal memorandum describing steps to be taken against the Black Panther Party, included a plan to release false police films 'indicating electronic surveillance where none exists'.[16] Another spoke of the need 'to get the point across that there is an FBI agent behind every mail-box'.[17]

This attempt to stimulate 'over-awareness' of surveillance activities fits in well with the general policy, outlined in earlier chapters, of using techniques which have maximum disruptive impact on the target community. The obsessive secrecy of the intelligence apparatus is the other side of this coin – an intention to keep everybody else in ignorance of what is going on. As one American document puts it, operations should be conducted most discreetly lest they create 'an awareness of surveillance operations in the general public which is detrimental to maintaining the confidentiality desired in intelligence operations'.[18]

Of the communications interceptions, the simplest technologically is that of letters. In the United States, there are two levels at which this operates. The lower is the 'mail cover' – a record of names and addresses from the faces of envelopes going to individuals or groups. The higher level is 'covert coverage', which means screening the mail and examining it with special devices, or opening it. Mail cover is less useful in Britain, where the US habit of writing the name of the sender on the outside of the envelope has not caught on.

The mail cover provides masses of low-grade information. (In this respect it resembles the information the British Special Branch gains from raids on the homes of political activists. Address books are always prime targets for removal.) How the system can work (or rather fail to work) is illustrated by the case of Lori Paton, a sixteen-year-old New Jersey high school student. As part of a school essay project, she wrote a letter in 1973 to the Socialist Labor Party, requesting information. But in error she sent it to the address of the Socialist Workers' Party, and so got caught up in the FBI mail cover of that harassed organization. The FBI activated a 'subversives' file on her, and started a full field investigation – interviews with the school principal, and so on. It took a court order to get the FBI to desist and to destroy her file – the first time that the FBI had been so ordered. The US Postal Service agreed to over 8,500 requests for mail surveillances (of which level is unclear) during 1973–5.[19] It is a lucky coincidence that William J. Cotter, chief inspector of the Postal Inspection Service, is an ex-employee (of eighteen years' service) of the CIA.[20]

In Britain, the Post Office needs no warrant to open mail.* The 1969 Post Office Act gave them *carte blanche* 'to do what is necessary to inform designated persons holding office under the Crown concerning matters and things transmitted or in the course of transmission'.

*For more extensive coverage of British operations, see Tony Bunyan's *The Political Police in Britain*.

Mail-opening is basically a one-sided surveillance method. You can intercept all letters which a person receives, but it is impossible to trace every letter a person sends. In Britain, incoming letters are usually intercepted at the local sorting office serving the person under surveillance. These letters are sent by special courier to the local surveillance office. In London, there is an area surveillance office for each of the seven major postal districts. There they are opened and photocopied. (The Xerox has taken a lot of drudgery out of mail surveillance.) This makes it possible to get the letters back to the local post office before the postman starts his next delivery round. The Xeroxes go to the headquarters of the Post Office Investigation Branch, for forwarding to the agency which asked for the interception.

It may not be necessary to open the letter: an American source states that a needle-thin flashlight can be inserted into a sealed letter to illuminate the writing for quick reading or photography.[21] The process in Britain has been described in some detail by the Hampstead Committee of 100:

The security services have a special apparatus for examining letters ... the device they use being rather like the viewing screen found in X-ray departments of hospitals. If this method proves unsatisfactory, then the contents of an envelope can be extracted through one of the holes left at the top of the gummed flaps. An instrument resembling a pair of long-nosed pliers is used to wind the letter into a tight cylinder and to extract it without visibly disturbing the sealed flap. (We understand that it is rather more difficult to replace the letter.) The commonest method is to use the bottom flap rather than the top one.[22]

If this method does not work, the letter may simply disappear. Or it may arrive but looking rather worse for wear and with an 'Opened in Error' or 'Misdirected' label. 'If all else fails, the bottom of the letter can be slit, the letter photocopied, then the letter resealed using woodpulp and a cooker that restores the texture of the envelope paper.'

One of the incidental results of mail interception is that letters do not always get to the right address. (Whether this is a shrewd plot to generate paranoia on the left, or just the result of bungling inefficiency is not clear.) With poetic elegance, this happened to one of us while writing this book. A letter concerning the book, clearly addressed to one of our home addresses, turned up instead in a bundle of normal mail at work. The Post Office offered no explanation except to assure us that this was one of those one-in-a-million chance happenings.

Telephone-tapping is far more convenient for the security forces than any other form of communications interception. It can be done officially by showing a warrant; or unofficially without much danger of the Post Office (or the telephone company in the USA) knowing anything about it. If the wire-tap is official and legitimate, monitoring can be performed at very 'safe' central telephone office locations. Thus in Britain the Post Office Investigation Branch listens in to calls within the local exchange. This can be done using 'TKO (Trunk Offering) boards' or monitoring boards. TKO boards, found in most auto-manual exchanges, are operated manually. They are used to check calls in progress and faults, to break in on a call in emergencies – and obviously for tapping. The operator simply plugs into the subscriber's exchange circuit and dials the subscriber's number. The tap is then in place until the plug is pulled out. However, this method is not really suitable for long-term tapping – for example, of political groups. It is labour-intensive, random and can be noisy.

Long-term tapping is likely to be conducted by monitoring boards to which particular subscriber's lines can be permanently wired (or at listening posts, as described below). Every time a wired phone makes or receives a call, a light goes on; the operator need only listen in at these times, and so can attend to many lines. Further economies of labour can be obtained with the use of automatic recording equipment, for example a tape-recorder which switches on only when the telephone under surveillance is being used – a switch is activated by the voltage drop caused by lifting the receiver. A recent telephone development will give the security forces a new tapping facility. A new transit system for STD calls, MF2 (to which some exchanges are already being connected), will eventually allow a 'special class' of user to carry out diallable TKO-ing, on any exchange with MF2 transit access.

Serious long-term tapping for political or operational intelligence is likely to be conducted at a 'listening post' established and run by the intelligence agency, to which the lines can be connected. Scotland Yard's listening post is believed to be based in a telephone exchange near Chelsea Barracks and to be able to service up to seventy-two taps at any moment.[23] Students at Copenhagen University discovered fifty Danish Post Office men in a listening post in the university basement. They were busily monitoring and recording international calls out of Denmark – for NATO.[24]

A good deal of information on telephone calls can be collected without any need to tap at all. The device which makes this possible is the printometer. When attached to a line, it automatically records the telephone numbers dialled on each outgoing call, together with details of duration and cost. The printometer is used to check customer complaints about bills, but it also provides a very useful source of low-grade information for the intelligence services. And it is widely used by the Post Office Investigation Branch to track down 'phone phreaks'. The Post Office can easily detect if a printometer is attached to a line, so it is unlikely to be used without their permission. One drawback about printometering is that it requires daily servicing – the tape on which the information is recorded has to be changed every day. However, there will soon be no need for printometers on many phones. The new TXE2 and TXE4 exchanges are equipped to record automatically every telephone number dialled. This will make billing easier – but not only that.

Tapping without a warrant has to be done without the Post Office knowing. But this is not very difficult. A telephone can be tapped anywhere along the line from the phone back to the local exchange. One particularly vulnerable spot is the green box along the road where many Post Office cables come together. Tampering with the telephone itself is not required; often, in blocks of offices or flats, access can be obtained to the terminal box located in a semi-public area. And an extension phone from a multiple-line office system is not immune. The tap can be made between the office switchboard and the extension, or all the main telephone lines entering the switchboard can be tapped. Access in private houses is not so easy, so that a line may need to be tapped after it leaves the house. A competent professional can trace the line back and choose a tapping location where an extension drop wire will be inconspicuous, or where a monitoring post can be established. Impudence is a feature of this profession. In 1973, two FBI agents were caught red-handed with a brief-case full of electronic equipment in the Federal courthouse in Gainsville, Florida. They were busily tapping the offices of the lawyers of seven anti-Vietnam war veterans then on trial on conspiracy charges in the same courthouse.[25]

All taps are basically extension telephones. But they can be connected in a variety of ways. They can be in parallel with the telephone (that is, across the pair of lead wires), or in series with it. Or a self-powered 'inductive' tap can be installed by suction caps in the phone itself, or anywhere within its immediate magnetic field, where it will pick up signals without any direct metallic contact.[26]

The telephone is also a popular way of bugging a room. In this case, it is used to listen not just to telephone conversations, but to any conversation in the room where the phone is. The popularity of the telephone is that its wires provide ready-made channels for smuggling signals out. Other methods (laying new wires or installing a radio-transmitting bug) offer more possibilities of detection. All methods which work when the phone is not in use require access to the room.

Like the tap, the bug may be in series or parallel. The series transmitter does not need a battery, but will operate only when the phone is off the hook. The parallel transmitter does so continuously, and so shortens battery life. There are many ingenious variations.[27] On the pretext of making a phone call, the mouthpiece can be unscrewed in a matter of seconds and the telephone microphone replaced with an apparently identical one which will broadcast continuously, using the phone's electric power, with a range up to 300 feet. The bell unit can be slightly adjusted and made to perform as a microphone transmitting continuously down the line, where a tap can pick up the signal. An elegant micro-miniature bug exists which can encode the audible sound it receives (so that it will sound like static to a counter-bugger) and transmit it up to twenty-five miles to a listening post. It is powered from there.

And there are 'third wire' or 'hot-mike' systems, in which the telephone is rewired to add an extra wire or component which is always live, with the transmission slipping out inside the telephone cable. But most fascinating is the 'infinity bug'. This is installed in the telephone instrument and can be activated remotely in the most flexible way. At a telephone anywhere in the world (with direct dialling), the number of the target telephone is dialled. When the call is answered, the would-be eavesdropper apologizes for a wrong number and then keeps the line open by not hanging up when the subject does. He or she then feeds in an audible tone which activates the bug. (With the American telephone system this form of bugging is a little simpler.) There is now an open audio path from the bug to the listener, and it will transmit any sound in the room. If the receiver is picked up, the bug disconnects. And the calls will not register on anyone's bill.

Room-bugging can also be achieved without using the telephone equipment. A battery-powered microphone may be hidden, to pick up any sound and send it out along carefully concealed wires. Or a tiny radio transmitter may be concealed in the area, broadcasting to a receiver somewhere in its range of around 300 feet. Sound-operated relays can be fitted, which switch on the device only while sound impinges on it. This preserves battery life and lessens the chance of accidental discovery. (It was this system which Nixon used to bug his own White House.)

The art here lies mainly in concealment. There is a device known as the 'spike' microphone which is invisible to the room occupants because the spike is driven into the wall from outside. The spike carries the wall vibrations caused by sound in the room to a vibration microphone, rather in the way a gramophone needle operates. Within the room, microphones can be – and have been – hidden in doorframes, mouldings, ceilings, bookcases, light fixtures, in heating ducts, under wallpaper and in television sets. Wires can be embedded in carpets or disguised as other types of wiring. Signals can be fed out over the mains electricity wires and picked up at some external socket. Or magnet wire may be run along the wall and then painted over to match the other walls. The same procedure can be used with 'silver-print' conducting paint instead of wire. Or (but this is very expensive) the two 'wire paths' can be painted with transparent paint, avoiding the need to redecorate.

In order for a transmitter to achieve a useful range it must be connected to a structure which can serve as an antenna, or have its own. Hiding places include picture frames, lamp bases, hollowed-out books, bookends, brooms and staplers. Professionals regard it as a challenge to develop creative innovations in concealment. And no detail is too small. When working in areas which are not kept clean, all traces of disturbance to dust and dirt must be removed. There are spray cans of artificial cobwebs for the finishing touches.

Bugging and tapping do not exhaust the ways in which people can be overheard. Directional microphones, like the parabolic reflector and 'machine-gun' microphones, can pick up conversations at distances of several hundred yards, either in the open air or through an open window. At less than fifty yards they can even be effective against closed windows. A continuous-wave laser beam bounced off the vibrating window of a room can reproduce the sound within at ranges measured in miles.

Bugging is not cheap. In Britain simple but effective bugs were advertised for purchase by post for as little as £7.81 in 1975.[28] In the United States, despite the 1968 Safe Streets Act, it was still possible in 1975 to buy over the counter a bug which would work for as little as $10. However, it would be rather bulky, and a professional unit bought under the counter might cost $250 or more. Perhaps the largest expense is for the services of a professional bugger, which would run to $5,000 for the job – and that does not include doing the listening or changing the batteries.

What can be done to find out if you are being tapped or bugged and to stop it? One remedy is to call in the professionals. The counter-buggers offer complete services to sweep any premises clean. But they are expensive. Prices are tailored to the size of corporate pockets. One US firm in 1975 charged $600 per day plus expenses, and in one day they could cover perhaps three or four office rooms. In 1973, a British firm was reported to charge £50 per day.

A thorough search is quite an expert job. The Post Office engineers test codes published quite widely in Britain several years ago do not, in fact, detect taps on the phone. Telephone lines can be tested by a 'telephone analyser' which detects any tell-tale voltage differences, listens in for any minute signs of transmitted audio, and sweeps the lines with variable sound frequencies to activate any audio-triggering devices. The most sophisticated – at a cost of £2,200[29] – is the Dektor telephone analyser. Telephones can be permanently and fairly effectively protected by elaborate 'wire-tap defeat systems', but at a cost in 1975 of $2,700 or a related rental charge. There are even high-voltage devices which will cause any unauthorized attachments to explode. Searching for transmitting bugs is conducted with equally complex equipment, which can search the radio frequency spectrum for clandestine transmissions. Hand-held devices were available at prices between £50 and £850 in 1975. If the transmitter sends out its message by wire, only a physical search will find it – and you have to know what you are looking for.

For most private people and political groups, it will not be worth the expense and trouble, particularly in view of the low probability of any individual phone or room being tapped or bugged. But no one with electronic expertise need pay the fancy prices of ready-made gadgets. 'Screamer' devices (working on a feed-back principle) capable of detecting bug transmissions could be assembled for as little as £20. And several of the 'telephone analyser' tests could be reproduced with standard engineers' equipment.

In the absence of such services, there are still a number of possible counter-measures, both defensive and positive. Possessors of phones thought most likely to be 'hot' may have to make crucial calls from phone-boxes (not always the same one). It goes without saying that people should be careful about what they say on the phone. If you think anyone might go to the trouble of installing an infinity bug in your phone, simply pick up the phone again after each incoming wrong number. This will cause the bug to disconnect. For a home-made anti-bugging device the stratagem of the detainees in Long Kesh could be imitated. High-acquisition directional microphones on watch-towers round the camp beamed into the detainees' hut and picked up the conversation inside. The response of the inmates was a devastating secret weapon – 'a steady, unvarying dosage of Radio One and particularly Tony Blackburn' at full blast. This was supposed to have put the microphones off their stroke.[30]

One more counter-measure is, if you find a bug or tap, not to interfere with it. It can be used to relay false information to whoever is listening at the other end. The Provisional IRA were still more enterprising. In 1974, they successfully tapped the phone in the operations room at Lisburn of the 39th Infantry Brigade which covered Belfast. The calls were tapped from a Post Office telephone junction box, with the aid of a device to 'unscramble' the work done by the Army's scrambler. The tap lasted for several weeks and the operator was never caught.[31] But the Army are learning the lessons of electronic security. Late in 1973, a £100 million military contract was awarded by the government to Plessey Ltd, the electronics and communications company, for 'a secure tactical trunk communications system'. It will be for a 'mobile, secret telephone service for the Army, completely independent of Post Office lines'. The new system will provide the soldier in the field or on the move with the equivalent of the STD telephone service.[32]

Computers

The future effectiveness of the technology of political control will depend to a large extent on the development of the computer. Its capacity to store and analyse enormous amounts of data, and to construct operational models, could make it a powerful weapon in all stages of a counter-insurgency campaign. Like many of the other technologies discussed in this book, large-scale computer technology is a fairly recent development. Twenty years ago most computer systems consisted essentially of equipment for reading and processing punch-cards and paper tape. Today the widespread use of higher-speed storage devices, such as magnetic tape and discs, has made it possible to store very large amounts of data and process it very rapidly. Computer storage and 'real-time' (immediate response) systems are now used by every major firm, bank and insurance company in the world, and the computer industry has one of the fastest rates of growth.

The largest client of the computer industry in most Western countries is the government. In Sweden, the government has recently taken over the country's largest data bank (which was previously privately owned), containing personal files on every resident. In the USA, computerization receives more funds than any other type of project sponsored by the National Institute of Law Enforcement and Criminal Justice (a sub-unit of LEAA). In Britain, the government has played a major role in the development of the computer industry by giving financial support and opportunities for experimentation with new systems. In 1973, twenty-one central government departments had data-processing facilities; and nearly 500 local authorities used computers. A large proportion of government funding for computers in the countries we have mentioned goes towards the setting-up of data banks. If governments were committed to protecting the interests of individuals, it would not be a source of concern that they had control over information stored in data banks. However, even in 'normal' times, governments are more concerned to further corporate interests than they are to protect those of individuals. Now, at a period of severe economic, social and political conflict, the primary interest of the government is in the survival of the state. In defending the state against those who threaten it, any government will use whatever available means it considers necessary – which will obviously include the computer technology at its disposal and the data banks to which it can gain access.

Most of the literature on the dangers of the computer society has tended to miss the point. The debates have centred on the question of privacy of the individual, and the ways to build safeguards into data-bank systems so that only authorized bodies have access to the data. The issue of privacy, and the right of every person to know what information about her or himself is on file, is, of course, important. But the vital question to ask is who has control over this information? Even if technical safeguards are built in (and many computer specialists regard the construction of a totally 'safe' system as an impossibility[33]) they will in no way prevent 'legitimate' government agencies from abusing confidentiality. The error stems from the belief that the government and its agencies are neutral. The safeguards which exist at the moment – such as code words for access to a data system, programmed checks to ensure that data are not altered illegally, and security measures around computer installations – only prevent the small-time crook from stealing information. Meanwhile, the big-time crooks (like the CIA and FBI in the USA) can enter, process or look at almost any information they please.

Our discussion on the place of computers in the technology of repression will therefore centre on systems controlled by government agencies. (In this respect we are rectifying an omission by the Younger Committee on Privacy, which reported in 1972; its terms of reference were restricted to the private sector and did not cover use of computers by any public bodies.) We shall first give an introduction to the use of computers in the preparatory period; then look at some examples of police use of computers, drawing on the experience of the United States, which is the leader in this field. Finally, we shall consider the use of computers by other government agencies.

Computers in the Preparatory Period

The major function of computers in the preparatory period is to lay the basis for effective police and possibly Army operations in the next phase of any counter-insurgency campaign. We do not expect the computer to be as central to this stage as say informers or electronic-surveillance equipment. In the first place, the greatest advantage of computers is that the time taken to retrieve any piece of information on the file can be cut down drastically. But it is in the later stages that such speed is essential, rather than in the preparatory period. In the case of political activists, the security forces are concerned with identifying them more for the future than for immediate action. Further, changes in the law such as the Prevention of Terrorism Act can make it possible for the police to detain people for a sufficient period to find out about their activities, without necessitating instant access to information about them on a computer. So on purely practical grounds there is not really any need for law-enforcement agencies to invest huge amounts of money in sophisticated computer systems for 'counter-insurgency' purposes at the present time.

The second limitation on the use of computers is a technical one: at the present stage of development of computer systems, it is not possible for them to operate as efficiently in most cases as the CID and Special Branch do already. Political groups in Britain are still small enough for their members to be recognized by police responsible for keeping an eye on them, and to do this more effectively than a computer (which could not at present, for example, match names to photographs).

The third limitation on the use of computers in the preparatory period is specific to Britain. In most other European countries, everyone has a personal number which is the key to every file kept on her or him by government agencies. This makes it a lot easier to follow the movements of individuals and relate information on them in different files – for example, health records and Social Security files. Thus there is a possibility of integrating information from different sources to build up a complete picture of someone. In Britain, where there has long been resistance to any idea of personal numbers, the difficulties of integration are enormous. A personal number on an identity card which can be forged only with difficulty and is used for most transactions with state agencies is much more suited to computerization. Thus the increased use of computers for political surveillance would be greatly facilitated by the use of identity cards with personal numbers.

However, these limitations on the use of computers in the preparatory period do not mean that they cannot perform very valuable functions: only that these functions are unlikely to extend far beyond present computer capabilities in crime-fighting. This is why we discuss the police system developed to fight crime in some detail. Many of their present applications could be equally useful for collecting information on people suspected of political activity. In particular, the most highly developed use of computers in British law enforcement at the present time is for vehicle tracing. (It is most highly developed because each vehicle has a number which must be registered and can therefore be tracked down.) Of more interest is the future development of research projects which are closely linked to the needs of the police in the preparatory period, such as the need to know who sees whom with what frequency. These projects are still in the early stages; but they are worth watching.

One far-fetched application of computer technology is relevant to the preparatory period. This is the development of models based on known facts which attempt to predict whether, for example, a person is likely to become a political activist or where a riot is likely to take place. Again, these projects are at an early stage, but they reflect the trend for the social sciences to be applied to the control of dissent.

The British Police National Computer

A recent advertisement in the national and technical press promised excellent prospects for successful applicants: 'You would be joining the formative stages of what will probably be the largest single computer-controlled network in the world.'[34] The Police National Computer Project, officially conceived in 1967, has been in operation since 1974. By 1976, the policeman on the beat will have access to the centralized information store at Hendon, north of London, via a nation-wide terminal network. This impressive project is the result of a partnership between the Home Office, local authorities and the police, under the overall jurisdiction of the Under-Secretary of State for the Home Office. The total cost to 1980, including running costs, hardware and staff wages, is estimated at between £30 and £40 million; and this at a time of sweeping cuts in social spending. There is no doubt that such a system is necessary from the police point of view, in order to prevent the breakdown of the

172 The Technology of Political Control

manual Criminal Records system. This comprises a Central Criminal Records Office (CRO) and Fingerprints Division at Scotland Yard, and ten regional offices each also housing a CRO and fingerprints file.

The major problem with this system was the amount of time it took to answer a query which required searching through the files – on average about twenty to forty minutes. Meanwhile, across the Atlantic, the success of computerization of police records and traffic-control systems was already being demonstrated in California. The imminent collapse of the British records system and the lessons of the California experience stimulated the initiation of the British Police National Computer Project. In 1970, the Home Secretary authorized the purchase of three Burroughs B6700 computers.

The PNC data base is maintained at Hendon on a twin Burroughs B6700 large-scale computer system which provides for a central file of about 5,000 million characters. (Each character can be one of 256 different letters, numbers or symbols.) It is planned that the file will eventually hold about 25 million vehicle owners' names, coded fingerprints of approximately three million people, some five million criminal names, about 200,000 stolen vehicles, and still have space left over.[35] However, the Project is not attempting to computerize all the information housed by CROs – only information needed by policemen on the beat in order to take operational action will be transferred to the data base at Hendon, together with the main indices to the manual file in the CROs. So when a file is accessed, it will refer the inquiry to the relevant CRO file for more detailed information. The computer is equipped with amending and updating facilities, so that new information can be incorporated in a matter of seconds.

In the initial stages of the project, three types of records are being held on the Hendon computer: a motor-vehicle owner's index; an index of Scotland Yard's fingerprints file; and an index of stolen and suspect vehicles. Information on vehicle registration is transferred from the Department of the Environment's new computer centre at Swansea to Hendon. Each record in the stolen-vehicles index contains the registration number, vehicle type, make, model, year and colour, together with information about where and when it was reported missing and which police force is involved in the case. Theoretically, the stolen-vehicles index can handle an average of 8,000 inquiries in a peak hour. In his 1975 Annual Report, the Chief Inspector of Constabulary describes how the finding of stolen vehicles has been speeded up by the computer; in one case he claims that a stolen vehicle was recovered before the owner, on reporting the theft, had left the police station. Previously it could have taken up to ten days for information on stolen vehicles to reach all police forces. By the end of 1974, there were particulars of about 120,000 stolen vehicles on the PNC file.[36]

The national fingerprint collection held at New Scotland Yard will be the computer's next major acquisition. At the time of writing the fingerprint files are not as well developed as the vehicle ones. But it was planned that, by the end of 1976, police forces would have access via computer and television to any of the 3.5 million sets of fingerprints at present on manual files.

The ultimate goal is to provide a national computerized criminal-records system accommodating up to 38 million files of all types, and answering an average of 20–25,000 inquiries in a peak hour, mostly concerning vehicles and criminals' names. By the end of 1974, 375 terminals in local forces were already operating and by the end of 1976 there will be over 1,000. When the system is fully operational, the policeman or woman on the beat will be able to obtain answers to queries by using a lapel radio to contact the terminal operator at the local police station. (In Washington, DC, in 1975 police patrolmen were given their own portable 'data-access terminal' so they can access the computer directly.) Police are already being trained to operate the terminals – two operator training schools have been set up, at Hendon and Durham, administered by the Home Office. Between September 1973 and December 1974 over 2,000 police and civilian terminal operators passed through the two schools.[37]

At the present time, the PNC is not really much more than a giant store which can handle information much more efficiently and quickly than manual filing systems. From the point of view of political surveillance, the vehicle application is by far the most useful. Storing names and other details of political activists is really useful only if there is a long-term prospect of rounding up large numbers of people with great speed, but even then it is not likely that the Special Branch or MI5 will need a computer to tell them who the 'leaders' are. In the preparatory period, it is far more important to prevent political groups from gaining support and to find out the rate at which they are building up their membership. A project which is currently under experiment in the Thames Valley area, if successful, will be much more useful for their early stage of operations in the preparatory period.

The Thames Valley Project

The idea of using the computer to establish links between people, places and vehicles is not a new one: indeed, it seems almost the obvious thing to do after collecting large amounts of information. In 1967, Paul Baran let his mind wander amid such possibilities: 'I visualized the growth of a large network of interconnected computers able to recall any selected information on any individual. The computer could perform cross-file examinations, studying, and looking for relationships between individuals suspected of conspiratorial activities.'[38] In 1972, a Home Office project was set up to do just that: a terminal at Slough police station was linked to a computer in London, and the *Police Review* described the project as follows: 'The automated detective will be making logical deductions by piecing together scraps of information gathered over months of painstaking investigation. Such a fact as a subject having lunch with a man with no criminal record may lead to the build-up of a picture that no detective could hope to piece together.'[39]

In July 1974, the Honeywell computer firm announced that it had won a £500,000 contract from the Home Office to continue this pioneering work. A Series 6000 computer has been installed near Oxford with visual display units to access it at police stations all down the Thames Valley. The essence of the project is to feed into the computer information from police notebooks, which in many cases amounts to little more than gossip, rumour and suspicion, in other words the type of low-grade information that Kitson is so insistent upon. This dubious information gathered by the uniformed police will thus be instantly accessible to specialist forces such as the CID, Special Branch and Bomb Squad. Apart from the possibility of linking together scraps of circumstantial evidence gathered in different places at different times, the project will also prevent uniformed police from keeping information for themselves in the hope of solving a case and thereby improving their chances of promotion. On the other hand, it has yet to be proved that the amassing of a lot of seemingly unconnected facts and then connecting them by computer will yield much. According to Honeywell, the system will be reviewed after the Oxford experiment 'with a view to making recommendations that might be applied more generally'.[40] Neither Honeywell nor the Home Office are willing to give any information about the relation of the project to the PNC.

Since both the PNC and the Thames Valley project are new developments in British law-enforcement, it is necessary to look across the Atlantic if we are to be able to evaluate the usefulness of computerized law-enforcement (and possibly anti-subversion) techniques. Present US experience could point to future British developments in this field.

The US Experience

In 1967, at the height of the anti-Vietnam war and black civil rights movements, the Institute of Defense Analyses (IDA) published its *Task Force Report: Science and Technology*. The report, which was the IDA's submission to the Commission on Law Enforcement and the Administration of Justice, set up by President Johnson, recommended that all police records should be stored in computers and these data banks should be interconnected so that police in one area should have immediate access to information stored elsewhere. The centre of this system would be a national file on computer in Washington,

DC, linked to regional files for individual states or groups of states, and local files for major cities. LEAA was to be the co-ordinating body for this project.

Before this time, a few states had already set up centralized files of criminal histories. New York for example had a system called NYIIS (New York State's Identification and Intelligence System) which had more than three million fingerprints and 500,000 summary criminal histories on computer, with additional information on manual files; it was used by over 3,600 local law-enforcement agencies. At the national level, the FBI maintained the National Crime Information Centre (NCIC) which operated through local law-enforcement control terminals.

In 1969, LEAA began funding Project SEARCH (Systems for Electronic Analysis and Retrieval of Criminal Histories), a 16-million-dollar demonstration project, in which twenty states shared criminal histories through a computerized central data index. SEARCH was intended to be a prototype for a national computer file which would facilitate 'prompt apprehension of interstate felons'. It consisted essentially of a computerized central index, with individual criminal history files and user terminals.[41] The initial design of the system followed the decentralized model proposed by the Presidential Commission on crime, but in 1970 the then Attorney General, John Mitchell, decided – despite objections from the LEAA and many liberal quarters – to transfer the file system from LEAA to the FBI.

The variety of agencies which previously participated in the NCIC system can be judged from a list published as early as 1972. This included the Secret Service, the Internal Revenue Service, the Alcohol and Tax division of the Treasury Department, the Immigration and Naturalization Service, the Bureau of Prisons, the US Courts, US Attorneys and the US Marshals. Official estimates of the number of people who will eventually be on file range from 5 million (FBI estimate) to 20 million (LEAA estimate). The number of files in the total system, including all the state files, will be much greater.[42]

The FBI's central computer is in Washington and has more

than 7,000 teletype terminals located throughout the US, primarily in local police stations. The system is heavily used: for instance, in July 1973 the central computer handled over 109,000 transactions daily, including inquiries, updating and entries. In 1971, the national data bank of criminal histories based on the results of SEARCH was added to the NCIC. This is the CCH (Computerized Criminal History) system which contains a 'rap sheet' on everyone who has committed a crime. The FBI rules for safeguarding the system from abuse include the right of every individual to see the information on her or his file – providing of course she or he goes down to the local police station in person, presents appropriate identification and submits to fingerprinting. There are no civil or criminal penalties for misuse of data; everybody is safe, because the FBI promise that they will not 'knowingly act in any manner which would infringe upon individual rights to privacy'.[43]

As we have said, the collection of large amounts of information on data bases is only a first step towards the use of computers to counter political dissent. With their information systems already fairly well developed, the US police are branching out into correlation. The leading project in this field is PATRIC (Pattern Recognition and Information Correlation), which will provide 'tactical information derived from crime and crime-related reports for use by investigative and uniformed personnel.' The Los Angeles police department intends to use PATRIC to extend the investigators' access to files, by correlating the components of various crimes to isolate those appearing to have been committed by the same person. Possible suspects will also be identified.[44]

An ambitious system was advertised by IBM at the 1972 'ON-LINE' exhibition in London. Developed by the police in Kansas City, Missouri, the 'ALERT' system provides each patrol car with a terminal and radio link to the central computer. On receiving a police inquiry about a particular address, the computer will send back 'the names of all persons on file living at a particular address or in the immediate locality. This type of information is particularly useful when a call is made to investigate a disturbance at a particular locality.' The IBM handout concluded by explaining how they intend to expand the system in the future:

- Project patterns of criminal behaviour.
- Analyse trends that, if not altered, will result in future social problems.
- Create systems to deal with unacceptable behaviour patterns before crimes or accidents are caused.
- Develop individual patterns of persons having trouble functioning in society.

... A police information system cannot be judged a complete success until all the above objectives have been met.[45]

It is as well to be cautious about what is claimed by IBM when it is trying to sell systems. However, if it did manage to bring such a project to fruition, a potential for its application to repression would be enormous. There are already signs that this US technology is coming to Britain; the Thames Valley experiment is only the first step.

Central and Local Government Data Banks

In Britain, the scale of police computerization is tiny compared with the number of computers in local and central government, many of which have files on individuals. The major user of computers in government departments is the Ministry of Defence: *Computer Survey* reported that in 1972 it was using 500 computers. It is naturally more reticent about what it is doing with them than the police force. It is, however, almost self-evident that the police and Army, as the forces responsible for an internal defence campaign, will amass data on people and use them. It is less obvious that data collected by other government agencies can be used for similar purposes; yet the second largest users of computers after the Ministry of Defence are local authorities. It is difficult to imagine that they would refuse to give information to the police or Army in, say, a state of emergency.

One of the most highly developed applications of computerized data collection in Britain is the medical records system maintained by the Department of Health and Social Security.

98 per cent of inpatients are now recorded; further, in 1972, the details of all inmates in psychiatric hospitals were entered on a government computer file. A special project being carried out in Oxfordshire is designed to build up a lifetime medical history of every individual. Part of the scheme is a plan to record every visit to the GP on the computer.[46]

If all the information stored in data banks belonging to different government departments were integrated, it would be possible to build up comprehensive personal files on everyone in Britain. But the portents for integration are not promising, because each department has installed different computer systems at different times. In 1972, a government study concluded: 'Our general review of departments ... has brought to light comparatively few indications of systems integration either within government or with external organizations ... these are limited in scope and lie mainly in the future.'[47] Given the problem of integration, if the government decides to set up a national personal data bank, it seems much more likely that it will start from scratch.

It will, however, be able to draw on the experience of other countries which already have national personal data banks, such as Sweden, Finland, Denmark and Belgium. In Sweden, each person has a national personal number which is the key to a record in the Basic Information Register, with details such as name, address, marital status, residence code and taxation district. The national register is the centre of a series of special registers covering education, taxation, health, employment and crime. Work is going ahead on the assembling of a series of registers which will house details of institutions, each with an organization number. Finally, the Basic Information Register and the Organization Register will be cross-related to a third register, based on the geographical location of the people and institutions in other registers.[48]

The Swedish and Finnish system depends on the use of a national personal number, and the fact that every time a person changes his or her address he or she must register the new address with the police – both practices which are alien to Britain and would require a basic reorientation on the issue of individual rights (though of course we cannot rule out the introduction of such practices as emergency measures). But there will certainly be pressure on the British government to bring its computer system into line with other countries. The OECD recommends that 'Central co-ordination should be established to ensure that programmes once developed are made available to all government agencies, maybe even on an international level.'[49] It is difficult to tell whether the government will yield to this pressure or to that of civil libertarians opposed to any greater infringement of privacy.

Finally, private data banks should be mentioned, if only to get things into proportion. Credit bureaux, for example, have far more computerized personal files than any law-enforcement agency. It has been estimated that the Associated Credit Bureaux have computerized files on about 110 million people in the USA.[50] One British credit firm alone has boasted that it will have 90 per cent of the nation on computer files by the end of this decade.[51] And many of these agencies are prepared to give information to the police in return for information on police files.[52] In the USA, the trading of information between government agencies and credit bureaux is established practice. The New York Credit Bureau, for example, has supplied data to the FBI and the State Department.[53]

The police (and possibly the Army) thus have access (or potential access) to large amounts of information about people stored in data banks. There is no doubt that they will make use of it if they need to. And once information on people is stored in data banks there are very few safeguards against abuses. The only way to ensure that it is not used against political dissenters – other than the creation of a society where there is no necessity to suppress anyone – is to try to ensure that those who operate such systems, the technicians and engineers, will refuse to allow information to be used by the security forces. It is also necessary to know what computer technology is capable of – and to be wary of the claims made for its effectiveness by those who are interested in creating paranoia. The value of amassing low-grade information can be greatly overexaggerated; and the computer applications which would be really effective in the preparatory period have yet to be fully developed. On the other hand the very fact that governments are putting money into such developments is an indication of the extent to which they feel threatened – and not by the rising crime rate alone.

14
Monitoring Militant Action

In the 'non-violent' phase information gathering will be concentrated much more on collection of operational information. With strikes, factory occupations and mass demonstrations breaking out in different parts of the country, it is essential that the security forces are able to take rapid action. They must have equipment which can see and hear what is happening and relay it instantly, by day or night. They must be able to dispatch men and vehicles to the scene of an incident before it develops into mass effective action. In this chapter we shall describe some of the equipment the police and Army have or are acquiring to deal with militant action.

Radio and Telephone Communications

Police radio and telephone systems have been developing so rapidly in Britain in the last few years that the Chief Inspector of Constabulary complained in his 1974 Report that the Police Directorate of Telecommunications 'has been fully stretched in its efforts to provide more and increasingly sophisticated communications equipment for the police service'.[1]

Accompanying this development is the improvement in methods to prevent interception. Some radio enthusiasts make a habit of listening in on police transmissions. The French Journal *Interférences* says that in France, as in the USA, this has become a national hobby. For those not initiated in the sport, it goes on to explain how to listen in to police wavebands.[2] In Britain, all police VHF systems were studied in 1975 'with a view to providing better cover'.[3]

Apart from the problem of how not to be listened to, the police have the problem of how to listen in to illegal transmissions, especially where they suspect that demonstrations or disturbances are being controlled by radio. The military have long employed electronic counter-measures to monitor and 'ferret out these illegal devices', but they have only recently become available to the police. There were receivers that could cover the entire radio frequency range and also permit a user to tune into a specific frequency.[4]

The police are also concerned to prevent unauthorized access to their telephone systems. In 1974, a new automatic telephone network linking all the main establishments in the Metropolitan Police area was established. It provides fast communications over private lines with alternative access to public telephone networks. A special feature designed 'for use in emergency conditions' is a system being incorporated at each of the twelve switching centres in which 'least essential connections can be quickly disconnected'.

These developments in telecommunications are largely internal to the police, to enable them to communicate more easily. To collect information about the activities of militants they will use all the devices developed for the preparatory period – bugs, transmitters, telephone taps and so on, as well as informers and infiltrators. But the 'non-violent' phase requires further technology. In particular, the police (and possibly the Army) must be able to *see* what is happening.

Optical Devices

The Report of HM Inspector of Constabulary for 1974 simply records 'development, testing and evaluation of equipment and techniques' for optical aids.[5] It is, however, possible to fill in at least some of the details behind this officially vague statement. As well as incorporation of relevant Army-type equipment, the British police – in the wake of their American counterparts – are acquiring devices which will monitor activity above the city streets.

Cameras are now standard equipment for most police forces, and, if some riot-control experts have their way, video equipment will soon have the same status. But what the police really need in order to counter militant action are devices which will give real-time intelligence so that they know where to deploy their forces. The solution is provided by TV cameras at strategic points, linked to central control rooms at police stations. Most of these systems have been developed for traffic control in congested city centres. But the police have been quick to spot the application to crowd control and monitoring.

In early 1972 a study prepared by the US Committee on Telecommunications of the National Academy of Engineering and funded by the Justice Department recommended twenty-four-hour television surveillance of city streets.[6] Closed-circuit television is now being adopted rapidly by US police-force systems. Three US towns already had round-the-clock television surveillance in downtown areas as early as 1971.[7] New York has a very interesting system. The City Police Department uses closed-circuit television cameras to monitor demonstrations and civil disorders. Cameras have been installed at traditional trouble spots: City Hall, Times Square, the United Nations Headquarters and so on. Operators in the control room monitor the progress of the demonstration and feed information into the computer, which is linked to a deployment system.[8]

Police in the University area of Cleveland, Ohio, are going one better. They are introducing a closed-circuit TV system using laser beams rather than cables for transmission. The fixed cameras, with tracking and lens manoeuvrability, are monitored at the police station. With these cameras, they are able to monitor 80 per cent of the areas where 70 per cent of 'street crimes' occur. Often the cameras can monitor the flight of suspects; the advantage of laser beaming is that the cameras need not be permanently located – they can be shifted around if one area becomes the focus of disturbances. The cameras are in operation twenty-four hours a day.[9]

The British police are still a long way off from laser-beam closed-circuit TV systems. The first major British innovation in the field of TV surveillance is the Greater London Council's CITRAC (Central Integrated Traffic Control) scheme. It is run jointly by the Metropolitan Police, the City Police and the GLC. A pilot experiment was carried out in 1973 over the West London area, which monitors $6\frac{1}{4}$ square miles with eight cameras. The success of the scheme persuaded the GLC to

Monitoring Militant Action 185

extend it to cover the whole of London. Forty-five cameras connected direct to Scotland Yard are to be installed in Central London streets, probably by the end of 1975. In the control room, operators can adjust the cameras by means of teleshift controls – zoom, focus or tilt. Further developments may include another 150 cameras in Outer London, and the Post Office is already developing cheaper closed-circuit TV systems to suit the smaller city. The *Post Office Telecommunications Journal*, reporting on progress of the experiment, was hopeful that, 'within the next decade, many of the larger towns in this country will have computer-controlled traffic lights and television surveillance'.[10]

The claim that the system is only for traffic control is somewhat undermined by the development of another network, used specifically by the police for crowd control. TV cameras have been installed by the police on top of high buildings at strategic points in London. These include the top of the National Gallery in Trafalgar Square (a traditional rallying point for demonstrators); on top of the Privy Council building in Whitehall (the route of many demonstrations and near most government ministries); and on the top of the Duchess of Argyll's house near Grosvenor Square (the location of the American Embassy). Scotland Yard's spokesman told *The Times* in 1973 that they were 'part of a traffic scheme planned with the Greater London Council'. The Duchess of Argyll had a different story. She said that she had agreed to have a camera installed on the roof of her house 'to help the police with the demonstrators in Grosvenor Square'.[11] The *Post Office Telecommunications Journal* claims that the traffic and crowd control systems could be interfaced at any time – though at some technical inconvenience.

Television surveillance has its drawbacks. In the first place, it is expensive. But, more importantly, it is labour-intensive. TV surveillance requires operators constantly monitoring screens in the control room. Even though in some places an operator monitors up to eight screens at a time, it is a tedious business.*

---

*The Home Office is sponsoring research to determine the optimum number of screens an operator can watch at any one time.[12]

The next set of devices we shall consider have been developed to overcome this problem.

Sensors and Intrusion Devices

Sensors are electronic devices which detect people or vehicles passing within a given range. In 1967 sensors were planted along the MacNamara Line in Vietnam and, although the experiment had to be abandoned, the military were not discouraged. Later, sensors were used along the Ho Chi Minh trail. Battery-operated sensors relayed information to a relay platform which flew overhead twenty-four hours a day. In the relay aircraft, the data was processed by computer and usually transmitted to the Air Force computer in Thailand. The computer would print out activation patterns of the sensors at high speed and show updated sketches of the area on TV screens. The operator could then track the movements of people crossing or moving along the trail. But the military were forced to admit that traffic was never more than slowed down on the Ho Chi Minh trail, despite the total expenditure of $2,000 million on the sensor programme.[13]

Nevertheless the US Army, Navy and Air Force have set up organizations for exploiting the existing technology.[14] One of the things they came up with was a sensor system modelled on the Ho Chi Minh trail development, for patrolling the Mexican–American border. This was one of the first applications of sensors to law enforcement.

The British Army have been quick to see the usefulness of sensors in Northern Ireland. The *Land Operations Manual* lists six different applications for remote sensor devices, including 'early warning for other devices' and 'prisoner cages — escape routes'. The IRIS equipment consists of four infra-red fences connected with cables. TOBIAS is a seismic detector which can sense people at up to 150 metres and vehicles at up to 500 metres, and can also detect animals. The latest types of sensor can detect the vibrations of marching troops or trucks on the move, and are sensitive to metal, heat, sound and even the smell of urine.

The sensors used in Vietnam were designed mainly for rural

Monitoring Militant Action

areas. Developments since the end of that war have, by contrast, been directed largely toward the use of sensors in urban areas, usually to guard buildings and key installations. They are still sponsored by the military, who have adopted four different approaches to improving the probability of detection. 'Smarter' sensors electronically classify the input they receive from the target, or exclude unwanted noise. Sensors with different capabilities (for example, magnetic and seismic) can be combined. Information received from many dispersed sensors can be processed by inserting logic into the information flow. Finally, experiments are being made with sensor interaction, in which the sensors are physically separated so that they provide complementary information.[15]

Despite these impressive developments, the Mitre Corporation, which is responsible for them, is not satisfied. A great deal of time spent watching nests from which the birds have flown could be saved by a device which will detect the presence of cars behind a closed garage door. The corporation also feels the need for a 'remote car motion indicator' and devices for 'inconspicuous remote viewing' so that agents will run less risk of detection.[16] The 'motion detector' may improve the possibilities of this. It is hooked into a closed-circuit system taking a static picture of an area. Any motion inside the range of vision of the camera triggers an alarm which can show as a flashing marker on a remote monitor display.[17]

Electronic tracking devices are already, of course, a valuable aid to security and intelligence operations. A sensor can be attached to the car to be followed; or it can be attached to a tailing car so that other members of the force can follow out of sight. The sensor, when it is switched on, acts as a radio beacon, transmitting a characteristic signal over ranges of at least a mile or two. Cars following at a distance can detect from the signal how far away the sensor is, and in what direction it is travelling.

A variant of this approach is the 'electronic number plate', originally designed to catch lorry hi-jackers. Trials of this system have been successfully completed by the US Department of Transportation. A battery-operated transponder is fixed inside the vehicle. Each vehicle has a unique code assigned to it (from a pool of 100 million codes). To track down the vehicle, a police helicopter broadcasts a radio signal addressed 'personally' to it, using its code. When the helicopter is in range the signal switches on the transponder to transmit a characteristic signal. This enables the helicopter to tell how far away the vehicle is and in what direction it is travelling. Clearly, a system of this kind can easily be adapted for other purposes, such as tracking vehicles belonging to suspects. Or beyond. The Raytheon Company of Wayland, Mass., has developed a device called Raytag. This has inspired a Raytheon scientist to the following vision: 'Looking still further ahead, the possibility of having every motor vehicle equipped with such an "electronic license plate" certainly has profound law-enforcement implications.' Indeed it does.

Night-Vision Devices

Many of the activities carried out by militants in the 'non-violent' stage of a crisis – clandestine meetings, factory occupations and so on – will take place under cover of darkness. The evidence of Paris in May 1968 and of Northern Ireland shows that night-time activities grow in importance as the conflict mounts towards 'open insurgency'. Police and Army effectiveness – in information-gathering, riot control or lethal fire – can be drastically curtailed by darkness. The problem is an old one, not confined to 'internal security' operations. But it took the US weapons development programme for the Vietnam war to find an effective answer – night-vision equipment. Declassified in 1969, these devices are now being snapped up by US police departments.

The British Army has its own night-vision devices, which have seen active service in Northern Ireland. The *Army Land Operations Manual*, in a series of amendments dated January 1973, lists five different types of image-intensifiers and two types of thermal imagers; it also notes that these new devices are rapidly replacing active infra-red (IR) equipment. Among them is the 'Twiggy' image-intensifier, a tripod-mounted surveillance device with a range of up to 600 metres against men in starlight. More mobile is the Individual Weapon Sight, which can spot men in starlight at up to 300 metres and is small enough to be fitted to rifles. There have been reports of widespread destruction of street lights in Republican strongholds by British soldiers, partly to take advantage of the tactical edge such devices give them, and partly for technical reasons, as we shall see later.

The British Army has also used thermal viewers with infrared cameras mounted on an RAF Phantom jet to detect escape tunnels being dug out of Long Kesh by internees. Every few days the jet would fly over the camp photographing every inch of ground. There have been stories that the Army would allow the men to dig almost to the perimeter before stopping them, or watch them digging in completely the wrong direction. It seems that infra-red tunnel detection has had a very high success rate in Northern Ireland. Helicopter-mounted thermal viewers have also been used to detect buried road-side landmines.

Having proved their worth in Vietnam and Northern Ireland, it is hardly surprising that night-vision devices are beginning to look attractive to the British police. By 1973 they were using two types of night-vision equipment: passive image intensifiers and active infra-red viewers.[18] Passive intensifiers operate by using an objective lens to receive the low level of illumination available outdoors at night. By passing this light down an intensifier tube, an image up to 50,000 times brighter can be produced. Even if there is no moon or artificial lighting, but only stars behind cloud cover, this image can be easily observed through an eye-piece. Under average conditions, most intensifiers can detect a person up to 200 metres away and recognize him or her at 50 metres. Most image-intensifiers can be adapted for TV or 35-mm. camera. The problem with using them is that the degree of brightness and quality of image are adversely affected by the presence of bright lights within the field of view.

The second, less portable, type of night-viewing device – the active infra-red viewers – incorporate an infra-red spotlight. This is used to illuminate the scene, which can then be viewed through an infra-red converter which makes it visible to the human eye. The quality of the picture produced is good (up to 150 metres with a hand-held viewer), but the image is confined to the area illuminated by the infra-red spotlight.

A third type of night-vision device has only recently come into service – the thermal viewer. The chief advantage of the thermal viewer is that it can give images at up to twice the range of the other types we have described. Furthermore, the image is not affected by other lighting in the field of view, as it is in the other types; indeed, it can be used in the daytime to distinguish between warm and cold objects. Thermal viewers depend simply on their ability to pick up the heat emitted as infra-red radiation by a person or vehicle. The average temperature of a person's head and outer clothing is always several degrees above the background temperature, so that the person stands out 'thermally' from his or her surroundings.

Commercially available thermal cameras are not practical for police use because of their bulkiness, high cost (about £10,000 apiece) and lack of portability, and because they require liquid nitrogen for cooling the detectors. The only truly portable viewer tested by the Police Scientific Development Branch was the US Army model designed by Hughes and made by Phillips, which weighs only five pounds and had very simple controls. The detectors reach operating temperature fifteen minutes after they are switched on, and the equipment is cable-connected to a battery which powers it for twelve hours. This it seems, 'closely approximates to a suggested specification for a police thermal viewer'.[19] The Home Office has commissioned a prototype chest-mounted thermal camera for trials with the Fire Service, and it may be possible to modify this for police use.

The principal application of thermal viewers is for night surveillance of people and vehicles. The main operational advantage of thermal imaging comes in built-up areas, where street lighting makes other night-vision devices ineffective. As we have noted elsewhere, many of the new technological developments for police use are directed towards tracking vehicles. Thermal viewers can help here, too:

A thermal viewer makes it possible to pick out recently driven vehicles from a large number of vehicles. The tyres provide the best means of comparison and they stay warm for over an hour after the vehicle is parked ... It is possible to drive along a road or round a car park and quickly identify all recently driven cars, when, for instance, there is a search for an abandoned car.[20]

We have already seen how aerial surveillance thermal imaging has been used by the Army in Northern Ireland for tunnel detection – it works on the simple principle that freshly disturbed soil is warmer than the earth around it. It is also possible to detect people and vehicles by thermal viewers placed in helicopters. From a helicopter flying at 200–300 metres, targets over an area of one square mile can be observed with thermal viewers. The development of thermal viewers thus adds to the versatility of the next item of police equipment we shall consider – the police helicopter.

Helicopters

The helicopter is a mobile and agile observation and communications platform – and at times can be more than that. It can cover a wider area more quickly than the patrol car on the ground. Its bubble enclosure permits an unobstructed line of vision. In urban areas it can skip over traffic which could block a patrol car.

The incorporation of the helicopter into police systems has accelerated rapidly since the mid-1960s; one survey found that the number of police helicopters in the USA had risen by one third in 1970–71 alone.[21] By 1973 there were over 150 in use by a total of sixty-three US cities and counties. By 1967, the Home Office Police Research and Development Branch was already studying police use of helicopters in Britain.[22]

The first regular police helicopter patrol (as opposed to earlier search and rescue operations) began in Lakewood, California, in 1966, after the successful use of Army helicopters in Vietnam. It was called 'Project Sky Knight' and was funded by LEAA's predecessor organization. In 1968, the project was given a glowing report,[23] and police chiefs all over the US began to investigate the possibilities of launching similar projects. By 1971, LEAA had awarded some one million dollars in discretionary grants to help the purchase or lease of police helicopters.

The Hughes Sky Knight model is designed specifically for use in urban areas. Normal patrols fly at a height of 400 to 500 feet and it has been estimated that they can patrol an area seven to sixteen times faster than a car.[24] Communications with police cars are carried out by radio; some helicopters have a communications mixer panel so that the observer and pilot can transmit and receive simultaneously on different frequencies.

Kansas City's 'ALERT' (Automated Law Enforcement Response Team) is a fairly typical police-car patrol system to which helicopters have been added. The city has six Hughes model 300 helicopters and at least one is available twenty-four hours a day. In 1972, the unit logged 5,794 flying hours on test flights, surveillance, photo flights and covering demonstrations.[25] About 65 per cent of the helicopter patrol time in most systems is in support of ground patrol cars or police on the beat. At night, they can illuminate the area using powerful searchlights or practice covert surveillance.[26]

The most important application of patrol helicopters in the 'non-violent' stage is to riot control. Helicopters were used at Berkeley to spray CS gas at demonstrators in People's Park. They were used by the military in the 1967 march on the Pentagon, and in the November 1968 march on Washington. In Cleveland, police helicopters with searchlights patrol the city's ghettoes at night; and in Philadelphia, police were secretly trained to fire guns from helicopter platforms.[27] New York completed a test survey in 1968 of helicopter surveillance using closed-circuit television. The test system comprised:

A TV camera, zoom lens, image stabilizer and microwave transmitting equipment installed in a helicopter. The signal is received in the Empire State building via antennae. The signal is then relayed via microwave TV relay links to police headquarters. The signal can be distributed to various offices throughout the building including the Command and Control Centre, where the information can be evaluated and manpower and equipment assigned to cope with the problem. This installation is equipped with recording equipment so that a permanent record can be made of transmitted audio and visual signals. Live TV images can be provided on a six-foot by eight-foot screen for close observation.[28]

The fact that in many ways patrol helicopters operate like aerial patrol cars makes the link with command and control systems an obvious future development. Not so obvious is the use of helicopters prescribed by Congressman James Scheuer in his book, *To Walk the Streets Safely*[!], which bears a strong imprint of the Vietnam experience:

In view of helicopter mobility and versatility, city officials should re-examine the techniques used to deploy personnel. Situations calling for large numbers of troops and policemen might be handled by heavy personnel-carrying helicopters. To accommodate such transports, perhaps docks could be built at convenient points in midtown. Our military experience demonstrates that men can also be landed on unusual terrain by means of ladders or portable landing docks.[29]

With all these operational advantages, the place of helicopters in the police arsenal is assured. The rapid rate of acquisition continues: Hughes Helicopters of California, the supplier of 70 per cent of patrol helicopters, forecast in 1973 a total worldwide market of 8,000 police patrol helicopters by 1980, with an estimated 3,000 going to US agencies.[30] In Britain the Commissioner of Police of the metropolis wrote in his 1974 report that increased use of helicopters for police duties had provided 'assistance at everyday incidents'; they had supplied aerial photographic evidence and helicopters had been used to deal with 'widespread traffic congestion caused by a major demonstration'.*[31] There are very few sour notes among the songs of praise for police helicopters; but an LEAA official responsible for evaluating and assessing them described the helicopter 'the post-computer status symbol for some police departments' and suggests that patrol cars are cheaper and probably just as effective. And the Baltimore police department, scorning this new technology, purchased bicycles for patrol purposes in 1972.

*Although the Scotland Yard Press Bureau informed us in July 1975 that the Metropolitan Police only had one helicopter!

Computer-Assisted Police Operations

All the devices we have discussed so far in this section are designed to help the police and Army to gather information about and watch over criminal actions or civil disturbances. Real-time information, such as that provided by optical equipment, sensors and helicopters, is essential when the police need to act rapidly to prevent escalation of militant activity.

Once a riot, demonstration or strike is happening, the police or Army normally have one main objective: to cool things down as quickly as possible. Immediate and efficient deployment of resources is of primary importance. The military are much better trained at this than the police. But the latter have recently begun to borrow military methods for deployment, using computer-assisted command and control systems. These are especially important when disturbances are breaking out in different parts of a city. As the US Institute of Defense Analyses explained in its report to the Presidential Commission on Law Enforcement in 1967 '"Command and Control" is military terminology for the planning, direction and control of operations. It involves the organization of personnel and status monitoring, decision-making and execution.' [32]

Most command and control systems are used for ordinary crime-fighting. One of the first sophisticated computerized systems is New York City's SPRINT (Special Police Radio Inquiry Network). This refers all incident information to the police department computer, which looks for further useful data in its memory bank and then sends a message to a radio dispatcher at headquarters. The message is displayed on a TV screen and shows such information as the exact location of the incident and the three nearest patrol cars. The radio dispatcher then tells one of the patrol cars to go to the scene.

A different system operates for riots:

> In a riot or other emergency situation, an emergency communications centre must be established to transform a police department from a loose collection of independent units to a cohesive coordinated force ... Means must be provided to collect and display, rapidly and continuously, all the varieties of tactical intelligence

relating to the location of events and the disposition of forces ... Contingency plans for situations that might arise ... must be developed and stored in readily accessible form.[33]

The New York City computerized riot-control room was set up in 1969 and uses closed-circuit TV cameras, as well as helicopters and the fixed cameras described earlier. It is linked to local precincts by a special twenty-four-hour 'hot-line'. A computer hook-up also links it with the SPRINT system so that patrol cars can be deployed. When he opened the command post, Mayor Lindsay filled in some interesting historical background. 'Our people visited the Strategic Air Command in Omaha, the Space Center in Houston, and the Pentagon, and this extraordinary command center came out of it.'[34]

The city of Los Angeles is currently experimenting with a totally integrated command control and communication system. The operator at the 'complaints board' will enter incident data into the computer using a display terminal. The computer can then transmit the message to a terminal, in the appropriate car or helicopter. Meanwhile, sector co-ordinators in the control room will be tracing the course of events on graphic display terminals, which can show street maps, incident locations and where the available police vehicles are stationed.[35]

In Britain, the Police Scientific Development Branch of the Home Office set up a project in 1968 to determine the usefulness of a small computer in the police control room of a typical British city. Birmingham was selected as the typical city, and the system became fully operational in 1972. An ARGUS computer was installed in the central control complex, and operators in the control room and each of the twelve police subdivisions have access to it via visual display units. Details of an emergency call are fed into an 'incident pro forma' as soon as they are received. All subsequent action is largely automated.

Patrol cars have been installed with data input devices so that they can inform the computer of their location and movements. This system is centrally controlled but operationally decentralized, so that police are dealing with a situation in their own locality and know the nature of the area and population. The system appears to be a success, and the results of this pilot scheme have been encouraging enough for a second project to run in Glasgow. A third system, in Staffordshire, will develop the application of these techniques to a county police force.[36] A fourth is planned for the new West Midlands police force, which will study the feasibility of developing a system for a larger force. All these projects involve the development of management information systems to extract the maximum effectiveness from the resources of the force.[37]

Associated with police command and control systems are automatic vehicle-location systems which can track down and direct patrol cars. In London, the Metropolitan Police tested one such system in 1974. Called 'FLAIR' (Fleet Location and Information Reporting), it is based on the principle of dead-reckoning navigation. The *Daily Telegraph* reported the results of tests carried out in Hackney: 'a Rover 3500 on "security runs" was accurately tracked over routes completely unknown to the "Flair" staff ... Scotland Yard's head of telecommunications reported a maximum error of only 33 feet to 34 feet using the system.'[38] The article concluded: '... remote monitors in offices away from the control centre will help control large police operations such as civil disturbances, disasters and VIP escorts'.

15
Riot Control

We have argued throughout this book that the threat of internal disorder is increasingly replacing the Soviet threat as the bogey of advanced capitalist countries. The strongest evidence for this shift is the mushrooming of new technological developments for riot control.

The need for governments to suppress demonstrations and strikes is by no means new. Nor have British ones ever been especially squeamish about it. The 'Battle of Peterloo' in 1819, in which a peaceful meeting calling for parliamentary reform was the object of a cavalry charge (score: 11 dead, 400 wounded), is just one example. Throughout the nineteenth century, deaths resulting from Army or police intervention in strikes occurred frequently.

British colonial history shows a good deal less restraint. The classic massacre in the old tradition was carried out at Amritsar, India, in 1919. A force of British and Gurkha riflemen opened fire without warning on a packed, peaceful crowd attending a meeting in support of independence. In ten minutes some 300 were killed and 600 wounded. The outcry in Britain over Amritsar showed that, even in the colonies, the time for such outright brutalities had passed.

It is easy enough to kill people. It is harder *not* to kill them, but to stop them all the same. 'Non-lethal' riot-control technology provides governments with sophisticated methods for controlling unruly populations. At the same time, it avoids the public outcry which results from outright massacres such as Bloody Sunday.

Already in 1912, the Paris police had developed the concept of using chemical weapons to subdue 'criminal and riotous individuals or groups'. They used bombs filled with ethyl bromacetate, an early tear gas. It was not until the fifties that the British began using 'non-lethal' riot-control technology extensively in the colonies. In the 1960s the USA, confronted with insurrections in its domestic colonies of Watts, Newark, Detroit and Chicago, moved decisively in the same direction. By 1968, the author of a US study on riot prevention and control was already arguing that the project of controlling and preventing riots called for 'a dedication and level of effort truly comparable with the Manhattan Project'.[1] In the same year, the Law Enforcement Administration Agency (LEAA) was set up to supervise the spending of federal funds for 'law and order'. Its budget rose from $63 million in 1969 to $856 million by 1973.

Only a part of LEAA's funds are devoted directly to the control of riots and civil disorders. (The rest goes for more conventional law enforcement activities and weaponry.) And some of the results are simply new variations on an old theme, such as SWAT, the Special Weapons and Tactics section of the Los Angeles Police Department. SWAT teams are heavily armed and specially trained for counter-urban-guerrilla activities. It was their massive fire-power which in 1974 roasted to death the surrounded members of the Symbionese Liberation Army. The new aspect of SWAT is that it is part of a police department — its weapons and methods of operation would be far more at home in an Army setting.

Justifications for the New Technology

The need for governments to employ the new riot-control technology signals the breakdown of attempts to control dissent by the usual methods. As Major-General Deane-Drummond puts it: 'The object is not suppression, but the avoidance of conflict.' But when avoidance fails and riots occur, we are entering Kitson's second, 'non-violent' phase of the crisis. If force is to be used to quell non-violent action, then the government must educate the public to accept it through 'programmes of advance public information and community preparations'.[2] Any adverse publicity must be promptly countered.

In order to reduce public outcry against the methods it intends to use, the state must prepare the ground by justifying their necessity. There is a range of attempted justifications for the use of riot-control technology, from conventional weapons downwards. The toughest line is to proclaim the trouble to be a rebellion. For instance, in the USA, analogies have been drawn between ghetto riots and 'insurgency' in Vietnam. This definition, if acceptable to the public, justifies the application of almost any level of force.

The second line of approach is to claim that 'what the rioters do is worse than what we do'. For an example, take this response to an inquiry about Ireland from a Ministry of Defence official: 'You mention the injuries apparently caused by rubber bullet rounds ... but you do not mention the number or nature of casualties among either the security forces or the civil population, not only those killed by shots or explosions but also those seriously injured and maimed by nail bombs, stones and so on.'[3] The implication that deaths had occurred as a result of demonstrators' actions prior to August 1970 (when rubber bullets were introduced) is false. But in any case the asymmetry between the two sides, one backed by all the resources of the state, precludes any facile comparison between the actions of demonstrators and those of the security forces.

A further justification for the new riot-control technology is: 'If we weren't using gas (or rubber bullets, or whatever) we would have to use guns.' But we have seen from the case of Northern Ireland that it is not gas *or* guns but gas *and* guns. The new technology supplements the old: it does not replace it. As another Ministry of Defence official has admitted: 'CS gas is rarely of use against gunmen; its application comes ... at a lower level of violence, in circumstances in which the use of firearms by the troops would be inappropriate if not unlawful.'[4]

The final justification for the new riot-control technology is that it is harmless, except for marginal effects or rare coincidences. In fact, there is no such thing as a 'non-lethal' riot-control weapon. The Americans have recognized this by substituting the term 'less lethal'. As a report to the United States National Science Foundation states: 'All weapons, and a wide variety of objects that are not intended to serve as weapons, create some primary or secondary risk of death or permanent injury.'[5] All effective riot-control agents are inherently unsafe, even if used as instructed. For one thing, their recipients are not all healthy twenty-five-year-olds. For another, they are seldom all standing at the 'correct' distance. And there is no way to deliver a measured dose to each individual in the target area. (The US Food and Drug Administration has taken the position that non-lethal weapons based on tear gas 'are not intended for the benefit of the persons to whom applied and do not fall within the statutory definition of drugs contained in the Federal Food, Drug and Cosmetic Act'.[6]) In any case, they are not used as directed. Deliberate abuse is so common as to constitute a rule rather than an exception. One (albeit atypical) police chief in the USA actually refused to issue Chemical Mace (see p. 213) to his men because he felt they would use it to 'torture people'.

Later in this chapter we shall show that all the riot-control agents used by the British Army in Northern Ireland are inherently unsafe. But this conclusion necessarily applies to all 'less lethal' weapons. Every weapon is a trade-off between safety and effectiveness. From a safety point of view, it has been suggested, the ideal weapon would be marshmallows delivered by parachute.[7]

Purpose and Characteristics of Riot-Control Weapons

The aims of modern riot control, in a nutshell, are to contain the disturbance by getting the crowds off the street; to punish and harass the insurgent population enough to make them disown their front-line activists, who can then be mopped up; and to conduct this operation with the appearance of minimum force so that any adverse reaction from unaffected sections of the population can be avoided. This is a delicate balance, and keeping on the tightrope is a difficult job for any government concerned to maintain at least a façade of liberal democracy and due process. The need therefore for an elaborate armoury of sophisticated riot-control weaponry becomes clear. Different 'riot' situations have different tactical characteristics, and the political environment within which the the violent encounters occur can change almost from week to week. What is required is the availability of 'a suitable range of graduated alternatives'.[8] Kennedy and MacNamara called it 'graduated response' – in Vietnam.

But the principle is not really one of minimum force, but of minimum political reaction. That is why the government is so determined that the public should believe that their riot-control agents are safe, but is much less concerned that they should actually *be* safe. As an American official report[9] puts it, 'it is preferred that onlookers not get the *impression* that the police are using excessive force or that the weapon has an especially injurious effect on the target individuals. Here again, a flow of blood and similar dramatic effects are to be avoided' (italics added). This 'minimum force' is the minimum force which *enables the state to win*. The way is open for a series of phased escalations, until (so the theory goes) the disaffected section of the population decides it is not really worth all the suffering. History has rather discredited this theory: just as in Vietnam, the 'controlled response' campaign in Northern Ireland during 1969–73 produced unintended results. A process of escalation was started which raised the stakes to the level at which domestic anger against the government was intensified and the political gamble of 'minimum force' failed.

The riot-control arsenal is never complete. Much of its effect lies in uncertainty and fear of the unknown. 'As soon as a new non-lethal weapon has been used, the shock effect will be reduced in the future.' Familiarity breeds a less wary response. To maintain even the same level of deterrence, constant innovation is required. New weapons 'can be kept in reserve for the moment when their employment might gain tactical surprise'.[10]

Handling a Riot

Owing to the secretive habits of British authorities, most of the available information on the handling of riots by the security forces comes from American sources. However, the brief discussion of this subject in Volume Three of the British *Army Land Operations Manual* seems to indicate that the tactical principles differ only in detail between the two countries.

The first essential for the security forces is good intelligence (in the military sense). This starts before the demonstration. A US Department of Justice publication advises:

> Factions often develop among groups that are planning either political demonstrations or actual violence. One faction will sometimes wish to undermine the success of the planned event in order to embarrass the other faction. The jealousy between the subgroups may enable police to elicit information from each about the other ... In some cases, jealous members have enabled plainclothes officers to obtain entry into meetings of the dissident groups.[11]

For the demonstration itself, one leading riot-control authority recommends the maintenance of an 'automatic pick-up list' of people who should be arrested at the start of any civil-disturbance operation – 'within the bounds of law', naturally.[12] At the site of the demonstration photographs may be taken of leaders and lists made of the number plates of cars; plainclothes officers and informants 'should mingle with the crowds and enter into the mob to gather intelligence, identify leaders, ascertain their plans, and, if at all possible, photograph and record their orders and statements'.[13] The same procedure of course applies to intelligence operations for industrial disputes, especially where mass picketing to close the gates of a factory or 'flying pickets' are used.

For the police (or Army) 'a candid and close working relationship with news media'[14] is of prime importance in all disturbances. They must ensure that the media disseminate the security forces' version of the incidents. They may also be able to borrow photographic equipment or make use of information collected by journalists. One enterprising US police department worked out an ingenious arrangement with the TV and film vehicle covering the head of the march. Unknown to its organizers, the police controlled the speed of the march by signalling to this vehicle to speed up or slow down.

The way in which the security forces break up a demonstration or riot depends on the nature of the crowd. A large, disciplined demonstration can present fewer technical problems than do several smaller groups moving swiftly and simultaneously along different routes. To deal with the smaller groups, the security forces must also break into smaller, more mobile groups – losing some of their advantage in discipline, resources and concentration of forces. (However, small groups are also more vulnerable to arrest.) A number of harassing tactics have also been employed in riot situations to reduce the effectiveness of the police. The FBI lists (among others) false calls to say that 'an officer is in trouble' resulting in the diversion of resources, and blocking police switchboards by calling and leaving the line open or by flooding it with petty calls.[15] Colonel Applegate even records a range of home-made weapons (and methods of manufacture) which have been used against the police – including incendiary devices and fuse mechanisms.[16]

When confronted with a riot, the security forces have three objectives: Contain, Isolate, Disperse. That is, to stop the 'contagion' from spreading out of control, prevent reinforcements from reaching the demonstrators and destroy the crowd as a purposeful entity. For dispersing the crowd, Coates cites the full military sequence:

1. An overwhelming 'show of force'.
2. The use of organized formations of men to break up and disperse the mob.
3. The use of 'less lethal' weapons.
4. Selective fire by marksmen.
5. Use of full fire power.[17]

Other writers more tactfully omit the last two stages. Deane-Drummond adds a very British preliminary operation: try to persuade the crowd to go home.

The 'show of force' should be a rapid and impressive display of police power and resolve. The aim is to convey an overwhelming impression of the power of the state which will persuade the crowd of the futility of its enterprise. Its members may shred away at the mere sight. However, this does not always happen. So the officer in charge may then order the crowd to disperse. Should they still resist, they should be made to go.

The first aggressive move by the security forces will generally be a move by foot formations.[18] There are three basic types: the skirmish line, the wedge and the diagonal. The skirmish line is used when confronting the crowd or advancing on it, or blocking off an area, but not actually in contact. From this formation, gas may be lobbed into the crowd and a wedge may be swiftly formed. (Changes in formation take place quickly to surprise the crowd.) The wedge is a formation shaped like an arrow-head pointed at the crowd. It is an offensive formation and can advance on the crowd to split it and clear the streets. The open base of the wedge can be filled in to make a triangle or a diamond when, for example, entering the crowd to make an arrest. The diagonal is another offensive formation – a group of men in a line slanting at an angle towards the crowd. The diagonal advances on the crowd in order to drive it in a particular direction. During combat in any of these formations, the officer in charge will be in the rear of the line of contact with the crowd. If any members of the crowd get behind this line, the unit is supposed to withdraw.

When dispersing the crowd, it is essential that the security forces leave escape routes open. If not, an unpleasant mêlée is likely to develop. This is, in fact, what happened at the Red Lion Square fracas in June 1974, when one of the demonstrators was killed. The absence of exits, coupled with the omission of any broadcast warning, are indications that the violence on the part of the police was not entirely unplanned. If gas is used, the need for exits is particularly great – in some conditions, gas may otherwise send crowd members rushing blindly into the police or Army lines in an attempt to escape.

If the initial strength of the security forces is too small, they can hold the situation by firing gas or other riot weapons from a safe distance until reinforcements arrive. An ingenious variant of this approach has been used by the British Army in Belfast. In August 1973 a crowd of 3,000 demonstrating on the second anniversary of internment was brought to a halt at an Army barrier. Rubber bullets and water cannon were used, not to disperse the crowd but apparently to incite them to action against the troops. The proceedings were carefully videotaped and later used in conjunction with intelligence material to identify 'ring-leaders' and active participants for retrospective arrest. Eventually one-third of the 'active rioters' were charged and convicted with the video record as evidence.[19] Gas has a number of tactical advantages. It can be employed to block off a street or deny access to some area. And there is also the surprise attack. 'The least violent and courageous members of the mob will be found in the rear, where there will also be spectators. It is often a good tactic to launch a surprise attack by gas against the rear elements.' Such attacks will usually cause panic, and panic is contagious. The sight of the rear in flight can be quite demoralizing even to the hardier souls.

The security forces, as we have noted elsewhere, have a high regard for the importance of 'leaders'. Without them, the crowd is thought to be reduced to a confused, bewildered group. If leaders can be lifted from the crowd, concerted action on the part of the remaining demonstrators is regarded as impossible. So, as a US police manual puts it: 'Agitators should be arrested or removed from the scene of the disturbance as soon as possible.' Hence the value of 'snatch squads'. But such squads have their drawbacks: being lightly dressed for rapid movement they are exposed to unfriendly missiles and the result may be 'unseemly brawling, few prisoners and high tempers',[20] not at all what is wanted in a well-managed riot. (The Irish have countered with their own anti-snatch snatch squads.) Arrests are not always feasible. The FBI recommends: 'It may be advisable at the time to only identify and photograph the leaders, hotheads, psychopaths, demagogues, and others, making the arrest later out of sight of the public.'[21] The British police followed this policy with the leaders of the Shrewsbury pickets.

The available 'less lethal' weapons fall into two major groups, plus a scattering of miscellaneous gadgets which vary from the banal to science fiction. The two major groupings use, respectively, the kinetic energy of impact of a projectile, and the irritant properties of a gas or spray for their effects. We discuss these groups in turn.

Impact Weapons

Only one of the impact weapons uses its energy (or, more precisely, its momentum) to knock people down. Paradoxically, it is the mildest of the group. This is the water cannon, used in Derry in October 1968 to hose demonstrators across Craigavon

Bridge. It was anything but new. The British Army had used water cannon in Cyprus in the 1950s. It has also been used against civil rights demonstrators in the USA, in South America, Germany and Paris. Basically, it is a motorized water-tank equipped with a high-pressure hose. It can be used in two ways: operated with a flat trajectory, it has an effective range of 40–50 yards; at a range of 30 yards or less, it can knock a person over. Using a higher trajectory, it can achieve an effect like heavy rainfall, providing a thorough soaking at 50–75 yards. Water cannon are employed to break up demonstrations through the force of the jet itself, the discomfort of a drenching or the slipperiness of the ground underfoot.

Water cannon are frequently used with brightly dyed water. The dye is a concentrated edible vegetable dye, non-toxic but difficult to wash off the skin and impossible to get out of clothes. The Army in Northern Ireland claim that this is done to identify the rioters for subsequent arrest. However, although many are dyed, few are arrested. A more plausible explanation is that the dye is used as a form of punishment – victims suffer the expense of stained clothing or possibly the criticisms of parents or employers. The dye currently used in Northern Ireland was specially developed at the chemical-warfare establishment at Porton. The Army gave Porton a tight specification on colour. Not red, since it looks like blood on colour television. Not green or orange, for obvious reasons in the Irish situation. So this dye is various shades of blue. (Future additives to the water may well include CR gas, which, unlike CS, is water-soluble.)

The early water cannon used in Northern Ireland (and in other countries) were made by Mercedes-Benz, but these have been replaced. The current version has a 22-ton Foden chassis, modified and fitted with a pyrene body, made to Ministry of Defence specifications by Chubb Fire Security. The design improvements are intended to reduce its vulnerability to demonstrators – there are now no lengths of exposed hose, no ledges where petrol bombs could lodge and few handholds to help the agile climber. The cab and 'gunners' windows are covered with protective wire-mesh. Ten feet high, seven feet wide, and over twenty-one feet long, it looks like a bizarre combination of armoured car and furniture van. Each vehicle carries five tons of water, which it uses in 5½ minutes.

Vehicles of this size are hard to manoeuvre against small, highly mobile groups. Also the short duration of one tank load imposes severe limitations on their use. To provide a more continuous cover, two cannon can be used in tandem, one re-loading while the other fires. But this still requires easy access to copious supplies of water. This, and their poor manoeuvrability, makes them suitable only for set-piece confrontations. And water cannon have other tactical drawbacks of which the demonstrators can take advantage. Unlike gas, the water cannot go round corners, so that even a small obstruction will provide a shield from its force. It does not cause pain or discomfort comparable with other major riot-control agents. And once someone has been drenched, there is nothing to lose by remaining in the area. For more determined people, more powerful riot-control technology is needed.

This is not to say that water cannon are safe – the experts have been united in warning of their dangers. The reason for this is the massive kinetic energy of the jet. People who have fallen may be rolled along the ground by the force of the jet, and there is also some danger from flying debris and glass if the jet hits buildings or loose material.

Designing riot-control weapons is a delicate business. There is no way to avoid 'undesirable effects' completely, because a perfectly non-hazardous weapon cannot be made. The effect of any 'less lethal' impact weapon can only be made through pain, or fear of pain: 'Transitory pain is apparently the only safe mechanism for achieving desirable effects from blunt-trauma, less lethal weapons.' So US military scientists working on the problem for the civilian LEAA came up with a scientific-sounding objective that weapon techniques should be 'optimized to maximize pain while constrained to minimize hazard levels'.[22] Research on these methods has involved finding out how great an impact the body can stand without suffering 'undesirable effects'.

The British government claimed that intensive tests were

carried out under medical supervision before rubber bullets were introduced in 1970. Yet when the US government began its own research programme into the effects of impact weapons, also in 1970, 'very little quantitative data on blunt trauma to the body' was available.[23] This is curious, since Britain and the USA have an information-sharing agreement which covers such matters. (Co-operation is close. For example, two US Army researchers recently attended a symposium on riot control sponsored by the British Army.) It seems that the British testing of rubber bullets was a good deal less thorough than the government would wish us to believe.

The American research project, carried out for LEAA by the (now-defunct) US Army Land Warfare laboratory, studied seven different projectiles. These ranged from a half-inch paintball (a soft plastic shell filled with an oil-based paint) weighing three grams to the 191-gram (6¾-ounce) 'Stun-Bag'. Each projectile was fired against the heads of baboons and the bodies of small pigs – tests which were thought to be reasonable predictors of the effects on humans. The major conclusion of the study was that an impact weapon with an energy level below 15 ft lb.* is 'safe' or of 'low hazard', provided the projectile is large enough not to damage the eyes; between 30 and 90 ft lb. is a dangerous area; and impacts above 90 ft lb. are in the 'severe-damage' region. Injuries caused include serious skin lacerations, massive skull fractures, rupture and destruction of of the kidney, fracture and fragmentation of the liver and haemorrhages, necrosis and rupture of the heart.

The rubber bullet was not among the weapons studied, but it is similar to the Stun-Bag in several important respects. The Stun-Bag is a soft canvas pouch filled with metal buckshot. It is packed into a cartridge which can be fired from a variety of weapons. The pouch is spin-stabilized in flight and spreads out into a three-inch diameter 'pancake'. It weighs between 5½ ounces (157 grams) and 6¾ ounces (191 grams). Here we will consider only the 'Super Long-Range Round' with an initial velocity of 230 feet per second. Tests using the 5½-ounce Stun-Bag showed that

*1 ft lb. is the amount of energy required to raise a weight of one pound through a distance of one foot.

a hit on either the head or the rest of the body was almost certain to cause 'undesirable effects' at ranges of up to 40 yards and with very high probability at up to 50 yards.[24] A single impact can damage several organs, not all directly under the point of impact. The initial energy of the Stun-Bag is 288 ft lb.; at 25 yards it is 150 ft lb. and at 50 yards 81 ft lb. It was rejected by the US study as 'unsatisfactory at all ranges'.

The rubber bullet is a little lighter (149 grams) than the Stun-Bag, but it is fired at a higher speed. Its muzzle velocity is 240 feet per second (over 160 mph), giving it a muzzle energy of 293 ft lb. If the decline in velocity during flight is similar to that of the Stun-Bag, the impact energy of the rubber bullet would be around 153 ft lb at 25 yards, and still over 86 ft lb at 50 yards. Possibly the unstable flight of the rubber bullet causes it to slow down more quickly than the Stun-Bag. Nevertheless, the conclusion must be that for much of its effective range the bullet causes impacts in the 'severe-damage' region. Of course, rubber bullets are supposed to be fired at the ground in front of the demonstrators, but soldiers facing a hostile crowd obviously want to make full use of their 'less lethal' weapons. This has been demonstrated many times in Northern Ireland, where we have seen that rubber bullets have frequently been aimed directly, sometimes at point-blank range. Other forms of abuse of rubber bullets were described in Part One.

How did such a dangerous – and apparently under-tested – weapon come into service? The story begins in 1958 in Hong Kong, where the police developed a way of striking demonstrators with wooden sticks without the inconvenience of a baton charge. The new device, called a 'baton round' was a fluted cylinder made out of teak, just over an inch long, which could be fired into crowds. (It also whistles on its way to the target, an additional psychological deterrent.) A heftier version, $7\frac{1}{2}$ inches long and weighted with a metal core, was also developed. The baton round was adjudged a great success in the Hong Kong disturbances of 1967, so it was naturally considered for possible use in Northern Ireland. But it was rejected for use there on the grounds that it was too dangerous – it could cause serious injuries both from impact and from splintering. (In fact it killed a girl in Hong Kong.) Apparently what is good enough for use against 'foreigners' in the colonies is still not acceptable against English-speaking whites – even in Ireland.

However, something was clearly needed to put down the 'unruly Irish'. A nine-month research effort produced an adaptation of the Hong Kong projectile using rubber instead of wood. The bullet itself is a blunt-nosed cylinder, 5¾ inches long, 1½ inches in diameter, and weighing 5¼ ounces. It is fitted into a cartridge with a small gunpowder charge. It can be fired from either the US-designed Federal Riot Gun or from a standard 1.5-inch signal pistol, such as the Verey pistol, modified with a lengthened barrel. (This is the same riot gun as is used to fire CS canisters.) The gun and bullets are all manufactured by the Charterhouse Subsidiary Company of Schermuly Limited,* Dorking, Surrey. Recovered rubber bullets can be reloaded into live cartridges – so the Belfast children's pastime of collecting spent rounds makes a good deal of sense. By the end of 1974, over 55,000 rubber bullets had been fired in Northern Ireland.

In Northern Ireland, seasoned demonstrators have by now learnt to take their chances with rubber bullets. But it is still clear that they are dangerous and can be lethal. The energy level in comparison with the Stun-Bag gives us indirect evidence. And a report to the US National Science Foundation (the principal US science agency) warns that rubber bullets carry 'some risks of internal injury or death'.[25]

There are also hard facts on the injuries caused by rubber bullets in Northern Ireland in the Belfast surgeons' report. Over a two-year period, ninety patients received hospital treatment as a result of injuries caused by rubber bullets. (Undoubtedly many more were injured, but for obvious reasons either did not go to hospital at all, or went to hospitals in the Republic.) Forty-one of these people required in-patient treatment.

Over 50 per cent of the injuries were to the head. Twenty-one patients had between them thirty-five fractures of bones in the head, including three of the skull. Twenty-four patients had a

* Schermuly also produced a British version of the Stun-Bag. It was evaluated for use in Northern Ireland, but was rejected as too risky; the manufacturers admit that it is 'likely to be lethal' at ten yards or less.

total of twenty-eight damaged eyes. Two people were blinded in both eyes; seven suffered complete loss of vision in one eye, and a further five suffered severe loss of vision in one eye. Seven victims lost consciousness, and three of these are known to have suffered brain damage, leading to death in one case. There were also seven cases of lung damage, and cases of injury to the lower spleen, intestine, liver, legs and arms. In addition to the death referred to above, a second death was not investigated as the victim was taken to hospital in the Republic. A third and fourth death occurred after the report was completed in May 1973.

How does the British military feel about this weapon? Apparently, that it is 'one of the most valuable ever produced'.[26] The main defect for the security forces is that current guns are single-shot weapons with a slow rate of fire. Schermuly Ltd has already developed and test-fired a prototype of a new device which fires three projectiles from one cartridge.

Another version of the rubber bullet was introduced by the British Army for use in Ireland as early as August 1972. This is the plastic bullet – basically a shorter rubber bullet with a PVC outer layer. It is harder, a little lighter, faster and more accurate than the rubber bullet. It was apparently designed to complement the rubber bullet at ranges of over fifty yards. It is also less susceptible to abuse by soldiers, since its hard plastic outer layer prevents objects being inserted. However, it has not found favour with the Army. It was not used in action until 7 February 1973, and by the end of 1974 only 259 bullets had been fired.

The US Army is also developing a new impact-energy riot-control agent – the Sting-RAG projectile.[27] ('RAG' stands for 'ring airfoil grenade'.) This is an annular-shaped projectile (like a broad bracelet) made of soft rubber, $2\frac{1}{2}$ inches in diameter and weighing 34 grams (rather over an ounce). A launcher is attached to the barrel of a standard rifle, and a blank cartridge provides the propulsion. Sting-RAG has a flat trajectory and improved accuracy – it can be aimed at individuals at 45 yards, or at small groups at 65 yards. It works by pain of impact – the muzzle velocity will be in the region of 200 to 240 feet per second. Sting-RAG went into full-scale development stage at the end of 1974. A companion Soft RAG is also under development: this releases a cloud of CS gas when the force of the spin strips off a paper breakband round the outside of the annulus.

Irritants and Gases[28]

In 1871 a German chemist, Carl Graebe, synthesized some white crystals with a stinging smell. This compound, chloroacetophenone – better known by its code name CN, or simply as 'tear gas' was the first standard gas adopted for riot control.

Gas warfare was introduced in the First World War, with the use of the lethal gases chlorine, phosgene, mustard gas and the rest – but irritants were also much in evidence on both sides. The French started by using ethyl bromacetate, the same gas as the Paris police had been using since 1912. It was the Americans, however, who took up CN as a lachrymator. They were actively developing it in 1918, but the end of the war came too soon for it to be used.

The Geneva Protocols of 1925 banning the use of chemical and biological weapons in warfare were drafted to cover 'the use in war of asphyxiating, poisonous or other gases, and all analogous liquids, materials or devices'. The British and French (and almost everybody else except the Americans) subsequently confirmed that the 'other gases' included harassing and irritant gases. The reason why this clarification was thought necessary was that between the wars tear gas (CN) was proving itself invaluable round the world for quelling civilian disturbances.

This widespread use of CN was possible, despite the Geneva Protocol ruling, because the ban on the use of gas in war in no way precluded its use on a country's own citizens – or those of its colonies. CN soon became the pre-eminent irritant gas and secured a niche in the armouries of riot police throughout the world. It remained the standard riot gas until the 1960s, when there were two new developments – Mace and CS gas. CS is a distinct chemical formation which will be discussed in detail later. Mace, however, is of interest mainly because it introduced a new way of getting the irritant to the people.

There are a number of ways of projecting harassing agents,

all of which produce a blanket of harassing agent over a crowd or area. Developed in 1965, Chemical Mace (to give it its registered trade name) is a method of putting the agent into solution so that it can be dispersed from spray-cans using conventional aerosol-spray technology, in a directed stream of liquid droplets. A succession of as many as fifty one-second bursts can be used on selected targets at ranges of up to twenty feet. In the USA, Mace, initially using CN, has become the most popular new police weapon since guns were invented. By 1972, some half-million units had been sold to over 4,000 police departments. It has never been issued to police forces in Britain.

The CN formation of Mace can cause serious damage to the eyes, though this should not occur if the agent is projected from the recommended range. However, twelve cases of chemical burns to the cornea examined by the Public Health Service in Berkeley in late 1968 were all found to have been caused at ranges of between six inches and two feet. Abuse of Chemical Mace, as a weapon of close-range retribution, especially on helpless criminals, is well documented. The US Army apparently decided that the CN-based Mace formation was too risky and developed its own liquid-stream projector based on CS. This has also been adopted for civilian use, so that there are now both CN and CS Mace formulations.

The beginning of the end for CN as a standard riot gas came in 1956, when the British Chemical Defence Experimental Establishment (CDEE) at Porton initiated a search for a substitute. CN was unsatisfactory for a number of reasons. It is too dangerous – at high dosages, blistering of the skin and serious lung damage can result, and quite a number of deaths have been recorded. It is not effective enough – people exposed to it develop tolerance, so that doses of a given size do not make them feel so sick. It is not sufficiently fast-acting. And it is not persistent – its effects decline rapidly after dissemination.

These are the technical reasons why Porton started looking for a suitable alternative to CN. But there are also political reasons. Manufacture of CN in Britain started as long ago as 1923. Why then did the need for a stronger agent arise only in 1956, after over thirty years' experience with CN? It is reasonable to suppose it was the times, not the gas, which had changed. 1956 was the year of Suez; it was also the year which saw the beginning of the Campaign for Nuclear Disarmament. There was an upsurge of anti-imperialist struggles abroad and political struggles at home. Foreign bases would need protection; and the withdrawal from the colonies in favour of local ruling classes had to be accomplished delicately. The logic of Home Office instructions to Porton becomes clearer against this background.

Porton's search came up with CS gas, orthochlorobenzylidene malonitrile. Its abbreviated name came from the initials of the two American chemists, Corson and Stoughton, who synthesized it as a chemical curiosity in 1928. But it was not given much serious atttention until the search for a CN substitute was initiated in 1956.

CS is a stable, off-white powder with a faint peppery smell.[29] It produces its effects by settling on the skin or being inhaled or swallowed. Porton itself provided a summary of these effects when filing for a patent (no. 967660, awarded in 1964) for a variety of dispersing cartridges and grenades:

In addition to causing pain in the eyes, tears, and spasms of the eyelids, [it] also produces a sharp pain in the nose, throat and chest, which becomes worse and causes choking sensations as exposure continues ... When [CS] is experienced in high concentrations, the violent coughing which is set up may induce vomiting. Stinging occurs on the shaved areas and on any exposed abrasions and there may also be irritation around the neck ... This irritation passes off rapidly as do the other effects ... The result of this combination of effects is ... [that] a concentration of between one part in 10 million and one part in a million is enough to drive all but the most determined persons out of it within a few seconds.

On 23 July 1970, British MPs got first-hand experience of these symptoms. Frank Roche threw a canister of CS gas into the chamber of the House of Commons to give members a taste of what Belfast was like. Two MPs were taken to hospital and one had to have a chest X-ray. The Serjeant at Arms, Admiral Gordon Lennox, complained that 'my face was smarting, my eyes running, and I was retching'.

The effects of CS are more severe than those of CN for comcomparable concentrations, and they are experienced almost instantaneously. The effects of CS wear off quite rapidly when the victim leaves the contaminated atmosphere, and within fifteen minutes he or she will probably be back to normal, except for the skin irritation. There are also, as will emerge, possibilities of more serious health hazards.

The use of CS gas in Derry in August 1969 was more of a shock to the British public than it should have been. The British Army and colonial police forces had been using irritants routinely in British colonies for years. For example, between 1960 and 1965 CN and CS were used on 124 separate occasions, two thirds of them in Guyana (then British Guiana). It was Cyprus which had the doubtful honour of being the first customer for CS. The effectiveness of CS there in 1958-9 clearly demonstrated its operational superiority over CN, and led to its rapid adoption by security forces throughout the world, notably the US Army in 1959.

Subsequent developments were rapid. By the end of the 1960s, CS had virtually replaced CN as the standard riot gas in Britain and elsewhere. Porton's 'pilot plant' at Nancekuke in a remote part of Cornwall set up a facility for batch production of CS with an estimated output of over five tons annually in the late 1960s. CS is packed into grenades, made to government-patented specification by Schermuly Ltd. Grenades are supplied to British police forces and the RUC, as well as being exported – reportedly – to over sixty countries, including South Africa. Much of the export trade is in fact carried on by Civil Protection Ltd using American-made CS powder.

Information about CS went to the USA by way of an information-sharing agreement (the Quadrapartite Agreement with the USA, Canada and Australia), and manufacture started there in the early 1960s. The US Army began using CS in Vietnam in 1964. By mid-1969, almost 7,000 tons of it had been employed – which would have been enough to fill more than 200 million of the cartridges which the British were beginning to use in Northern Ireland.

By January 1968 reports of deaths following exposure to CS

in Vietnam were beginning to appear in the British press. When it was revealed that CS was a British development, the then Secretary of State for Scotland, Mr Buchan, stated that CS would be used only 'to deal with armed criminals or violently insane persons in buildings from which they cannot be dislodged without danger of loss of life, or as a means of self-defence in a desperate situation, and that in no circumstances should it be used to assist in the control of disturbances'. Such government statements are not to be relied on – only a year later CS was to be used against the Catholic citizens of Derry.

A similarly cynical approach was demonstrated by the government assertion in February 1970 that CS was not covered by the Geneva Protocols. The argument advanced for this reversal of a position held by all British governments for over forty years was the legalistic one that CS was not, after all, a gas, but a 'smoke'. The true reason for the decision to redefine CS was its much publicized use in Northern Ireland. It does, after all, look bad to use on your own citizens devices which are held, under international law, to be 'condemned by the general opinion of the civilized world'.

In Vietnam, the Americans were rapidly developing CS weapons for every delivery system in use. By 1970, the US *Army Field Manual* listed nineteen CS munitions. Weapons range from a pocket grenade (XM 58) holding two grams of CS, to the vast XM 28 dispenser – a metal box three feet square and eight feet long, slung under a helicopter – which drops a stream of 2,090 individual paper bags containing in all 760 lb. of CS.[30] (There is even film of GIs using 'Mity Mite' CS dispensers like portable gas chambers to kill people hiding in tunnels and caves.) The Americans have also developed a number of different types of CS, to make it 'waterproof', or to enable it to fly better. CS2, for example, persists for thirty days or more in open terrain. It is used to contaminate particular areas and so deny them to the enemy.

Riot gases are almost always used in combination with other weapons. In Vietnam, CS was used to drive out NLF forces or civilians from cover, so that they could be machine-gunned in the open. As the *Field Manual* states: 'The employment of the agent is limited only by the availability of the agent, means of delivery (either ground or air) and the imagination of the commander and his staff.'

The British Army uses a number of burning-type CS weapons.[31] Since 1970, the standard equipment for patrols in Northern Ireland has been the 1·5-inch L3A1 cartridge, which is fired from signal pistols or riot guns – the same ones which are used to fire rubber bullets. The propellant charge ignites a fuse which gives a two or three second delay before the CS mixture itself is ignited. The cartridge then gives off CS for between ten and twenty-five seconds. Another much-used munition is the L1A2 hand grenade, which emits gas for between ten and forty seconds.

The Army has also developed a rubber cartridge containing CS mixture in the form of 400 pellets coated with sulphurless gunpowder, weighing 285 grams in all, of which 71 grams is CS. On impact, the grenade bursts and scatters the burning pellets over a fifteen-yard-diameter area (with increased danger of eye injury). There are two reasons behind this particular development. Firstly, it covers a greater area than does the conventional cartridge. Secondly, it stops demonstrators from picking up the burning canister and throwing it back. This was a common practice, for example, in the Derry confrontation. (The US Army have another way to get round this problem – a grenade which 'skitters' over the ground, so that it is difficult to catch.)

British police have been extensively supplied with CS cartridges and grenades. As early as 1968 stocks were held by thirty-six different police forces. So far they have only used them to remove armed criminals who are barricaded in. In July 1971, the Commissioner of Metropolitan Police repeated the earlier government assurance that the gas would not be used against demonstrators (except in Ireland, of course).

The original patent for CS declared that 'no permanent harm is caused'. This was deduced on the basis of research which would never have been acceptable if the agent were a new food additive or drug. For instance, the claim that CS did not harm the sick or those with breathing disabilities was made on the basis of studies of two bronchitic rabbits; while effects on the foetus were tested simply by injecting CS into fertilized chickens' eggs.

The only British government report on the use of CS is the Himsworth report, commissioned after the public outcry following the use of CS in the Bogside in 1969. Two of its eight members were on the Porton Scientific Advisory Committee, which had cleared CS in the first place; others were known to be very close to Porton. The Committee drew heavily on research done at Porton itself (though it did commission further studies). It concluded that, despite some minor hazards, CS should continue in service. The committee accepted that CS could cause death in people. But it maintained that since the dose required to kill is several thousand times greater than the dose which causes maximum irritant effects, there is no danger of demonstrators receiving a lethal dose.

The safety of the drug is much more open to doubt than the Himsworth Committee would have us believe. CS is more toxic in long exposures to low concentrations (as in operational use) than it is in the short periods of high concentration used in most laboratory testing. Further, the level of exposure which is likely to cause death is certainly lower for the weaker members of the community – the elderly or sick (particularly those with breathing problems), pregnant women and young children. Many of these people will not be in the 'front line' of the conflict, but trapped in their own homes they will be subjected to the build-up of quite high concentrations. And experiments have shown that significant lung damage can occur at one one-fiftieth of the expected lethal exposure dose accepted by Himsworth.

In any case, demonstrators in Northern Ireland have proved able to stand up to higher doses than Himsworth thought possible. Porton paid Army volunteers £1 per minute for the length of time they would remain in the smoke. Elsewhere, Himsworth has even described Highland soldiers being tempted by a five-pound note and a bottle of whisky to pass through a concentrated cloud – and being unable to do so. However, with gradual exposure, people are able to tolerate higher and higher concentrations, and demonstrators fighting for a cause they believe in are able to tolerate higher doses than soldiers volunteering for money. This makes demonstrators more vulnerable to the toxic effects.

Certainly high levels of exposure may lead to non-fatal injury. Even Himsworth was forced to admit a few blemishes on the record of CS. It may cause acute episodes of bronchitis and asthma in chronic sufferers. There was inadequate evidence on its effects on those suffering from heart complaints. And experiments to determine possible carcinogenic (cancer-inducing) effects from the gas had not been completed – this *two years after* it had been introduced in Northern Ireland. Neither had any tests been done to examine the effects of interactions with other drugs – such as alcohol or tranquillizers. Other physical effects include prolonged diarrhoea, allergies resulting from skin inflammation caused by CS, and possibly burning of the skin in wet weather.

The greatest hazard from CS undoubtedly arises when it is used in confined spaces. Reports from Belfast and Derry (as well as Paris in May 1968) repeatedly describe how CS canisters have been fired through doors and windows of houses. In the Paris troubles a woman died after heavy exposure in this way to both CS and CN. And in Vietnam many deaths have been reported from congestion of the lung, sometimes complicated by pneumonia – apparently from the build-up of CS in shelters.

When gas was used in Derry, BSSRS sent its investigating team of clinicians and scientists to Northern Ireland. It took evidence through less official channels than did Himsworth. So whereas Himsworth had failed to find any cases of loss of consciousness from the gas, the BSSRS team found three. They also found that a fourteen-month-old child developed acute bronchial disorder, a four-month-old baby suffered from a tight chest, while a five-year-old and a nine-year-old needed treatment for eye-burning. Dr Ray McClean (later to become Mayor of Derry) also reported a case of lung damage following the Derry attack. By sticking to official sources, the Himsworth Committee had cut itself off from evidence about those sufferers who, for totally understandable reasons, preferred not to present themselves for medical care while bearing the symptoms of exposure to CS.

There have also been several possible cases of death in Northern Ireland due to CS – one a 'cot death' of a baby who choked during the Derry attack. These are all discounted in official reports because of inadequate clinical evidence. In fact, a standard of proof is being demanded which, in a conflict-racked community, frequently cannot be met.

For a supposedly harmless weapon, this is quite a catalogue of ill-effects. But there are more, since riot gases can kill or injure as a result of crowd panic, direct impact of containers, asphyxiation or fires caused by burning-type grenades, and blast or fragmentation from bursting-type weapons. Another highly unpleasant effect of CS is contamination. Once the inside of a building receives a heavy load of CS dust, it is very hard to get it out. Stores in Washington, DC, which received heavy CS concentrations during April 1968 had to remain closed for several weeks. No easily available chemical decontaminant is known. Hard surfaces can be washed or vacuumed, though the dust bag must be kept wet to prevent the powder seeping through. Unfortunately for the ordinary home-dweller, these operations have to be performed wearing a gas-mask, protective clothing and rubber gloves. The only alternative is to leave the doors and windows open for long periods to air the place, and to move furniture into the open. One note of comfort is offered us by the Himsworth Committee: there is apparently no danger of harm caused by eating contaminated food. The slightest trace of CS makes food or drink so repulsive that no one could possibly swallow it.

There are a few things that people who face exposure to CS can do in the way of home-made protection.[32] An improvised gas mask, made from a cloth surgical mask with a small gauze sponge soaked in vinegar inside it, will reduce the effect of the gas by 50 to 70 per cent if worn with airtight goggles. Smearing one's face with a mixture of beaten egg and bicarbonate of soda has also been recommended, though there have been mixed reports of its efficiency. But even clothing which keeps as much skin well covered as possible will help. Effects are also reduced if you spend long periods continuously in the CS haze – but leaving the gas for even ten minutes may destroy this tolerance. Of course Bogside volunteers also used more direct methods against CS, such as protecting their hands and throwing the burning canisters straight back.

People suffering from the effects of exposure to CS should be removed to clean air and should on no account rub their eyes. Victims should stand facing into the wind with their eyes forced open if they are suffering from 'streaming' eyes. They should avoid strenuous exercise (to reduce sweating) and affected skin should be exposed to the air. They should avoid taking a shower for several hours, and then use cold or cool water to start with. In cases of severe contamination the skin should be washed with cotton wool soaked in a 2:1 mixture of water to alcohol (whisky is ideal) to which 10 per cent conventional ammonia solution (i.e. 23° strength) has been added. (An alternative treatment is to wash the skin, avoiding the eyes, with ethylene glycol – anti-freeze – followed by copious amounts of water.) A steroid or anti-histamine ointment (available at chemists without prescription) can then be applied. The eyes may be washed with water to which a few drops of ammonia has been added. This solution should be poured from the inside corner of the eye down, and out to the outside corner, to avoid infection of the tear ducts. Alternatively, use plain water or a one per cent solution of baking soda.

As we saw in Part One, CS did not prove to be the expected miracle cure for the 'law and order' problem in Northern Ireland. Hardened demonstrators can stand it, and its effectiveness is too dependent on the wind and weather. Porton was instructed to find yet another, improved riot-control agent. Just as CS was supposed to have all the answers to the defects of CN, so CR is now supposed to remedy all the deficiencies of CS.

The effects of CR are apparently dramatic: 'FIRE GAS' shouted the *Daily Express* in a front-page banner headline. It is highly irritating to the skin, eyes and mucous membranes of the nose and throat, and can cause loss of muscle co-ordination. The effect has been variously described as 'making people feel as if they are on fire' or 'producing a nettle-stinging sensation'.

These symptoms persist for up to twenty minutes. Porton admits that owing to the severe irritation and temporary inability to see clearly, some individuals might be expected to develop hysteria'.[33] Such people will be unable to run away, and so will be exposed to heavy concentrations of CR and thus to greater probability of injury.

The chief tactical advantage to the security forces of CR (dibenoxazepine is its chemical name) is that it is more easily soluble in water. Its history is like a speeded-up version of that of CS. It was discovered by two chemists at Salford Technical College in the 1960s. The discovery was published in the chemical literature, where eagle-eyed Porton scientists spotted the description of its 'intense lachrymatory and skin-irritant properties'. It was then developed by Porton, and in Britain the gas is produced at Nancekuke, along with CS. Information on the gas was given to the US Army, who adopted it for use in 1972. This is confirmation of the long-held view that, in the relationship between Porton and its US equivalent, it is Porton which is 'the brains of the outfit'.

In November 1973 CR was authorized for use in the UK 'in certain special circumstances' by the Ministry of Defence, and it was secretly authorized for use in Long Kesh some time before March 1974. The Army denied that CR has yet been used, though Long Kesh detainees claim that a new chemical irritant agent was used by the Army during the prison riots of October 1974. CR is stockpiled in Northern Ireland and in certain places in Britain.

The US Army has developed a hand-held weapon for CR (the XM36 dispenser) which is only six inches long and 1½ inches in diameter. It can be used in short or long bursts, 'by individuals engaged in riot-control operations and normal police duties for their own protection'. In other words, it is to be used like Mace. It has an effective range of fifteen feet and a total discharge time of twenty seconds. It is reported that the British Army has its own 'Self-Protection Aid Device', so that very soon we may see 'macing', with all its abuses, in the UK.

In Britain, we can expect that CR will be used in the future in the stream of water cannon and in a kind of jelly to make foam riot barriers. The solubility of CR gives it a major tactical advantage over CS. It can be directed much more effectively (in a jet or jelly) to just where the security forces want it. This means, among other things, that it will be much less harassing to the community surrounding a riot situation. Whether or not this is an advantage will depend on the political circumstances. The logic of the situation would suggest the retention of both CS and CR in the armoury – CS for use when population harassment is thought likely to separate the militants from the rest of the community; CR for use when harassment is likely to have the contrary effect of increasing solidarity. Elsewhere, a speedy decision to abandon CS has been predicted.[34]

Very few of the research findings on CR were published prior to its authorization – in blatant violation of the recommendation of the Himsworth Committee that research on new riot-control agents should be published in the appropriate journals. Only a limited number have been published since. Even *Nature*, the most prestigious general scientific journal in Britain, described the research done on long-term effects as 'entirely inadequate'. The government, of course, claims that, although CR has a more intense effect than CS, it is 'no less safe'. Even though the research results are not publicly available, we are asked to accept that CR's safety has been thoroughly established. So it was with rubber bullets. So it was with CS. Ministerial blandness to sedate public awareness. Over CS, James Callaghan (then Home Secretary) claimed that he was 'misled by scientists'. What will Roy Mason and Merlyn Rees be telling us in a few years' time?

Other Weapons

Most of the new riot-control weapons produce their effect by impact or chemical harassment. But the technological/political imagination has not been idle. Other devices have been proposed, developed or marketed in these boom years of law-enforcement technology. For instance, there is scope for the use of sound for riot control. Birmingham University seriously considered using an 'alarmingly loud' bell or a (scarcely audible) ultrasonic device to make life unbearable for students occupying the administration offices. They eventually decided against it. Not so the British government. In January 1973 they adopted an American gadget called the 'Sound Curdler' for operations in Northern Ireland (although it does not seem to have been used there). The Curdler (also called 'Super-Sound' and 'People Repeller') is a set of portable loud-speakers which can produce an intensely loud 'scientifically designed, shrill shrieking, blatting noise'.[35] Thirteen Curdler systems were bought from Applied Electro Mechanics of Alexandria, Virginia, at a cost of £2,000 each. The Curdler is normally mounted on an armoured vehicle or helicopter, though a portable version exists. The original, officially inspired story was that it would be used to blanket out all communication between people in the crowd and so prevent an organized attack on the security forces.[36] More recently, the story had changed – the 'noise facility' is apparently only to be used 'to gain the attention of the crowd'.[37] American sources scarcely mention this as a possible use – they talk instead of 'creating temporary disability' or of irritating and dispersing.

In fact, the intensity of the sound is so great that it would produce at least severe physical discomfort. The maximum output power of the loud-speakers is 350 watts (compare this with the 30-watt output of a really powerful hi-fi set. It has a gain power of 90 decibels. It has been claimed that the noise produced at thirty feet is rated at 120 decibels. Such intensities are certainly painful, and can cause disorientation and nausea. Used at close range, it could well lead to some permanent loss of hearing. An idea of the volume can be gathered from the fact that when the equipment is used as a loud-hailer it is clearly audible at ranges of up to 2½ miles. The US National Science Foundation Report concluded that, at the level of sound which creates physical distress, there was 'severe risk of permanent impairment of hearing'.[38]

The sound curdler seems not to be the only riot-control agent the Army has tried which makes use of sound. In the summer of 1973, the *New Scientist* claimed that the Army had tested a new sound device – the 'squawk box'. One military expert at Lisburn Barracks was reported as saying that tests conducted on soldiers had been highly successful. The prototype model used was said to consist of two speakers mounted on a three-foot cube. These emit ultrasonic sound of frequency 16,000 and 16,002 cycles per second respectively – too high to be audible to most people. These combine to produce a beat frequency of 2 cps, which is too low to be heard. This infra-sound may cause the victim to feel giddy and nauseous and, in extreme cases, to faint.

The squawk box is said to be highly directional. It could be focused on individuals within a crowd, causing distress in the victims, creating panic in others who would see the apparently inexplicable effects. This has been described as a ' "spooky" psychological effect'. The Ministry of Defence have denied owning any such equipment. After the Army trials were described in the *New Scientist*, the Army held a press briefing to demonstrate its new sound equipment. By an 'unforgivable oversight' – according to the Army – the *New Scientist* reporter, well known to the Army's press office, was not invited. This was, perhaps, not surprising, since instead of revealing the equipment he had described, the Army gave a demonstration of the *sound curdler* – which had already been reported in the press several months previously. The squawk box quickly faded out of the news: it appears it has never been fully developed. Its effects could probably have been overcome by wearing earmuffs.

The squawk box was apparently designed to be used in conjunction with another device, the 'photic driver'. This uses a flashing light to disturb the electrical activity of the brain – causing disorientation, nausea and even fainting. The most critical flash frequency appears to be about 15 cycles per second, but unpleasant effects are experienced over a range of about 10–30 cps. (Because of this, the frequency of strobe lights permitted in discotheques by the Greater London Council is restricted to a maximum of 8 cps.) This use of strobe lights seems to have come from an idea of Lindemann – Churchill's main scientific advisor in the Second World War. Lindemann wanted to put strobes on the top of tanks to disrupt enemy infantry as the tanks advanced. But nothing came of the idea. The present device was developed by Charles Bovill of Allen International (a London firm which specialized in bugging equipment) with the help of research facilities provided by an Army neurologist. Bovill claims to have tried out a prototype on some students who were making too much noise outside his home – with apparent success.

Flickering lights produced even by television or by sun reflected on ripples in water can induce epileptic fits in a small number of people who suffer from photosensitive epilepsy. The intense beam of the photic driver would be highly likely to stimulate fits in these people. It might even induce a fit in a person who had previously never suffered an epileptic fit. One of the few papers in the literature that describe experiments using exposures to intense photic stimulation of more than a few seconds found that as many as 14 per cent of normal children showed brain activity characteristic of 'petit mal' epilepsy.

An epileptic attack is a highly distressing and potentially dangerous experience. So, when the photic driver was first advertised by Allen International, it met with sharp criticism from epilepsy experts as well as from the more usual quarters. Bovill responded with a reference to the 'puke ethics' of his critics. Nevertheless, he did announce modifications to the device: lower-frequency beams 'which would not produce the highly distressing effects of earlier designs'. The Army claimed that 'we have no equipment which remotely resembles what we have heard of the Allen International photic driver',[39] but a *Times* reporter stated that 'military experts have been kept abreast of developments in its manufacture'.[40]

It is likely that the equipment will never be fully developed, since simple counter-measures would probably be very effective. Simply putting a hand over one eye, or wearing an eye patch would probably be sufficient to prevent abnormal brain activity, and so counteract the unpleasant effects. The effects can also be diminished simply by looking away from the source of the light or by wearing polaroid spectacles. So the 1970s version of the photic driver may already have suffered the same fate as Lindemann's proposed invention.

Even if the squawk box and photic driver are not brought into service, we can be sure that new weapons will be produced,

Riot Control 227

Research into them is certainly proceeding in the British government's secret research establishments. (In the US at least one other liquid irritant – code-named EA 4923 – is under study, and research is being pursued into chemical agents which will combine a surface irritant effect with 'central' effects.) We pointed out earlier that a steady stream of new agents will be needed because, despite their dangers, much of the effect of any new agent is psychological. As people become more accustomed to a new weapon, its deterrent effect is drastically reduced. There is also the constant pressure from the military to increase the strength of existing riot control weapons. (American Army scientists claim that the current non-lethal weapons are of the 'powder-puff' variety.[41])

Some further ideas for such 'less lethal' weapons may be gleaned from the US National Science Foundation Report. Altogether, it lists thirty-four different weapons, including many of those already discussed in this chapter. Here are just a few others:

electrified water jet: A mobile unit like a water cannon, only the water carries a high electric voltage. Could be used as a barrier or to disperse crowds.

cold brine projector: This fires a slug of icy liquid. On impact, the shock of the cold blow incapacitates the body.

dart gun: The projectile is a drug-filled syringe. On impact an incapacitating drug is injected.

stench: A pot or grenade giving off an obnoxious odour. (Deane-Drummond is not in favour of this because he says it is liable to cause ridicule!)

instant banana: Makes road surfaces so slippery that they are impassable.

instant mud: Makes the road surface so sticky that movement is very difficult.

taser: Fires two small barbed electrical contacts with up to 500 feet of trailing electric wire. The barbs catch in the victim's clothes or skin and he or she is paralysed until the current is disconnected.

Many of these weapons are only partly developed, or have

tactical inadequacies or problems of public acceptability. They are included here only because they give a vivid picture of the amazingly varied ways in which new techniques may be thought up to keep people down. If there is still any doubt about the thinking behind such devices, Congressman James Scheuer is anxious to dispel it with the hard (if exaggerated) facts:

As a result of spin-offs from medical, military, aerospace and industrial research, we are now in the process of developing devices and products capable of controlling violent individuals and entire mobs without injury. We can tranquillize, impede, immobilize, harass, shock, upset, stupefy, nauseate, chill, temporarily blind, deafen or just plain scare the wits out of anyone the police have a proper need to control and restrain.[42]

16
Torture and Interrogation

The evidence of the black civil rights movement in the US and the Northern Ireland conflict shows that, in the non-violent phase and even more in the phase of armed insurrection, far more arrests of political and trade-union activists are likely to occur than at present. The emphasis placed on intelligence-gathering by military theorists indicates that arrests are likely to be followed by lengthy interrogations. A considerable increase in the number of militants in prison, and the resulting strong politicization of prisoners, could well see the increased use of scientific techniques of prisoner control. This chapter and the next two are primarily concerned with interrogation and prisoner control. However, there is a considerable overlap between the techniques used in the two situations. Any one of these techniques can have a number of different functions. The distinction we make here between torture and prisoner control is to a considerable extent for convenience in describing and analysing them.

The oldest technique, both of interrogation and prisoner control, is the infliction of severe physical pain and/or mental stress on the prisoner against his or her will. This is torture. Over the last few years there has been a worldwide increase in the use of torture. It is so marked that Amnesty International recently likened it to a 'social cancer'.[1] This tendency seems likely to continue. Reports of hideous tortures from Brazil, Chile, Uruguay, Iran, Turkey and other such countries are all too frequent. But the practice is not limited to extremely authoritarian states in the Third World. Britain, France and the USA have all carried out torture in their colonial wars in Aden, Algeria, Vietnam and elsewhere, while the American training of torturers for Latin American police states has been denounced by no less a person than Ramsay Clark, Attorney General under President Johnson.[2]

More recently, liberal democracies such as Britain, USA and Germany have been devising new methods of imposing extreme stress on prisoners suspected of belonging to dissident groups. These methods are torture because of the stress they induce in the victim. Yet they are designed either to appear relatively harmless (as in the hooding torture used in Northern Ireland) or to lend support to claims – using medical language – that they are for the benefit of the prisoner (as in some of the prisoner-control techniques developed in the USA). Torture techniques, like riot-control techniques, are being increasingly designed for political acceptability as well as for technical effectiveness.

The Functions of Torture

Torture can be used on a prisoner to achieve one or more of four purposes – extraction of information from a determined person, preparation of the prisoner for a 'show trial', ending (or even reversing) the political effectiveness of the prisoner, and the inculcation of a climate of generalized fear among certain sections of the population. The standard method of achieving any of these goals has been, and generally still remains, the 'breaking of the prisoner' through a process of mounting stress, imposed classically by physical means, but more recently by psychological ones.

Extraction of information is always the *post hoc* justification for torture. This is hardly surprising, as it is the only function of the four which can be admitted by the state, if details of the methods used should leak out. We have already seen how Lord Parker and Mr Boyd-Carpenter justified the Northern Ireland hooding tortures in terms of the amount of information gained through interrogation.

Pragmatic arguments about the need for information can seem on the surface very compelling. Thus Roy Hattersley, Labour Minister, when asked on television whether it was ever justified to cause pain to a suspect to make him talk, replied, 'Let's imagine 250 people in an aeroplane. Let's say we know some terrorists mean business because one bomb has gone off already. Let's assume we've got a man who we know to be the terrorist who planted the bomb and could save 200-odd lives by finding out where the second bomb is. If he wouldn't tell me I'd have to think very hard before I said don't bring any pressure to bear on that man that might cause him pain.' To this sort of argument Amnesty say, 'As soon as its use is permitted once ... it's logical to use it on people who might plant bombs or who might begin to think of planting bombs. The example of Algiers is a classic case. Torture began under certain restraints and then it spread into an indiscriminate orgy of brutality.'[3] Nor need it stop at bombers. As we have seen, the label 'terrorism' can be applied to include all types of severe threat to the state. It is quite conceivable that the British government, following the example of many other countries, could use a similar logic to extend the range of torture victims.

Preparation for a show trial is the second function of torture. The classic example of this function was the preparation of former leaders of the Bolshevik Party for Stalin's Moscow trials of 1936–8, in which they publicly admitted their own guilt to charges of which they were totally innocent. The main factor in producing a confession was the totally broken state of the prisoner, following a very lengthy pre-interrogation breakdown process, based on isolation and sleep deprivation. This left the victim highly suggestible and totally lacking in will. The author Ilya Ehrenburg, who knew them and was present at the trial, told Roy Medvedev, 'They gave their testimony in a kind of mechanical language, without the intonation and temperament peculiar to each of them. Although each used some of his stylistic peculiarities, for the most part they used the language of an average office clerk, with turns of speech they had never previously employed.'[4]

It has often been assumed that the Chinese 'brainwashing' methods were closely related to these Russian techniques. In fact they differed both in technique and in function. The primary function of the Chinese method was *to end or reverse the previous political effectiveness of the prisoner*. In the Chinese method, torture was part of producing a new belief system in the prisoner – a process known as Thought Reform. So, unlike the Russian prisoners, people who underwent Chinese Thought Reform defended their new ideological position in most unmechanical ways.[5] The Chinese method did involve physical coercion – sleep deprivation, being chained up and possibly being beaten – but less so than the Russian methods. However, it relied far more on social pressures – the prisoner was exposed to a continual attack on his beliefs by cell-mates, as in certain Western psychiatric methods, such as Synanon Games, though far more intensively. The breakdown that ensued was followed by a lengthy relearning process – both highly social and highly intellectual – involving mainly extended group discussion.

Thought Reform depends upon the replacement of a partially contradictory world-view by a more coherent one. Western capitalism, by common consent, no longer has a coherent and confident world-view to offer. Moreover the methods were most likely to be effective in China with people who were initially not unsympathetic to the Chinese Communist position. So, to end the political effectiveness of a prisoner, Western methods would probably rely on creating a psychological incapacity so intense that the victim would find it very difficult to take up an active political role again.

This was an important function for both Portuguese and Greek torturers under their respective dictators. In Greece 'from 1971 to 1974 the purpose of torture became increasingly one of intimidation and terrorization with the specific aim of destroying the student movement'. In Portugal 'the PIDE understood that if a victim could be broken and made to talk, he or she became forever useless to the underground opposition movements since the latter would no longer be able to rely on him or her'.[6]

Breaking a prisoner by a combination of increasing physical pain and/or anxiety effectively neutralizes the victim even long after release. It produces a psychiatric condition similar to that occurring after excessive combat in wartime, technically known as 'anxiety neurosis'. An anxiety neurosis is a frequent after-effect of highly traumatic experiences and can take many forms. The distinguished psychoanalyst Fenichel describes it as including 'spells of uncontrollable emotions, especially of anxiety and frequently of rage, occasionally even convulsive attacks, sleeplessness or dreams in which the trauma is experienced again and again, also mental repetitions during the day of the traumatic situations and diminished sexual interest.'[7] One of us remembers vividly how in Northern Ireland, on visiting one of the victims of the hooding torture, the man spoke for hours in a torrent of words about his experiences three years before. He needed only the faintest hint of a question to set off a flood of words about another facet of the whole hideous memory. The after-effects are not only psychological. Anxiety can produce gastrointestinal, cardiovascular and genito-urinary symptoms and muscular disorders such as tremors. Studies of the after-effects of concentration-camp incarceration has shown that such symptoms may be very long-lasting, if not permanent.[8]

A life-long incapacitating neurosis is not an inevitable consequence of torture. However, long-lasting neuroses are common. Since such after-effects offer no visible signs it is easy to pretend they do not exist, as Lord Parker did in the Northern Ireland cases. This type of denial has many historical precedents. General Massu, commander of the 10th French paratroop brigade in Algiers in 1956 and the obvious model for the French commander in the film *The Battle of Algiers*, said on the World in Action film 'Year of the Torturer', 'The use of electricity if well controlled doesn't degrade the personality of the enemy, it shakes you up, which is obviously not very pleasant, but you get over it without any profound after-effects.' By contrast, Frantz Fanon documents in *The Wretched of the Earth* many psychological after-effects of electric shock torture administered in Algerian prisons.[9]

The fourth function of torture is *the inculcation of a climate of fear* in the general population so as to discourage it from providing support to the militants, and also to intimidate potential political activists. Amnesty International stresses the value to authoritarian regimes of such a climate of fear: 'For those who govern without the consent of the governed this has proved to be an effective means of maintaining power. To set torture as the price of dissent is to be assured that only a small minority will act. With the majority neutralized by fear, the well-equipped forces of repression can concentrate on an isolated minority.' Intelligence can be rapidly gained. According to the Amnesty report on torture, the Greek interrogators of a Wing Commander Minis claimed that they wanted him to tell people he was being tortured so that 'all who entered military police quarters would tremble'. This generation of a generalized climate of fear is perhaps one reason why the British Army were seemingly so unselective in the fourteen men they chose to be victims of their new torture techniques in August 1971.

How and Why Torture Works

Initial responses to stress are fairly well understood. When someone encounters a dangerous or frightening situation, the characteristic response of the body is to prepare itself for aggressive action or flight. The adrenal glands produce more adrenalin, and the muscles and brain work at peak efficiency. If the stressful situation lasts for a longer period of time, this typical acute response cannot be maintained. Provided individuals see themselves as acting purposefully in the situation they can maintain effectiveness (in military terms – morale) for a considerable period of time. But at a cost: they suffer anxiety, sleeplessness and loss of appetite. Eventually breakdown into a chronic state occurs. The person may behave entirely irrationally, for example, walking towards the enemy lines in wartime, or apparently becoming immune to highly stressful events and even retaining no conscious memory of them afterwards. The general aim of torture is to achieve a level of stress sufficient to break the victim.

In wartime this transition to a state of 'shell-shock' or 'battle-fatigue' has been very loosely estimated to take on average fifty days of heavy combat.[10] Towards the end of the sub-acute stage, soldiers become increasingly inefficient, easily startled, irritable and over-responsive. The transition produces a state of 'emotional exhaustion', where the person becomes listless and apathetic, and bizarre, contradictory behaviour occurs. The after-effect of this traumatic state is typically the type of anxiety neurosis discussed earlier.

Torture and Interrogation 235

This chronic traumatized condition is the end result of torture. We referred to it before as 'breaking the prisoner'. Traumatization occurs more quickly if one is tired, exhausted or sick, and if no adequate response to the situation is possible. So, the First World War, with its long periods spent under fire in wet, dirty, diseased trenches, produced vast numbers of 'shell shock' cases. The torturer achieves comparable exhaustion by continual torture sessions while the total helplessness of the victim ensures that no adequate response can be made.

The torture process need not involve physical methods for such a traumatized state to result. Thus the most frequently used KGB method involved a combination of isolation in a featureless 10 ft by 8 ft cell and the restriction of sleep. After an average eight weeks in this regime Hinkle and Wolff [11] describe the state of the prisoner as follows:

He sits and stares with a vacant expression perhaps endlessly twisting a button on his coat. He allows himself to become dirty and dishevelled. He no longer bothers about the niceties of eating. He mixes it [the food] into a mush and stuffs it into his mouth like an animal. He goes through the prison routine automatically, as if he were in a daze. The slop jar is no longer offensive to him. Ultimately he may lose some of the restraints of ordinary behaviour. He may soil himself. He weeps, he mutters and prays aloud in his cell.

The increase in stress necessary to produce traumatization is normally achieved by a combination of different stressors. When physical-torture techniques are dominant they are almost always combined with such stressors as isolation, sleep deprivation, squalid conditions, violation of legal rights and lack of knowledge of where one is. When psychological or physiological stressors are the main component, physical brutality normally exists as a sub-component. Moreover with both types of techniques there is the additional knowledge that the suffering is being produced by torture. Each stressor tends to increase the effect of the others, so that a positive feedback process of increasing stress is achieved, until, in the words of a Brazilian torturer: 'He'll be all broken inside.'

The number of ways of increasing stress is virtually limitless.

Many ways of causing physical pain are obvious. Others are less so, such as being forced to remain in a fixed position for a very long period of time. Still other stressors do not involve pain, but employ what may be loosely termed 'psycho-physiological' methods, such as isolation, sleeplessness, temperature manipulation, excessively salty diet, etc.

The hooding torture was the first well-documented use of these psycho-physiological tortures by an advanced capitalist state within its own borders. Already two new uses have occurred – the 'Tote Trakt' in German prisons and the Control Unit in British prisons, both using lengthy periods of solitary confinement as means of breaking prisoners. Psycho-physiological torture therefore needs special attention. Even doctors are not immune to the misconception that they are milder than traditional physical tortures. (In fact the Portuguese secret police, PIDE, had come to believe that psychological torture – in their case, sleeplessness – was more effective than physical torture.[12]) This sort of professional naivety is, of course, reflected in the views of the general population. Governments such as the British trade upon this fact when they adopt these more sophisticated torture techniques, which are far less liable to lead to public condemnation than the more obvious physical type. Their distinctive feature is the way they make use of mounting anxiety produced by psychological causes instead of the more obvious physical stressors.

One characteristic of anxiety produced in these sorts of circumstances is that it can feed on itself. For instance, the more anxious you are, the more likely you are to have a bizarre experience – hallucinations, paranoid delusions, inability to think – and the more bizarre experiences you have the more anxious you become. Emotional exhaustion increases and, as the anxiety levels mount, you will begin to develop symptoms similar to those found in acute psychiatric breakdown.

Psycho-physiological torture techniques probably date back almost as far as physical torture. While the conscious application of scientific knowledge to the improvement of these techniques is a post-war phenomenon, the 'craft' use of the techniques seems to have been developed by the KGB under

Stalin particularly in the period 1936–9. The two primary components of the KGB methods – isolation and sleep deprivation – remain the core of modern psychological torture techniques.

Isolation

Prolonged solitary confinement can have very serious psychiatric consequences. In the early nineteenth century it was widely used in prisons both in Britain and America. Prisoners were twenty times as likely to be diagnosed insane in Pentonville, where solitary confinement was used, than at other comparable prisons where it was not. After observing its effects on prisoners in America, Charles Dickens wrote:

> I hold the slow and daily tampering with the mysteries of the brain to be immeasurably worse than any torture of the body and because its ghastly signs and tokens are not so palpable to the eye and sense of touch as scars upon the flesh, because its wounds are not upon the surface, and it extorts few cries that the human ear can hear, and therefore I the more denounce it as a severe punishment which slumbering humanity is not roused upon to stay.[13]

The way solitary confinement operates can best be assessed by first examining sensory deprivation. This is the laboratory-developed analogue of the isolation component of the KGB techniques devised in the early 1950s by Canadian psychologists sponsored by the Canadian and American military. As we saw earlier, sensory deprivation has itself been used as the core process in a modern torture technique – the Northern Ireland hooding method. In sensory deprivation, isolation is taken to an extreme by reducing the stimulation of the sense organs to the minimum practicable. The term will also be used for the closely related technique, 'perceptual deprivation', in which the amount of change and patterning in the stimulation is greatly reduced.

Sensory-deprivation situations vary in their intensity. In a relatively mild situation, lying on a comfortable bed in a darkened sound-proofed room and wearing long cuffs on the arms and gloves, many volunteers have lasted as long as a week. In the most stressful, submersion in a tepid, darkened, sound-proofed water-bath, the average time a volunteer could endure was four hours. Even bed confinement can be made much less endurable by not allowing the subject to move much. Confined in an iron lung in a situation of perceptual deprivation, only 10 per cent of subjects could stand it for more than twenty-four hours.

During sensory deprivation, subjects suffer all manner of strange subjective experiences – disorders of thinking, hallucinations, 'body-image' distortions – 'my head is like a spinning cone going away from my body' – nightmares and paranoid fears. All produce anxiety, and the anxiety produces further bizarre experiences. The mounting anxiety results in a panic attack and the volunteer can only relieve it by ending the experiment. When release from the situation is impossible, so that helplessness is maximized and other stressors induce an initial high level of anxiety, a full-blown acute psychotic state can be reached within two to three days, as happened with the victims of the hooding techniques in Northern Ireland.[14]

The bizarre experiences that occur in sensory deprivation may very loosely be explained as a result of the need for the mental machinery to be relatively active the whole time. In this case, lacking novel perceptual input on which to work, it may substitute internally generated information. One would not expect a sharp break between normal situations and the sensory deprivation one, as this 'lack' of novel perceptual input can be more or less marked. It is not surprising that solitary confinement in a featureless environment, which lacks all forms of interesting stimulation including the most interesting and vitally satisfying source – other people – should produce similar effects, though on a different time scale.

Mild sensory deprivation is therefore characteristic of solitary confinement. One of the severest isolation cells known to exist is the so-called Tote Trakt in German prisons mentioned earlier. By the autumn of 1974 five members of the Red Army Fraction had been kept in a Tote Trakt during part of their three years in solitary confinement.

The most used Tote Trakt, at Ossendorf near Cologne, was officially the women's psychiatric section of the prison. It contains six cells and is relatively isolated from the rest of the prison. In late 1974, in response to a widespread protest campaign, two prisoners – Ulrike Meinhof and Gudrun Ensslin – were placed in the unit together. Until then there had always been only one prisoner on the Tote Trakt at any one time. Prison officials visited the prisoner only at set times, and never singly; they never talked to her. No other person came near the Tote Trakt at all. The normal direct route from the male psychiatric section of the prison to the exercise yard lay through it. But this route was never used when a prisoner was there. To add to the intense auditory monotony was visual monotony. The walls and furniture were all painted white and no pictures were allowed. The windows, which were barred, were also covered by a thick wire-mesh, which made it extremely difficult to see objects outside. In any case no one could ever be seen through the window, with the exception of a team of prisoners who once or twice a summer would cut the grass which lay between the Tote Trakt and the blank wall of the next cell block. The only relief from the monotony was provided by books and a radio on a fixed channel at fixed times. The radio and the books would be expected to reduce the isolation effects somewhat. But they would not eliminate them, as the German authorities like to suggest.

The symptoms produced by solitary confinement are similar to those of sensory deprivation. Albie Sachs, a young Capetown lawyer, was in isolation for 168 days in South Africa in the early 1960s under the 90-day Detention Act. He wrote of himself:

There are weird symptoms which, when taken in conjunction, present a picture of incipient mental disintegration. Often when I lie on my bed I feel as if my soul is separating from my body ... My limbs, my trunk and my head lie in an inert vegetable mass on the mattress, while my soul floats gently to the ceiling, where it coalesces and embodies itself into a shape which lodges in the corner and looks down at my body. Usually the shape is that of an owl which stares at me, calmly, patiently and without emotion. It is my own owl, my own I. It is I staring at myself. What's more I am aware of the whole process as though there is yet another self, which watches the I staring at myself. I am a mirror bent on itself, a unity, and yet infinite multiplicity of internal reflections.[15]

Even more clear evidence of the breakdown in normal mental processes comes from Meinhof's account, as one would expect from the greater severity of her situation – two years in isolation of which eight months were on the Tote Trakt. She describes her sensations:

The feeling that one's head is going to explode – the sensation that the cranium really ought to crack, break off – the feeling the spinal cord would be forced into the brain – the feeling the hemispheres of the brain would slowly shrink together like dried fruit, for instance – the feeling one was uninterruptedly, imperceptibly exposed to electrification, one was remotely controlled – the feeling that associations would be chopped off from one – the feeling one urinated the soul from one's body, as if one could not hold back one's water ... warders, visitors,* the yard seem to one like celluloid ... the feeling that time and space are joined into one ... the feeling of being in a distorted mirror.

In technical terms, this statement shows evidence of body image distortions, strong depersonalizations both of oneself (losing one's soul) and others (the celluloid), disorders of space and time, influences by machines; all are often found in schizophrenic breakdown. It says much for the basic strength of Meinhof's personality that after two years of this, she was capable of going on hunger strike as a protest against the conditions.

The pain of solitary confinement is resisted differently by different people. It is possible to resist the induced helplessness and create an intellectual defence against the situation by attempting to comprehend one's symptoms and by developing an obsessive routine. For instance, Edith Bone, while in solitary confinement for seven years, mentally catalogued 27,000 words.

As well as increasing the likelihood of a breakdown, isolation makes a prisoner much more vulnerable to interrogation. Sachs again describes it aptly:

The months of isolation have tended to wipe my mind clean of past recollection ... By isolating me from the world in which relevant events are taking place, they have succeeded in destroying my independent recollection of what happened. If I saw sentiments couched in a manner which I could recognize as being my own,

*The prisoners were allowed to see a visitor once a fortnight.

then I would have difficulty in deciding whether or not they are accurate. I could possibly even be persuaded that I gave a talk on a subject far more dangerous than that on which I did speak.[16]

Here we see the mechanism of confession manufacture laid open. Experiments have also shown that people become much more suggestible under sensory deprivation.[17]

This is probably a major reason why the German authorities imposed such a regime on the Red Army Fraction prisoners. 'Security' cannot account for the white walls and furniture, the lack of pictures, the wire-mesh, and the totally empty prison block – especially as they have now allowed two prisoners to remain together. Having held some of the Red Army Fraction for over three years without trial, the German authorities built a special courtroom near Stuttgart to hold a show trial which began in mid 1975. On Dutch TV, a Minister of Justice for the West German state of Hessen, inadvertently demonstrated the relation between the prison regime and the trial by stating: 'If necessary ... we must keep the person temporarily, mark my words temporarily [three years!], under isolation in order *to make it possible for the prosecution to achieve a proof without any lacunae so that it will stand up in court.*' If the defendants were to behave like revolutionaries, the rottenness of the German capitalist state would be partially shown up despite the irrelevance (to the working class) of the actions for which they were being tried. Although much affected by the prison regime, none of the prisoners confessed or agreed to testify. A new law was therefore passed allowing the state to exclude a defendant under certain conditions if his or her physical state would slow up the trial. Since psychiatrists appointed by the state testified that the prison regime had left them incapable of standing a full day's trial, the main defendants were excluded from their own trial! The Red Army Fraction trial is an excellent example of the way a modern capitalist state can integrate scientific and legal means of masked repression.*

*In May 1976 Meinhof died by strangulation. It is unclear at the time of writing whether this was murder by a guard or judicial murder by the state (suicide). Suicides resulting from the effects of solitary confinement occurred, for instance, in South Africa in the 1960s.

Sleep Torture

The other major technique of the new generation of torture methods is sleep torture. An important sub-component of the standard KGB technique, it was also the main component of the notorious 'Conveyor', continuous interrogation lasting several days, which was used for example by the Czechoslovak secret police in the 1950s. It was also the main method used by the Portuguese secret police – PIDE – under the fascist regimes before 1974.

The process used by the PIDE began with several weeks of isolation. Following this the victim was prevented from sleeping – usually for from five to eight days but on occasions up to eighteen days – initially by the endless tapping of a coin on the table and by being forced to walk round and round the room. Several teams of agents worked on four-hour shifts to keep the pressure up. When the victim began to doze, tapes were played of very loud noises – often screams – perhaps to be hallucinated as those of a member of the victim's family. They would also arrange readings of gibberish by agents outside the cell to make the victim think he was going mad.

Carlos Coutinho, a journalist, was a victim of the sleep torture in Portugal in 1973 – he was kept awake for 190 hours. He told reporters that after five nights of being kept awake he began to have hallucinations:

> I began to see marble plaques and posters on my back which disappeared as soon as I turned my head to read what they said. In the bathroom I began to see writhing masses of black maggots. They swelled up all over the bath and the washbasin.

After hallucinating a visit from his wife and daughter he said:

> From that moment until the end of the eighth night, the torture followed an apocalyptic crescendo which even now I find impossible to unravel as my memory for the event has remained very confused. In my hallucinations I began to see very refined machines, complicated gadgets for torture, great heaps of electric cables all tangled up, the cries of people being tortured, the voice of my wife, my daughter's cries, deafening sirens, explosions that blackened the walls of my room . . . I came to the conclusion I was going mad.[18]

He was then allowed to sleep, but months later was still suffering from continuous headaches, shouting in his sleep and inability to concentrate – symptoms similar to those of the Northern Ireland victim described earlier. Dr Afonso de Albuquerque, the leader of the team of Portuguese psychiatrists who examined torture victims after they were freed on the overthrow of Caetano in April 1974, says that, of the 90 per cent who had broken down under torture, 5 per cent are still psychotic. Many more will be suffering from anxiety neurosis.[19]

Laboratory research shows that symptoms of sleeplessness are quite similar to those resulting from sensory deprivation. According to Ian Oswald, Britain's leading sleep researcher, the most striking aspect of behaviour after 100 hours without sleep is the 'nightmare-like day-dream life into which some (volunteers) fall'.[20] Paranoid fantasies occur, often involving the experimenter plotting some devious scheme. Visual and auditory hallucinations also frequently happen in the laboratory situation, but they do not normally have the terrifying type of content that the Portuguese prisoners experienced – the emotional tone of a hallucination or a dream depends upon the anxiety of the person experiencing it.

Most laboratory experiments end after five days' sleep deprivation, yet the symptoms will get worse at an increasing rate as time without sleep is extended. In both sleep deprivation and sensory deprivation the ability to sustain normal thought breaks down in related ways. So it is to be expected that their effect will be greater when used in combinations than when used singly. These effects will be greatly intensified in the positive-feedback anxiety-increasing process. Initial beatings and threatening and humiliating treatment will pump up the anxiety levels, to give this process a head start. To break a person in this way is as easy as by physical torture. It has the great advantage for the state that it leaves no external scars.

Torture in Britain?

But wouldn't Britain be different? Surely a country famous for its political freedom would not indulge in such barbaric practices, at least not on its own citizens (not counting those born on the other side of the Irish Sea)? Any such sentimental view should be somewhat shaken by three recent independent developments concerning the prison service, the Army and the police respectively.

In August 1974 a new unit opened in Wakefield Prison that could house thirty-nine men. Soon another was to open in Wormwood Scrubs that could take twenty-eight. These were the 'control units'. Control units were designed for 'subverters of the prison order', a category with which we shall become more familiar in Chapter 18. The minimum time a prisoner was to spend in the control unit was 180 days, divided into two ninety-day phases. In the first phase he was kept in solitary confinement in his cell for twenty-three hours a day and allowed one hour solitary exercise. During the second ninety days he was allowed limited access to other inmates of the unit, but if he misbehaved in any way he could be returned to the first phase. To qualify for the second phase he had to sew mailbags for eight hours a day in the first stage. The system was designed so that 'opportunities for confrontation with prison staff are reduced', the staff anyhow being trained to be 'coolly professional', in the words of the Home Office. Privileges were very limited indeed and the cells were reputed to be featureless. In setting up the control units the Home Office had quietly increased the permissible maximum solitary confinement from fifty-six days to ninety days or more. Ninety days, strangely enough, was also the length of solitary confinement introduced by the South African government in the early 1960s. In South Africa the ninety-day detention system was being deliberately used to break the victim so as to obtain a confession. In Britain its function was also that of breaking the prisoner, and it appears to have been effective. Mollie Newall, whose brother was the first inmate at Wakefield, said after visiting him after he had been in for two months that for a normally cheerful well-built man he was 'nervous, disorientated, very depressed and had lost weight'.[21] There was a public outcry*, but solitary confinement is such a subtle torture that even such a famous liberal as Roy Jenkins was initially able to

* In May 1976, John Masterson, the first man to be released from prison after being incarcerated in a control unit, was admitted to hospital for psychiatric reasons, one month after his release.

ignore it. Eventually, in October 1975, when even medical experts were beginning to protest publicly, he announced that no more prisoners would be admitted to the Wakefield unit, but only because the unit wasted staff resources! This, of course, enables the Home Office to open it again 'should the need arise'. And it probably will. As we shall see in the next chapter, British prisons are overcrowded and understaffed and dissent, particularly political dissent within them, is very liable to increase.

The second alarming symptom is the revelation that the Army uses severe interrogation methods in military exercises. Thus in an SAS exercise in 1974 anyone 'captured' was stripped naked and rolled in the snow. On another exercise one 'captured' officer was thrown into a fast-flowing river with a rope tied to his leg. He was dragged out half-drowned and the process was then repeated. The hooding technique is regularly used in exercises, although for shorter durations than on the Northern Ireland internees, the maximum for a soldier being seventeen hours.[22]

Why is the Army using these techniques? William Rodgers, Minister of State for Defence, in letters to Mr Ive of the British section of Amnesty International, claims that it is designed 'to give servicemen a better chance of successfully withstanding interrogation', but says later, 'we simply do not have (and thankfully) any direct evidence but the professional advice tended to me is that the training is valuable'. Since the training 'has continued for many years', the fact that there is no 'direct evidence' must mean that very few soldiers have ever been interrogated by guerrillas – their only possible enemy. And which guerrillas are going to have noise machines available?

Could there be any other reasons why this training is used? One obvious purpose is for training interrogators. This would explain why the methods the soldier is 'trained to resist' are the sophisticated ones the British Army itself developed and still prefers. Secondly, undergoing a vicious interrogation is a very brutalizing experience; it has been used as such by the Greek police.[23] If the Army required soldiers to perform functions for which they need to be brutalized this could be attained by involvement in interrogation exercises.

Many of the functions of the SAS – the organization that features most in accounts of interrogation exercises – would seem to require brutalization. One function, for instance, according to *ALOM* is assassination.

That assassins have to be brutalized was amazingly clearly demonstrated in what the *Sunday Times* called 'the strange tale of Dr Narut'. Dr Narut worked for the US Navy as a psychologist. 'Trainees' there are forced to watch gruesome films with their heads bolted in a clamp and their eyelids propped open until they habituate to watching incredibly bloodthirsty scenes without stress. The trainees are then 'inserted' into US embassies under cover, ready to kill should the need arise.[24] Is it too far-fetched to assume the British Army actually use brutal interrogation for a related purpose?

The third of these ominous tendencies has been the way that police interrogation methods seem to be becoming more brutal. Virtually every one of the Irish bomb trials has been full of allegations of brutal interrogative practices on the part of the police. About the first of these trials, that of the Price sisters, Commander Huntley of Scotland Yard said: 'We have to admit to what was an assault – well, we shall say a technical assault – on Dolours Price. But desperate measures follow on desperate means ... The police occasionally have to use unorthodox – yes, unorthodox – methods.' Psychological interrogation techniques – isolation, sleeplessness, induced debility and exhaustion, threats and degradation – have no threshold which clearly separates torture from ordinary interrogation. They are ideal for a gradual escalation. The Prevention of Terrorism Act, 1974 gives the police seven whole days to use whatever strategies they like. There has been no public inquiry into any of these allegations. Commander Huntley's statement is a rare public admission, although the brutal beatings of the Birmingham bomb defendants by prison warders is widely accepted as fact. They fit the pattern of the Northern Ireland methods, the control units and the British Army interrogation training methods in showing a rapid deterioration in the British state's attitude to torture.

17
Scientific Interrogation

Information-gathering is a crucial component of the security forces' operations, so that technologies for information extraction are of obvious importance. Torture is effective, but it carries complex political consequences; and even psychological tortures can get a bad press. Are there no other ways of extracting an equal amount of information which would avoid the political drawbacks associated with torture? The simple answer is that there are not – although a number of innovations have been suggested. We will look here at three possible alternative means of extracting information from unwilling victims: the polygraph, drugs and hypnosis. Each of these may achieve some results; but, as we shall see, their effectiveness depends to a considerable extent on persuading the victim that they will work.

The Polygraph (Lie Detector)

The polygraph* is a device which can reputedly detect whether a person is lying. In the USA it has been in use since at least the early 1940s, although polygraph evidence is not generally admitted in court there. Recently the British authorities, too, have been showing an interest in the polygraph.[2] It was one of the technologies described favourably in a reprehensible little pamphlet put out by the British Association for the Advancement of Science.[3]

The polygraph works on the principle that a person who is lying will generally show an increase in anxiety and other emotional changes, which will be reflected in a number of physiological ('autonomic') changes. It is these responses which are

*We are considering here only the traditional polygraph – the 'lie detector'. There is also another device which is designed to measure the stress in a person's voice, but tests so far show it to be much less accurate than the polygraph.[1]

measured by the polygraph. Machines used by the police generally measure only three basic functions: blood pressure, rate of breathing and galvanic skin response (GSR) – the electrical resistance of the skin to the passage of a minute electric current. The more the subject perspires, the lower will be this resistance A polygraph described recently in *Police Review*[4] consisted of a cardiosphymograph – a cuff worn around the arm to measure changes in pulse rate, pulse wave amplitude and relative blood pressure; a pneumograph – a corrugated rubber tube of about two inches diameter, fitted around the chest to record changes in breathing patterns; and a galvanometer attached to the palm of the hand to measure GSR.

Once the victim is connected up to the polygraph he or she will be asked a number of questions, some of them 'neutral', others 'critical'. The neutral items will be ones which the victim can be expected to answer truthfully. Critical items are ones which the interrogator thinks the victim may lie about. By comparing the autonomic responses recorded for neutral items, the interrogator may be able to tell whether the victim was in fact answering truthfully.

The principle is straightforward enough, but in practice things are not quite so simple. There is no such thing as a foolproof lie detector. Individuals vary greatly both in their responses to neutral items and also in the way their responses change when they are lying. For example one individual might show a large increase in respiration rate and little change in blood pressure or skin resistance, while in others blood pressure might show the most change. And a relatively minor change in one individual might be more significant than a fairly large response in another. One way the examiner might try to overcome this problem is by getting the victim to lie about something trivial (such as which of a set of playing cards he or she has previously picked out) at the beginning of the session. This will give the examiner some idea of that particular individual's characteristic autonomic responses when he or she is lying.

Even with these preparations, the detection of a 'significant' change in autonomic responses can be difficult or impossible even for an experienced examiner. And it is also possible for the subject to confuse the examiner deliberately. The US Army is apparently teaching its soldiers to gain voluntary control over the responses measured by the polygraph by using biofeedback techniques.[5] This requires time and the use of equipment which is not generally available. For people without such advantages, cruder techniques can be used to beat the polygraph. The most obvious of these is to control the breathing rate. Shallow, slow breathing is often associated with lying; irregular breathing patterns will prove confusing to the examiner – and changes in breathing also have a disruptive effect on other autonomic measures. Any bodily movement – even an almost imperceptible one – is likely to disrupt the measurements, as will deliberately tensing and relaxing the body muscles at random intervals through the test sessions. A victim who can conjure up a strong mental image of anything which is unpleasant, frightening or erotic during the presentation of a neutral item will make it even harder for the interrogator to distinguish between responses to neutral items and those to critical ones. The more inconsistent the reactions are, the harder they will be to interpret.

Since such counter-measures are very simple to apply once the victims are aware that a detector is being used, it has been suggested that autonomic measurements could be taken during interrogation without the victim knowing about them. The BAAS pamphlet which we referred to above advocates the use of devices such as electrodes concealed in chair arms to monitor heart rate. And the Israelis were recently reported to be using a device which measures GSR at a distance in order to identify individuals crossing the border who have a higher than average anxiety level and might therefore warrant investigation. However, information obtained in this way is likely to be 'quite meagre and unreliable'.[6]

Truth Drugs

A persistent mythology has arisen about the existence of 'truth drugs' which make a person unable to conceal the truth. No such drug exists, although both drugs and the myths that surround them may be useful tools for interrogation. According to Amnesty International drugs were administered to some prisoners undergoing interrogation in both Greece and Portugal prior to the new regimes. There have also been allegations of amphetamines being administered to prisoners in Northern Ireland.[7] The CIA, too, have experimented with drugs for interrogation.

The first experiment in the use of a 'truth drug' was carried out in 1922 in the prison hospital in Dallas, using the drug scopolamine. The experiment was a success: afterwards the prisoner commented, 'I had a desire to answer any question asked, my mind would enter upon the true facts of the answer, and I would speak voluntarily, without any strength of will to manufacture an answer.'[8]

Although a few subsequent experiments were conducted on prisoners, most of our present information on 'truth drugs' stems from the use of drugs in psychiatric practice, to enable the patient to talk more fluently about painful experiences or to become conscious of experiences that have been repressed.

The two main types of drug used in psychiatric practices are short-acting barbiturates, such as sodium thiopentone and amylobarbitone; and amphetamines such as methadrine. Other drugs which have been used include amphetamine–barbiturate mixtures, ether, and hallucinogens such as LSD.[9] In each case the aim is to encourage the person to talk fluently, but the drugs achieve this result in very different ways. The barbiturates produce effects which are very similar to those of alcohol intoxication. Initially the person is likely to become more relaxed, then as more of the drug is administered there is an increasing loss of concentration, insight, memory for recent events and ability to think clearly. As with alcohol, inhibitions may be loosened, and the victim may be prepared to discuss some things which he or she wouldn't normally talk about.

Amphetamines produce a very different effect. They generally give rise to a sensation of well-being and alertness; speech may become very rapid and fluent. There may be an 'outpouring of emotions and memories'. With either of these drugs a co-operative subject may find it easier to discuss disturbing experiences; at very high doses abreaction may occur – that is, the person may become conscious of forgotten and traumatic experiences. But the situation is very different when the person is consciously withholding information. Slater and Sargant, two psychiatrists who pioneered much of the work on drug-induced abreaction, are adamant on this point: 'It is hopeless to expect a confession from the malingerer, who usually under this treatment becomes only truculent and abusive.' This would almost certainly also be true of interrogation victims.

Hallucinogens are unlikely to be used directly to obtain information, since a person sufficiently under the influence of the drug to be prepared to offer information would be likely to produce pure fantasy material rather than the facts the interrogator is seeking. This would also be true for very high doses of any of the other drugs mentioned above.

But this does not mean that drugs would be of no use in interrogation. Gottschalk has described a number of ways in which they could be employed.[10] Firstly, a victim who has been drugged would find it especially difficult to guard against the type of inadvertent slip which may occur in any interrogation, and combined with the other stresses of imprisonment drugs may serve to weaken the resistance of the person under interrogation. Secondly, if the victim believes in the effectiveness of the drug he or she may feel powerless against its effects – and therefore less guilty about anything said or done under its influence. Clearly, fear of betraying their cause is one important reason why interrogation victims withhold information; if this sense of guilt and personal responsibility is reduced, the victim may be more prepared to talk. A person under the influence of barbiturates, in particular, can be very open to suggestion; so a person who starts out convinced that the drug is effective is likely to become even more convinced of this during the course of the session. This in turn would reinforce the feeling of powerlessness – and make the victim even more likely to talk.

Gottschalk has also thought of a use for hallucinogens – to 'create an atmosphere of fear and terror in the informant, and the illusion of magical overpowering omnipotence in [the interrogator]'. Clearly this could prove a terrifying experience, and the threat of a repeat performance could be enough to persuade the victim to co-operate in providing information.

There is not much a person can do to counteract directly the effects of a drug, but there are ways of making sure that the interrogator gets as little information as possible. Since individuals react in very different ways to any particular drug, an obvious counter-measure is to exaggerate any effects which the drug has produced. Gottschalk recommends that a victim could 'simulate drowsiness, confusion and disorientation during the early stages of administration'. As the effects of the drug become more pronounced and genuinely disorientating, 'he can revel in fantasies; the more lurid the better. He can tell contradictory stories. He can simulate a psychosis.' The interrogator would almost certainly find it difficult to distinguish such a simulated response from one produced directly by the drug.

Hypnosis and Interrogation

The Israelis are reported to be using hypnosis in the interrogation of witnesses to a crime.[11] They claim that under hypnosis the witnesses are able to recall details which were never even consciously registered, for example a car number plate or the description of a person. This claim was repeated in the British Association pamphlet on police technology. It is a somewhat curious claim, since the published scientific literature indicates that people are no more able to recall such details under hypnosis than if they are simply encouraged to try hard to remember. However, such claims do tend to reinforce the idea in the public mind that hypnosis is a very powerful tool.

It would be a short step from interrogation of witnesses under hypnosis to an attempt to extract information from an unwilling suspect. Could this be achieved? Once again, there is nothing in the available scientific literature to suggest that it could, except possibly in very exceptional circumstances. Firstly, only a very small proportion of people can be hypnotized into a deep trance, and a number of sessions are normally needed before this can occur. Secondly, it would have to be possible to hypnotize a person against his or her will. Orne, who has published an authoritative account, intended for the military, on the possible use of hypnosis in interrogation, believes that this is very unlikely.[12]

But even if a person could be hypnotized, it is unlikely that an

Scientific Interrogation 253

interrogator would be able to persuade him or her to divulge information, since even under hypnosis people are still perfectly capable of lying.

However, Orne does describe a technique by which the interrogator can make use of the victim's own belief in the effectiveness of hypnosis to persuade him or her that he or she has been hypnotized and is unable to withhold information. This he calls the 'magic-room' technique. For instance, the interrogator may be able to make the victim believe that he or she is responding to hypnosis by suggesting that a cigarette will taste bitter – and then proffering a specially prepared bitter-tasting cigarette.

Another method might be to give the victim a sufficiently large dose of sleep-inducing drug to make him or her unconscious for a time. Following this period, the interrogator could read to the victim from notes supposedly obtained under the influence of the drug, but in fact making use of information obtained beforehand from sources other than the victim.

So it may be that the success claimed in Israel for hypnosis is little more than an attempt to persuade the public of the effectiveness and almost magical properties of hypnosis. If this is the case, their tactic can be easily countered by the simple dissemination of information of the kind in these pages.

18
Prisoners of the Strong State

The New Treatment

During the initial stages of a major political crisis in a Western liberal democracy, arrests and imprisonment of militants are likely to be comparatively rare and will mainly involve people suspected of violent or terrorist actions. But if the labour movement moves leftwards, the state may try to stem the tide by imprisoning some of the more left-wing and militant leaders. The calculation is that they will remain undefended by the 'moderate' majority. This tactic has had some success in the case of the Shrewsbury building workers, imprisoned on conspiracy charges arising out of the building workers' strike of 1972. It can also backfire dramatically, as it did when the imprisonment of the Pentonville Five dockers released a wave of trade-union solidarity which swept government policy aside. In general, such dangerous gambles can be taken as evidence of how little room for manoeuvre the crisis has left the government.

Nevertheless, as the economic and political crisis develops we can expect a gradually increasing number of explicitly 'political' prisoners in British gaols. At the same time, the growing political consciousness of society as a whole is likely to produce a generation of 'criminal' prisoners much more responsive to radical appeals. This development occurred among black prisoners in the USA, as can be seen in a quotation from George Jackson, writing from Soledad gaol in 1970: 'There are still some blacks here who consider themselves criminals but not many ... with the time and incentive these brothers have to read, study and think, you will find no class or category more aware, more embittered, desperate or dedicated to the ultimate remedy – revolution.' This tendency is not limited to the United States:

there have recently been a number of Marxist study groups in British prisons.

In this chapter we shall discuss some solutions to this problem which have been developed – primarily in the USA. In the late 1960s and the early 70s, with the rise of the anti-war and particularly the black movement, America was confronted with massive problems relating to prisoner control. A partial solution was found in the development of a 'therapeutic' model of prisons, which often had the additional (and perhaps unexpected) benefit of conferring an extra degree of control over the prisoner. The 'therapeutic' model appeared on the surface to be a 'humane' way of approaching the problem of increased crime rates; and so it fulfilled one of the major requirements of new techniques of repression – that they should appear relatively innocuous.

Clearly the British penal system will find its own specific ways of adapting to the new pressures, but at least one prominent British criminologist, Professor Stanley Cohen, has predicted that many of the US prison developments are likely to be increasingly used in British gaols. There are three separate, but related, problems facing the government with regard to political prisoners. Firstly, there is the damaging effect of publicity surrounding their trial and imprisonment. Secondly, there is the danger of *increasing* the political commitment of both political prisoners and the 'criminal' prisoners who are exposed to their influence, and of others not in gaol. This was the experience in the United States in the 1960s and early 70s when the imprisonment of black militants was an important factor in the development of black consciousness – and where radicalized ex-convicts played an important role in black movements. Thirdly, there is the danger that political prisoners will provide a focus for the organization of political movements within the prisons. The events in Attica in 1971[1] and in other US gaols showed how prisoners can organize mass actions around such demands as the right to be protected from racist attacks and the right to dissent. This function was certainly not lost on the Californian prison warders who (through their Correctional Officers' Association) cited 'the revolutionary movement, the existing conspiracy to destroy our system, as the prime cause of increased prison violence and murder. To reverse this trend, we recommend the housing of revolutionary inmates in a maximum-security facility. We do not see this as the ultimate solution.'[2] That phrase 'ultimate solution' carries with it unfortunate echoes from history.

In the USA the authorities attempted to find a solution to this problem by the use of the medical and related professions and the 'therapeutic model' of prisons. The doctors involved may be among the last to realize that the 'therapies' they have developed can be a technique of social control amounting to a refined form of torture. There are three main reasons why the therapeutic model for prisons has found ready acceptance. Firstly, there is the total lack of clear criteria for what constitutes 'mental illness' or a 'behaviour disorder'. Secondly, there are a small number of prisoners whose crimes can be understood primarily in terms of an individual pathological process. This provides a rationalization for extension of the model to other prisoners. Thirdly, unlike other techniques of repression, the advent of the medical profession into the penal field has been actively encouraged by many groups and individuals who see it as a way to *reform* prisons. Whereas warders are often expected to act in brutal ways, doctors are presumed to be 'above suspicion'. Their function is to 'cure'. If the initial remedies fail, it is only logical that harsher ones will be tried. Thus painful 'cures' may be justified as necessary both to the watching public and also to the doctor. So while a tight control over prisoners can be maintained by more traditional methods – such as inhuman living conditions, harassment, brutal treatment and physical torture – psychiatry has the decisive advantage for the state that it does not carry with it as many political drawbacks.

The origins of widespread psychiatric intervention in prisons date back to the 1950s and 1960s, the heyday of liberal reform when the medical profession attempted to introduce a therapeutic climate into prisons and borstals. They believed that, if only each offender could come to understand his or her motives for criminal behaviour, the excessively high recidivism rates could be reduced and the prisoners could learn to lead useful lives. Since the cost to the state of keeping someone in prison is very high – £2,210 per year in 1973/4[3] – it was obviously worth experimenting with these therapeutic endeavours.

Numerous reviews have been made of these attempts at therapy. Most reached a similar conclusion to that of Robert Martinson, who surveyed virtually all of the literature on prison therapy since 1945. He found that the programmes had 'no appreciable effect, positive or negative, on the rates of recidivism of convicted offenders'.[4]

However, while the therapies proved ineffective in changing the behaviour of prisoners after release, it became increasingly clear that some of the techniques could be used to change the behaviour of people still in prison. The behaviour technicians were retained, as Cohen says,[5] 'not because of some inherent superiority in their paradigm of crime, but merely by showing that they have the power to be more effective custodians'. This has been achieved mainly through the systematic application of so-called 'learning theory' – a branch of psychology whose principles have been drawn from laboratory experiments with animals, but which can also be applied to the modification of human behaviour. Other methods which the medical profession have to offer include drugs and the ultimate 'therapy', brain surgery.

The 'therapeutic' techniques used in prisons are obviously equally applicable in the setting of a psychiatric hospital. One of the drawbacks of imprisoning political prisoners is the adverse publicity which may surround an open trial. The purposes of the state can sometimes be better served if this can be avoided. One way of achieving incarceration without trial is to declare the activist 'insane'. So before going on to describe prison developments in detail, we will look at the phenomenon of the 'insane dissenter'.

The Insane Dissenter

What does it mean to say someone is 'mentally ill'? Where is the borderline which distinguishes, say, 'schizophrenia' from other less severe disturbances? If questions such as these could be answered with the same certainty as can questions about broken bones or measles, there would be little scope for the political abuse of criteria for diagnosis. In fact there are differences between the psychiatric traditions of different countries, between the same country at different times, and between individual doctors within a country at any particular time.

One study for instance found that 61·5 per cent of admissions to New York mental hospitals were diagnosed 'schizophrenic' compared with only 33·9 per cent of admissions to similar hospitals in London.[6] Another study in Britain found that only 54 per cent of patients kept the same diagnosis over four admissions in a two-year period. Using more narrow diagnostic categories (for example different types of schizophrenia), only 20 per cent kept the same diagnosis.[7] In both cases the authors concluded that it was the labels rather than the patients which had changed.

How can this happen? Most authorities agree that schizophrenia is a 'severe mental disorder' which may be characterized by 'loss of reality contact', 'disorders of thought', 'hallucinations' and 'delusions'. Any, or all of these features may be present at any given time, and the 'schizophrenic' person may well have periods when he or she behaves perfectly normally. Clearly what constitutes a 'disorder of thought' or a 'delusion' will depend on what the psychiatrist takes to be 'normality', which in turn must depend on his or her own view of reality. There is some point at which a patient's beliefs will be held to constitute a 'delusion' or 'loss of reality contact'. This point will be different for each psychiatrist. So with complacent psychiatrists or convenient definitions, psychiatry can be turned into an effective weapon against political dissidents.

In Russia the technique of declaring dissidents insane dates back to at least 1836.[8] The practice was used on a massive scale under Stalin in the late thirties, and has continued since his death – despite an official (secret) report in 1955 which condemned the practice.

The current use of psychiatry in Russia is interesting. It would clearly have been possible (as under Stalin) to secure the co-operation of certain psychiatrists in faking evidence to 'prove' that a dissenter was insane by almost any standards. But as one British psychiatrist who examined the 'symptoms' of Soviet dissidents given in their official hospital reports pointed out: 'These concepts go right outside the realms of any medically accepted sphere. These symptoms could include you and me as being schizophrenic.'[9] So in Russia the looseness of the criteria for defining 'mental illness', referred to above, has been exploited for political purposes. Of course, a number of Soviet psychiatrists have challenged this definition. Dr Semyon Gluzman, the author of a psychiatric report on one incarcerated dissident (Grigorenko) which declared him perfectly sane, was subsequently sentenced to seven years' forced labour and three years in exile.

Until 1961 people who had been committed to a psychiatric hospital in the Soviet Union against their will had the right of appeal (at least in theory) to a court of law.[10] In the new criminal code, introduced in that year, this provision was revoked, thus bringing the law in line with that of the USA and Britain. This coincided with the rise of the 'cultural opposition' which emerged in the aftermath of Khrushchev's 'secret speech' exposing Stalin's atrocities. By the end of 1972, as the opposition had become increasingly political, strict censorship and repression were reimposed.

Obviously most of the persistent dissidents could be tried on trumped-up charges of anti-Soviet actions. But some were prominent citizens, and open trials would have given rise to much adverse publicity for the state. One such person was Pyotr Grigorenko, a former Major-General in the Soviet Army. An old Bolshevik, he was head of the Cybernetics Department of the Frunze Military Academy and a prominent member of the Party. His activities in defence of democratic rights were clearly a great embarrassment to the Party leaders. In 1964, they solved the problem by having Grigorenko declared 'mentally ill'. He was incarcerated in a psychiatric hospital. At the same time he was expelled from the Party and his army rank was reduced. Following his release in 1965, he continued to campaign for socialist democracy and a return to Leninist principles, and was prominent in opposition to the Russian invasion of Czechoslovakia. In 1969 he was rearrested. He was beaten, went on hunger strike and was forcibly fed. He was given a psychiatric examination and found to be sane. However, following re-examination at the notorious Serbsky Institute in 1970, he was again declared mentally ill. The psychiatric report stated: 'Grigorenko is suffering from a mental illness in the form of a pathological (paranoid) development of the personality, with the presence of reformist ideas that have appeared in his personality, and with psychopathic features of the character and the first signs of arteriosclerosis.'[11]

Grigorenko is just one of a number of political dissenters who have been declared insane. His case is exceptional only in that unlike many others he was not declared schizophrenic. For example, in May 1970 the biochemist Zhores Medvedev was found to be suffering from 'incipient schizophrenia [accompanied by] paranoid delusions of reforming society'. Other particularly Russian forms of 'mental illness' include 'obsessive delusions of being a champion of truth and justice'; 'over-concern in his mental processes' and 'paranoid reformist delusions'.[12] Treatments for these 'illnesses' have included regular haloperidol and phenothizine injections – the drugs which schizophrenic patients normally receive in mental hospitals in the West. The dissidents have also been given 'insulin shock' and other barbaric physical 'treatments' which used to be common in the West, but are no longer in favour.

Psychiatry and Western Dissidents

Those who throw up their hands in horror at Soviet treatment of dissidents often neglect the fact that psychiatry has also entered directly into the field of Western politics. Thomas Szasz cites an American study in which each of the 12,356 American psychiatrists were sent a questionnaire asking: 'Do you believe that Barry Goldwater [then Republican nominee for President] is psychologically fit to serve as President of the United States?' As many as 20 per cent of the psychiatrists were prepared to offer an opinion on the matter, and by a majority of 1,189 to 657 they declared the Republican candidate to be unfit for the Presidency. Two typical replies were: 'Senator Goldwater impresses me as being a paranoid personality or a schizophrenic, paranoid type'; and 'Goldwater is basically a paranoid schizophrenic who decompensates from time to time'.

There is no reason to suppose that these psychiatrists would prove to be any more reticent in their 'diagnoses' of other political dissidents; revolutionaries have far more sweeping criticisms of American politics than anything Goldwater has proposed. But it is one thing to offer a psychiatric explanation for political behaviour, and quite another to suggest locking people up on the basis of this. Such a move would certainly provoke widespread reaction both on the part of psychiatrists and of others.

However, once a person has been convicted of a crime, there is much more scope for the abuse of psychiatry in the West. And political prisoners are certainly not immune from psychiatric 'diagnosis' and 'cure'. One psychiatrist, David Hubbard, who examined over forty captured hi-jackers claimed that their outwardly political motives were no more than a cloak for personal problems. 'Evidence' cited for this included frequent childhood dreams of being paralysed, an unhappy and unfulfilled sex life, an inordinate amount of time spent watching television, and – a dominant characteristic – frequent crossing of political borders.[13]

Another psychiatrist, who gave no indication of ever having met a hi-jacker, made the following contribution to their diagnosis: 'The destruction of aeroplanes it seems to me is then symbolically the destruction of the mother who threatens the Palestine guerrilla with loss of self-identity. Diagnostically we may then assume maternal deprivation and possessiveness, a lack of individuality and a conception that can only be accomplished by the destruction of the possessive mother.'[14] In the article the social and political factors which led to the hijackings were completely subordinated to presumed psychological inadequacies which left the guerrilla with no alternative but the destruction of aeroplanes.

One remarkable example of this increased tendency to see imprisoned political activists as 'abnormal' can be seen in a remark made by the Associate Superintendent of a Californian prison about George Jackson's moving book of prison letters, *Soledad Brother*. 'This book,' he wrote, 'provides a remarkable insight into the personality makeup of a highly dangerous sociopath.'[15]

'Sociopath' is roughly the American equivalent of the British label 'psychopathic disorder'. This is defined in the Mental Health Act of 1959 as 'a persistent disorder or disability of mind which results in abnormally aggressive or socially irresponsible conduct on the part of the patient, and requires or is susceptible to medical treatment'. In Britain a psychopathic disorder does not constitute sufficient grounds for compulsory detention in a mental hospital.

In Grendon Underwood Psychiatric Prison in Britain, the inmates, according to the Governor and Medical Superintendent, W. J. Gray, are a 'predominantly psychopathic population who are grossly disturbed in their capacity for interpersonal relationships.' Grendon provides therapy for its 'disturbed' inmates. But, Gray tells us, 'Medical and psychiatric treatment in a penal setting is fraught with difficulties, chief of which is the prisoner culture and code ... The Prisoners' Code is socially unacceptable and quite hostile to ordinary social standards; its rules are derived from the basic character of the prisoners who, as a group, are inadequate, aggressive, anti-social, preoccupied with immediate needs and unable to form any trusting relationship.'

And what is this devastating Prisoners' Code? According to Gray it 'supports the individual inmate when he is in trouble with the authorities, gives him a sense of belonging and a feeling of security'. It also 'compels him to take part in demonstrations against authority ... and can, at times, lead him to further violence when he is not so motivated'.[16] So it seems these 'grossly disturbed' people aren't always so bad at relationships after all; they just relate to the wrong people. No doubt many of the men at Grendon do have an unusually high share of problems; but it is easy to see how such a label could come to provide a very convenient psychiatric description for anyone who chose to organize dissent in a prison, possibly justifying an indefinite term of sentence and compulsory therapy.

Of course no reasonable person would wish to deny prisoners access to medical treatment – prisoners' organizations often claim that medical services in prisons are abysmal. But the labelling of prisoners as 'mentally ill' or 'disturbed' or 'psychopathic' may have far-reaching consequences. Take the case of one, by no means untypical, 'patient' – Roosevelt Murray in the Patuxent Institute for Defective Delinquents in the USA.[17] After serving most of his four-year sentence (for 'unauthorized use of a motor vehicle') in a conventional gaol Murray was psychiatrically assessed and found to be suffering from a 'sociopathic disorder – anti-social (with affinity for autotheft)'. In 1961 he was transferred to Patuxent, where he remained eleven years later. Since his transfer he had refused to co-operate with any of the therapeutic endeavours of the staff. At his annual review board in 1962 he 'launched an attack on the United States and said he wanted to go to Russia'. This incident was described by the psychiatrist as an example of his 'paranoia'. The original diagnosis of 'potentially violent' turned out to be a self-fulfilling prophecy. Disciplined in the early days for such offences as throwing a bag out of the window and fighting with another prisoner, Murray had since become increasingly violent, a trend which culminated in the stabbing of a social worker in 1972. When asked by the review board why he had stabbed the social worker, he replied, 'because I wanted to get out of this place any way possible'. He had repeatedly pleaded to be sent to a 'normal' gaol.

A reporter who was present at the review board asked if it were not possible that Murray was genuinely (and, by implication, not unreasonably) angry at being held for fourteen years on a relatively minor charge. The psychiatrist replied that it was 'a matter of projection ... many of these people like to blame anything instead of what really bothers them' – a reply which might easily have been made by Russian psychiatrists 'treating' political dissidents.

It is clear from these examples that there does exist ample scope for the use of psychiatry as a means of reducing dissent. This potential has been realized in one American prison in a way which puts even the Russian use of psychiatric diagnosis into the shade. Officials at the California Men's Penal Colony invented a new psychiatric classification of 'psychotic repression'. This means that the inmate is insane but that he is repressing the signs of his psychosis! This diagnosis was used to justify the administration of large doses of tranquillizers to the prisoners.[18]

In Britain, present prison therapies include the use of drugs, electro-convulsive treatment and behaviour therapy.[19] Each of these, as we shall see below, is open to considerable abuse. At present it seems that these techniques are used relatively infrequently, but Cohen predicts that a 'scenario which is certain to unfold itself during the coming decades is the rapid entry of psychiatric personnel and practices into the British penal system'. Evidence of a move in this direction can be seen from the Interim Report of the Committee on Mentally Abnormal Offenders,[20] which recommended the urgent provision of at least 2,000 secure places where prisoners and non-offender psychiatric patients alike would be treated. One illuminating reason they give for this need is that the demand for psychiatric places is increasing. Of course this could mean that more disturbed people are committing crimes nowadays, or 'need' to be locked away despite having committed no crime. A more likely explanation is that more of the people committing crimes (or not committing them) are being labelled 'disturbed' and in need of treatment.

We will look now at some of the implications of this new 'psychiatric imperialism', the therapeutic model for gaols, and the 'treatments' that go with it.

The Shape of Gaols to Come?

The incidents at Gartree prison during 1972 provide a striking example of the problems already facing prison authorities. In that year there were eight separate incidents involving work or food strikes by virtually the entire inmate population as well as numerous other protest actions such as sit-down demonstrations, fires and assaults on officers. Other prisons have faced similar, if less extensive, protests. An influx of political prisoners, well used to organizing and leading mass actions, could turn these protests into major battles. Cohen cites orthodox criminologists who believe that there will in any case be a major breakdown in the criminal justice system before the end of the century, if there is no change in penal methods.[21] So changes in the penal system have become inevitable.

First of all, there is a need to reduce overcrowding in the prisons. Partly this will be achieved by an expansion of prison capacity – an official policy which has, though, been held up by government cut-backs. It is also likely that there will be a major move towards alternative punishments for minor offenders through schemes such as 'Community Service Orders' which are now being tried experimentally in several parts of Britain. Prisoners remaining in gaol would then increasingly be those convicted of large-scale organized crime or crimes of violence, and what Cohen terms 'unambiguously political' prisoners.

The traditional methods for dealing with dissent would almost certainly prove insufficient in the face of widespread protest actions by prisoners. The problem for the authorities is to prevent protest actions from happening rather than to put them down once they are in full swing. In America one way this has been achieved is by offering major incentives for 'good' behaviour, coupled with severe punishment for 'disruptive' behaviour, all disguised with a therapeutic rhetoric.

One aspect of this which is used in most American states is the policy of Indeterminate Sentence, the IS. The most extreme form of an IS would be a sentence of 'one-day-to-life'. Such a sentence would permit the prison authorities, rather than the sentencing judge, to require the prisoner to remain in gaol for any length of time, depending on his or her behaviour in the gaol. In Britain there exists a very limited form of the IS – the parole system. This allows for any prisoner to apply for release after serving two thirds of his or her sentence. The British 'life' sentence, of course, carries no fixed term. The IS as it operates in California and other American States offers much more scope. In California, a conviction for second-degree burglary may carry a sentence of one to fifteen years, while robbery carries an IS of five years to life.[22]

The IS is in line with the 'therapeutic' model of prisons, according to which a person is 'treated' until he or she is 'cured'. Two basic models for a 'therapeutic' prison have been developed in the USA. The first which is fairly widespread depends mainly on various types of behaviour modification programmes, while the second, less common, is more akin to the Chinese method of 'thought reform' (although the therapeutic rhetoric is obviously different).

The simplest form of behaviour modification is one based on 'reinforcement' in which 'good behaviour' is rewarded by extra 'privileges'. The justification for calling this 'therapy' lies in the assumption that with continued application of such rewards, the person will become more and more likely to behave in a cooperative way; so it is not only one particular action which is being affected by the rewards, but, in theory at least, the prisoner's future behaviour too.

One way in which this has been brought about is through the introduction of a system of graded incentives. Sheldon Messinger, working in the Californian prison system, has developed a model for prisons using what he calls a 'complicated Chinese box effect'. On entering the gaol each prisoner spends a period of time in a unit of the gaol where he or she is accorded few rights or 'privileges'. Following a period of 'good' behaviour he or she is moved to another unit, where some of the most unpleasant features of the previous unit are eliminated and greater contact with other inmates is permitted. A further period of 'good' behaviour results in progression to yet another unit and further privileges. Release may only be secured when the prisoner has progressed to the levels of higher privilege. Conversely, uncooperative behaviour results in the prisoner being relegated to a less privileged level, with no immediate chance of release. There may be any number of levels, though the maximum so far seems to be eight. A typical system involves 'honour units' with maximum 'privileges'; 'non-honour units'; isolation cells with temporary isolation from other prisoners; 'adjustment cells' with more permanent isolation, where the prisoner will be put on arrival in the gaol; and 'indeterminate segregation units', where the most recalcitrant prisoners are deprived of all but the barest essentials. Even such basics as a varied diet or tables and utensils for eating may be withheld. In some cases prisoners have even been kept in darkness. So by making all 'privileges' dependent on 'good' behaviour, most of the prisoners will be highly motivated to co-operate fully with the authorities. At the same time the system of segregation ensures that the persistent trouble-makers can be separated off from the other inmates to reduce their influence.

In Britain, according to Cohen, the majority of prison reformers, official policy makers and prison staff at all levels are united in advocating a greater degree of segregation of inmates.[23] The reformers see it as a way of avoiding 'contamination' of the potentially 'reformable' prisoners by the hard core of recalcitrant criminals. Prison officers recognize the greater potential for control which such segregation offers. Following a riot in 1969 a special wing – 'C' Wing – was set up at Parkhurst gaol to deal with a potentially disruptive group and so relieve other parts of the prison of some serious control problems.* After the 1972 riots at Albany gaol, thirty prisoners were removed to a special wing there. The setting-up of 'control units' in Wakefield and Wormwood Scrubs gaols, which was described earlier, is further evidence of the move towards increased segregation of inmates along American lines. As the name implies, its mode of operation is in accordance with the same principles. It has been predicted that the 'planned incentive' scheme is likely to become the model for changes in the British penal system.

A second, totally different model for prison 'therapy' has also been developed in America. This one has nothing in common with behaviourist learning theory. The Asklepeion programme in Marion Illinois Federal Penitentiary uses 'treatments' which include 'transactional analysis'; 'Synanon games'; 'primal therapy' and 'attack therapy'; most of which rely heavily on bodily involvement and 'acting out' of emotions.[24] According to the originator of the scheme, Dr Groder, the

---

* The other reasons given for setting up the wing all related to treatment and included 'attempted suicide, mental breakdown, regular hunger strikes and chronic sick reporting'.

object of the 'therapies' is initially to 'unfreeze' the prisoner's formal organization of beliefs about him or her self (or, as Opton describes it, 'to degrade the self-concept and shatter his personal identity'). When this has been achieved, the person will then 'change' his or her personality and belief system. In the final stage the new personality will be 'refrozen'.

Some of these therapies have also been used since 1973 in the California Institute for Women. In one instance a politically radical woman refused to join in the all-night marathon session of 'attack therapy'. She was pinned to the floor by a guard, while another prisoner beat her, fracturing several facial bones. This particular outcome was certainly unexpected, but it is in the nature of such therapies that they are likely to lead to incidents of this kind. Despite this the Asklepeion programme was scheduled to be one of the primary programmes at the new – and notorious – Federal Research Center at Butner in North Carolina.

There is no doubt that such methods would provide a highly effective way of dealing with political prisoners. Matthew Dumont, the Assistant Commissioner for Drug Rehabilitation in the Massachusetts Department of Mental Health, has pointed out that 35 per cent of the men identified as 'special offenders' who were to undergo a new treatment programme in a New England gaol had been given that label for activities involving political protest. And in 1971 the *New York Times* reported that 'more and more prisoners are organizing politically, and their political organizing is bringing them closer and closer to the one objective prison administrators dread most: militant unity'.[25]

The events in Attica gaol in 1971 showed some of the potential for this unity. Following the killing in San Quentin gaol of George Jackson, the Black Panther leader, 1,500 prisoners at Attica participated in an open rebellion in support of a list of thirty demands. The authorities had to call for troops to be sent in to crush the rebellion. The troops launched a full-scale military attack in which twenty-nine inmates and nine of their hostages were killed and over three hundred were wounded. The prison authorities clearly cannot afford too many repeat performances of such a massacre. The new lines on which prisons are being run will be of enormous assistance to them in ensuring that such massive protest will not occur again.

The prisons just described, though, still rely on traditional high walls and barred doors. Some law-enforcement officials believe they have a better idea, more in keeping with the rapid technological developments in other fields. J. A. Meyer, of the US Defense Department, is one of them. He has outlined a sophisticated system of electronic tracking – not too far removed from Orwell's telescreens – to monitor people's movements.[26] This wouldn't prevent crime, but it would ensure that the person committing a crime could be easily traced. Meyer envisages that, as a condition of bail or parole, every prisoner would be fitted with an irremovable transponder, a small battery-operated device which would send out automatic radio signals giving a unique identification. The signals would be monitored by a massive country-wide network of transceivers, located at street corners, inside buildings – including the victim's own home – on public transport and at other strategic places. These would activate all the transponders in the area every few seconds, causing them to send in their coded characteristics. The information would then be sent back to a central computer which would keep a continuous record of all of the wearer's * movements. Then, if a crime is reported the police can check on all the transponder wearers who were in the vicinity at that time.

Transponders not in contact with any transceiver could be paged by the computer, and the wearer would then have to phone in details of his or her whereabouts. If a transponder went 'missing' the police would home-in on the suspect transponder's last position.

As a condition of parole, certain areas or hours could be designated out of bounds to any particular transponder, causing alarms to ring and doors to be bolted in front of the transgressor, or simply a police patrol to be alerted. And any attempt

---

*Meyer calls the victims 'subscribers', since they would have to pay for the doubtful privilege of wearing a transponder!

to interfere with the transponder would of course result in a warning signal being sent to the computer.

Meyer admits that 'outright revolt by 25 million arrestees and criminals [the number of people he estimates the scheme would need to cover] would be troublesome', but he reckons that more limited acts of sabotage could be easily detected and remedied. It is difficult to know at this stage whether such a foolproof system really could be designed. But there are plenty of American experts who have been pushing the idea. 'Electronic alternatives to prison', to use the words of one of its proponents, psychiatrist R. K. Schwitzgebel of Harvard University, could have a profound influence on the state's ability to control its citizens.

What Meyer calls an 'externalized conscience' could easily become a Big Brother. And, once the scheme was fully operative, it might not seem too big a jump to extend it to people with no criminal convictions.

But there would be major difficulties. As with the other technologies of political control, it would be necessary to introduce the scheme with widespread propaganda defending its 'humaneness'. This argument may prove acceptable to many people, including convicts faced with the alternative of a prison sentence. However, from the point of view of the state, the scheme has a major drawback. Unlike many other technologies of political control, it cannot be introduced by the back door. To be effective, there must be transceivers everywhere and sufficient parolees to justify their use. So the project will be very much in the public eye. And the field will be wide open to a massive political response.

Towards Clockwork Orange: Punishment-as-Therapy *

I believe that the day has come when we can combine sensory deprivation with drugs, hypnosis and astute manipulation of rewards and punishment to gain almost absolute control over an individual's behaviour. It should be possible then to achieve a very rapid

*The phrase punishment-as-therapy has been borrowed from Edward Opton's excellent article 'Psychiatric Violence against Prisoners', cited above. Much of our information is drawn from this article.

and highly effective type of positive brainwashing that would allow us to make dramatic changes in a person's behaviour and personality. I foresee the day when we could convert the worst criminal in the matter of a few months – or perhaps even less than that.[27]

So wrote one psychologist, James McConnell, in an article entitled 'Criminals Can Be Brainwashed Now'.

In describing the behaviour modification programmes now practised in some prisons, we have already come across the use of the controlled punishment of prisoners who fail to respond to the offer of 'privileges' for good behaviour. Solitary confinement can amount to torture, legitimized by the satisfying fiction of a 'therapeutic model'. In some of the cases we describe below, the torture is even more obvious.

The punishments-as-therapy used in US gaols have included drugs, in particular tranquillizing drugs, those which induce vomiting, and suxamethonium chloride, a compound similar to curare; electric shock; and even electro-convulsive treatment (ECT). Many of the 'therapies' described here were initially developed for use with mental patients, homosexuals or drug offenders. As Matthew Dumont, Assistant Commissioner for Drug Rehabilitation in the Massachusetts Department of Mental Health, points out: 'Drug abuse programmes offer the observer of American society a perfect laboratory for the study of social control capacities.'[28]

Tranquillizing drugs have been used widely in both American and British prisons. A number of ex-inmates of British gaols have claimed that daily injections of tranquillizers were given against their wishes. These help to make the prisoners more docile and less willing to protest against prison conditions. The use of drugs may also be seen as a punishment. In the USA, at least, they have been used not merely to tranquillize the victim, but also to punish him or her with a highly unpleasant experience. The threat of further administrations of the drug is likely to make the person much more co-operative in future.

One drug which has been widely used in American prisons is chlorpromazine (Largactil). It is the drug most often used with schizophrenic patients. A typical therapeutic dose given in hospitals may be between 75 and 800 mg.; but in prisons it seems that up to 3,000–4,000 mg. may be used.[29] Apart from the massive tranquillizing effect, there are a number of other highly distressing side effects which are extremely likely to occur at these high doses. In particular there may be a Parkinsonian-like tremor, involuntary movements and jerks, dizziness and restlessness. At these doses a person won't be able to move properly or to speak or think clearly. Further evidence that the drugs are used as punishment may be seen from the fact that some prisoners suffering these 'side effects' have not been given other drugs which would normally be given to counteract them.

Another drug which is chemically related to chlorpromazine is fluphenazine. In the form of fluphenazine ethanate (Prolixin or Moditen) one injection will last *for about two weeks*. While it has more of a tranquillizing effect than chlorpromazine, it has less sedative effect, so the person will be less confused about what is happening. He or she will be able to remember the experience more vividly at a later date. Because of this, fluphenazine may be more effective as a punishment drug. The 'side effects' of fluphenazine are very like those produced with chlorpromazine, and they are common even at low doses. Another very common effect of fluphenazine, which occurs after the main effects have worn off, is a period of severe depression.

These descriptions by prisoners who have been given Prolixin are a clear indication of why it is so effective as punishment:

> It seems it's destroying your mind. You can't concentrate. If you're thinking of three things at the same time, all those thoughts explode. If you're thinking of spaghetti for example, the spaghetti is blown up in your mind to the size of large tubes, snaking around every which way ... It seems like your breathing has stopped. Your eyeballs feel funny, feel like you're dying.

> I couldn't sleep – couldn't think – couldn't get comfortable – couldn't walk normally and my tongue thrust between my teeth. Prolixin is torture. It's called liquid shock therapy by the prisoners.[30]

One prisoner cited by Opton was given three such doses over a period of six weeks until his attorney intervened to stop the punishment. At that time some 200 men were undergoing 'treatment' with Prolixin in the same institution! They were hardly an exception. At Vacaville psychiatric prison (the gaol which gave birth to the Symbionese Liberation Army) Prolixin was administered to 1,093 prisoners in 1971.[31]

Another major tranquillizer, haloperidol (Serenace), is mentioned frequently in connection with the 'treatment' of Russian dissidents. For Leonid Pluysch (a case of 'creeping schizophrenia with paranoid reformist delusions'), prolonged treatment with the drug resulted in convulsions and temporary loss of speech and ability to hear.

Another type of drug which has been used is apomorphine. One injection induces between fifteen minutes and an hour of uncontrollable vomiting. It is not often used in clinical practice now, partly because of its toxic effects. Injections of apomorphine can produce 'side effects' including persistent nausea (vomiting which continues well beyond the usual period of up to one hour); depression of the central nervous system leading to muscular weakness; heart and respiratory irregularities; and dizziness. In extreme cases, deaths can also occur. A prison psychiatrist claimed that apomorphine would be given as punishment for such things as not getting up in the morning, giving cigarettes to other prisoners against orders, talking against orders, swearing or lying.[32] One prisoner at Vacaville gaol received twenty-eight of these treatments at two-hourly intervals for a period of five days. His 'illness' was homosexuality.[33]

A third type of drug used in punishment-as-therapy at Vacaville, Atascadero, and the Californian Institute for Women is the compound suxamethonium chloride (Scoline, Anectine or Midarine). It has effects similar to those of curare. About thirty seconds after injection, all the victim's muscles become completely relaxed for a period of about three to five minutes. One of the consequences of this total body paralysis is respiratory arrest; in other words, the person is unable to breathe voluntarily during this time, and oxygen must be administered. However he or she will remain fully conscious and will be able to see and hear normally. When the drug is used in clinical practice an anaesthetic is given as well, partly because the onset of relaxation may be accompanied by painful muscle twitching, and also because the experience of total paralysis is extremely disturbing. It has been likened, even in non-stressed voluntary subjects, to sensations of 'drowning' or 'dying'.

This effect is the reason why Scoline has been given as punishment-therapy in US prisons. While the prisoner is 'overwhelmed by a feeling of suffocation or drowning, of sinking into death' he or she is forced to listen to a confident and authoritarian voice repeating a description of the reasons why he or she is being punished, and is instructed to remember the experience next time he or she contemplates repeating the 'antisocial' act. Suxamethonium chloride alternated with sodium pentathol has recently become a familiar torture in Uruguay.[34]

Electric shock to the arms, feet or groin has been given as 'treatment' at Connecticut State Prison. But even more horrifying is the use as a punishment of electro-convulsive treatment (ECT), in which an electric current is passed through the brain. ECT was at one time a fairly common 'treatment' for schizophrenia, until it was found to be ineffective. It is still used fairly frequently in the treatment of severe depression. When it is applied bilaterally (that is the current passes through both hemispheres of the brain), as it generally is, it causes temporary loss of memory. On occasions some permanent loss of memory may occur as a result of brain damage.

As with the other treatments, the stated rationale for giving ECT is its therapeutic value. It could be argued that the disruptive behaviour of a prisoner was the result of 'depression', and therefore ECT would be 'needed'. However, there are good reasons to believe the prisoners' claim that ECT has been given simply as a punishment, since ECT has on occasions been given without anaesthetic,* which is not normal clinical practice. In some cases in the USA, not even a muscle relaxant has been given, resulting at times in bones being broken as a result of a violent convulsion. ECT was used explicitly for behaviour modification by one volunteer doctor in Vietnam. When the patients in the mental hospital where he worked for two months

*See for instance the *Revolutionary Action Committee for Broadmoor Manifesto*, published in 1972.

refused to work, they were told 'people who are too sick to work need treatment. Treatment starts tomorrow – electro-convulsive treatment ... The next day we gave 120 unmodified [that is, with no anaesthetic or muscle relaxant] electro-convulsive treatments.'[35]

One prisoner at Vacaville gaol described his experience of ECT: 'They hit you with the first jolt and you experience pain that you would never believe possible. At the same time you cannot breathe and they apply oxygen. During all this time you are in convulsions. This only lasts a few moments but it seems like a lifetime. A few seconds after that you pass out.' According to Vacaville's medical superintendent, ECT was given to 433 prisoners in the gaol in 1971.[36]

It is clear that such techniques provide an excellent means for exerting control over prisoners. They are torture – but heavily disguised by therapeutic rhetoric. The prevalence of such techniques is also a clear indication that it is useless to expect that prison doctors themselves would never sanction the use of torture. As we explained above, the medical personnel involved are likely to be among the last to recognize the implications of their 'treatments'; the language of therapy serves to mystify doctors too.

Physical Control of the Mind – Psychosurgery

Aversion therapy goes about as far as anyone knows how in the difficult task of trying to make people think and behave differently by applying carrots and sticks. The human mind being often recalcitrant, this can be a frustrating business for those who try to counter various types of 'anti-social' behaviour. Psychosurgery appears to some to provide an answer.

One line of argument has been to suggest that some aggressive individuals are the victims of brain damage. An example of this approach can be seen in a letter from a psychiatrist, Frank Ervin, and two neurosurgeons, Vernon Mark and William Sweet, published in the *Journal of the American Medical Association* in 1967.[37] The authors pointed to race riots in black ghettos and asked: 'If slum conditions alone determined and initiated riots, why are the vast majority of slum dwellers able to resist the temptations of unrestrained violence?' They went on to hypothesize that it might be that the violent minority were suffering from brain damage.*

Mark and Ervin even wrote a book about their 'successes' in eliminating violent behaviour by means of surgery to remove damaged brain tissues.† In this, they make great play of the supposed similarity between aggressive acts and certain forms of epileptic seizures. However, there is no direct evidence at all to connect the violence which occurs, for example, in race riots and brain damage. Indeed, one survey of especially aggressive prisoners concluded that these people had no more 'hard' signs of brain damage than anyone else.

But even if brain damage is not the *cause* of aggressive behaviour, brain surgery can still be an effective way of 'calming' people. So the second, increasingly prevalent, line of argument has been that psychosurgery may be a way to 'cure' the socially diagnosed disease of violence. Despite his claims about violence being caused by brain damage, Ervin has explained his real reasons for supporting research into the causes of violence in the following terms: 'We're not talking about being nicer to people. I make no human arguments at all ... we're really talking about being cost-effective'.[38] Another neurosurgeon, M. Hunter Brown, spelled this out in greater detail: 'Each young criminal incarcerated from twenty years to life costs the taxpayer perhaps $10,000. For roughly $6,000 we can provide medical treatment [psychosurgery] which will transform him into a well-adjusted citizen.'[39]

Psychosurgery is brain surgery performed to alter thoughts, social behaviour patterns, personality characteristics, emotional reactions or other forms of behaviour. Unlike other forms of neurosurgery, it is not performed to remove dangerous or

---

*The same sort of rationale was used by Professor Herman Witter when he proposed carrying out a forcible examination of Ulrike Meinhof's brain to try to obtain evidence that a brain tumour, which had previously been removed, had recurred.

† When another psychiatrist, Peter Breggin, did a follow-up study of one of Mark and Ervin's 'successful' cases described in *Violence and the Brain*, he found that the patient was not only still aggressive, but also psychotic as a result of the 'treatment' he had received.

diseased brain tissue, but entails the destruction of brain tissue which by any physiological criterion is perfectly healthy.[40]

The beginnings of widespread psychosurgery date back to the Second International Congress of Neurology held in London in 1935. At this conference, two American researchers reported that they had eliminated temper tantrums in a chimpanzee, Becky, by making bilateral lesions in the frontal lobes of her brain. One neurologist in the audience, believing that Becky's behaviour had been analogous to that of many chronic mental patients, suggested trying operations on them too. It was this grossly oversimplified and inadequate view of human behaviour which laid the basis for some 70,000 lobotomy operations performed in the USA and England between the mid-thirties and the mid-fifties.

There is no doubt that many of the patients were made less anxious by the operation and sometimes even scored higher on formal tests of intelligence, though usually they were in such a bad state before the operation that almost any change would have been an improvement. But the outcome was very unpredictable. A large number of the patients developed epilepsy following the operation. Many became asocial and apathetic, and showed loss of judgement and reduced creativity. Many surgeons considered that the loss of such abilities was outweighed by the lessening of anxiety or other positive effects. A few maintained that it might be precisely this 'blunting of function' which was responsible for the success of the operation.

Concern over the undesirable effects of psychosurgery coincided with the rise in the number of drugs available for treating mental patients; and so by the late fifties the boom in psychosurgery was over. But the research continued, and it became apparent that depression and anxiety could be relieved by making tiny lesions in particular areas, rather than the massive destruction which was a feature of earlier lobotomies. In addition, the development of stereotactic and X-ray equipment enabled surgeons to localize structures deep in the brain which had previously been inaccessible. Now it is possible to destroy a target area deep in the brain by the injection of a mixture of oil and wax, or by implanting radio-active seeds, or by using ultrasonic energy. Laser beam surgery has also been suggested.

Another technique (developed in Britain) involves the implantation of a large number of tiny electrodes. With the patient fully conscious, one of these electrodes is activated, giving rise to characteristic sensations – with a different effect being produced by each electrode. In one of Mark and Ervin's cases, responses to stimulation of adjacent electrodes in the temporal lobe gave rise to sensations varying from 'teeth ache, lose control, everything wild, speech trouble' to 'power gone, weak, weird' and 'nirvana'. After carefully charting the responses from all the electrodes, the surgeon can select those areas which when stimulated lead to an undesirable (for example, aggressive) response, and destroy them by increasing the current to coagulate the surrounding cells.[41]

Although this procedure may appear quite logical (if somewhat macabre), experimental and clinical evidence shows that it does not have the effect of selectively eliminating the response which was produced by the electrical stimulation.

In February of 1972 a number of surgeons estimated that 400–600 psychosurgery operations were being carried out each year in the United States,[42] and agreed that the numbers were rapidly increasing. But the new targets of the psychosurgeons are not restricted to deteriorated mental patients – they include neurologically normal 'hyperactive' children,[43] and 'violent individuals' – since it has been found that lesions in certain parts of the brain have a 'calming' effect. One Indian surgeon even calls his operations 'sedative neurosurgery'.

While it is true that destruction of tissue in certain parts of the brain may eliminate violent behaviour, this can be achieved only at the cost of disrupting many other functions. Those parts of the brain which are directly involved in the expression of aggression are also responsible for many other vital functions. Take for example the amygdala, a structure lying beneath the temporal lobe of the brain which has been a frequent target of psychosurgeons attempting to eliminate aggression. This is also an important discriminatory mechanism in such crucial behaviour as eating, drinking and sex, as well as in virtually all social activity.[44] A psychologist, Ruth Anderson, who studied some of the effects of amygdala operations, reported that the patients tended to become more inert, less creative and showed less zest and intensity of emotions. She remarked that the patients closely resembled those with frontal lobe lesions[45] (described above). Nevertheless, some psychosurgeons have continued to advocate psychosurgery for violent offenders. A number of American prisoners have already been operated on, although recent court cases have, at least for the time being, prevented further attempts. At least one British surgeon, Mr J. Brice, at the Wessex Neurological Centre in Southampton, has operated on people involved in crimes of violence.[46]

Destruction of brain cells is not the only way in which behaviour can be controlled directly. Mark and Ervin propose that a 'prolonged therapeutic effect [might] be obtained by the introduction of chemical agents into focal areas of the brain to produce a chronic stimulation over long periods of time'. The areas which might be stimulated in this way would be those which produce such feelings as relaxation and euphoria.

Already some patients with narcolepsy (inability to stay awake) or severe pain have electrodes implanted permanently in their brains which can be activated whenever it is necessary to keep themselves awake, or to control the pain. Two criminologists, Barton Ingraham and Gerald Smith, have recommended the extension of such techniques to prisoners on parole. Not for them simple monitoring of parolees' movements by the system of transponders we described above. They want a more direct form of control.

In fact the behaviour which could be controlled by implanted electrodes – at least in the foreseeable future – would be less selective than Ingraham and Smith seem to envisage.[47] It would not be possible, for example, to distinguish between an unprovoked aggressive impulse and a normal defensive response to the sort of aggressive acts anyone could be exposed to. However, the blanket reduction of all aggressive responses could well be achieved by such methods.

Electrical activity in the brain could be picked up by implanted electrodes, 'telemetered' to a distant instrument room and monitored by a computer. The computer would be programmed to respond to particular electrical patterns characteristic of, for example, aggressive behaviour and, if activated, would send back radio signals. These in turn would activate the stimoceiver (implanted beneath the skin, possibly in the shoulder) and apply electrical stimulation to another area of the brain. This area could be one of the 'punishment' centres, an area where electrical stimulation produces very unpleasant sensations. Alternatively, the rapid successive stimulation of different areas could lead to confusion, making any co-ordinated action impossible.

Further refinements could even eliminate the need for the computer monitoring of this process. The signal could be monitored by the implanted receiver itself, so that the effectiveness of the system would not be restricted to a limited geographical area. The control potential of such systems is clearly enormous.

The techniques referred to above are currently being advocated for control of violent offenders, including those involved in riots as well as in individual acts of violence. It is most unlikely that such techniques would be used in the near future on political offenders. The success of the opposition to psychosurgery in American prisons shows how little room for manoeuvre the state has with such techniques. Almost certainly they could be introduced on a wider scale only if the working class had already been soundly defeated and there was little chance of any political opposition to their use developing. Psychosurgery for political dissidents is perhaps the nearest that a state could come to eliminating 'thought crime'.

The Political Prisoner

When the state locks up political prisoners, it presents a challenge to the groups they belong to and those who sympathize with their aims. Sometimes the reaction is so strong that release becomes the government's best short-term policy. The vehement and sustained Irish reaction to internment without trial was effective in achieving a gradual reduction in its scope and its eventual elimination.

In the absence of such a show of solidarity, prisoners have at times demanded to be given 'political' status, a category which does not exist at present in Britain. However, this could prove a misguided policy. In many countries 'politicals' are treated worse than civil criminals. A more important dimension was brought out by the following paradox. At the same time as Irish Republican prisoners, including the Price sisters, Dolours and Marion, were on hunger strike for political status (and for return to a gaol in Ireland), members of the Red Army Fraction in Germany were using the very same weapon in order to bring about 'the abolition of separation between the political and all other prisoners'.[48] Similarly in America radical prisoners have fought to remain in contact with other prisoners.

The isolation of political prisoners is a way in which the penal system keeps the mass of prisoners leaderless. In a time of intense political activity the British government may prove all too willing to grant special 'political' status – though not exactly along the lines anticipated by the Irish prisoners.

The political prisoner may serve as a rallying symbol for protest outside the prison, but there is little he or she can do to influence events directly. Virtually the only effective action available is the hunger strike, particularly if the prisoner is in solitary confinement. The authorities recognize the political force of this weapon and fear what will happen if the strike ends in death. In Britain and Rhodesia, in the United States and the Soviet Union, in France and Germany, and in many other countries the answer of the authorities has been the same – forced feeding. In Britain the method of forced feeding has remained unchanged since 1909 when it was first used. The prisoner is held down with the head facing upwards and with a wooden block between his or her teeth. A large greased tube is inserted through a hole in the block, and down into the throat. A small quantity of water is then poured down the tube (to ensure that it has not been mistakenly pushed into the lungs), followed by the nutritive liquid. This process may have to be repeated several times daily, since it is frequently accompanied by vomiting. Uncooperative victims may have their gums pricked with sharp objects to make them open their mouths; a steel clamp may be used to keep the mouth open.[49]

Forced feeding of prisoners has remained in regular use in Britain from the time of the Suffragette movement. It became a live public issue again only in 1974 with the lengthy hunger strikes and forced feeding of Irish Republican prisoners in England, such as the Price sisters and Michael Gaughan. The physical dangers from forced feeding include damage to the mouth and gums and loosening of the teeth caused by the clamp; ulceration and infection of the throat caused by repeated passage of the tube; vomiting, with the risk of inhalation; pneumonia, which is sometimes fatal; and risk of suffocation if the tube enters the lungs in error. At the same time, the number of calories taken in is inadequate, so malnutrition still results. Even the former Home Secretary Robert Carr admitted that 'when accompanied by force against the wish of the prisoner [it] is a horrible and dreadful thing'.[50]

Following major protests about forced feeding – and refusal of Brixton doctors to continue the process when Marion and Dolours Price withdrew their co-operation – Roy Jenkins finally announced a change of policy on forced feeding. This was widely reported as a decision to end forced feeding in prisons. In fact, the policy announced was merely to release prison doctors from the obligation to force feed a sane person. This left the way open for the practice to be resumed when political circumstances permitted. This proved to be quite soon – by the end of 1975, cases of renewed forced feeding were being reported in the press.

In the USA the major battles against brutal prison treatment – particularly the new 'therapies' – have been fought outside the gaols. A number of organizations such as the Medical Committee for Human Rights, the Center for the Study of Psychiatry, and the American Civil Liberties Union as well as numerous other groups and individuals have organized highly effective protests about the misuse of psychiatry. Law suits have been taken out on behalf of prisoners subjected to the treatments, and against the setting-up of new 'therapeutic' prison projects. So, over the past few years, the legal rights of the authorities to administer the punishments we have described have been gradually reduced. As a result, in 1974 all Federal funding for psychosurgery was stopped, and the LEAA declared that it would no longer support any projects involving psychosurgery, medical research, behaviour modification or chemotherapy – affecting some 350 projects at that time. Similarly the new prison centre at Butner in North Carolina and other research centres have been forced to abandon proposed behaviour modification and psychosurgery projects. Martin Groder, the chief architect of Butner's therapy programmes, has resigned from the Bureau of Prisons in protest against the curtailment of therapy programmes.[51]

Finally in May 1975, Norman Carlson, the Federal Director of Prisons, announced a change in policy. 'Therapy' in US prisons is to be drastically curtailed. Prison is once again, according to Carlson, to become a punishment.[52] According to the American Psychological Association 'the banning of these [behaviour modification] procedures will result in a regression to outmoded unsystematic forms of inhumanity in prisons ... [and] will tend to stifle the development of humane forms of treatment that provide the offender the opportunity to fully realize his or her potential as a contributing member of society'.[53]

Just what the new US penal policy will be is at the time of writing unclear; certainly the state, faced with thousands of militant and angry men and women prisoners, will need to find some effective way of controlling them. One development is likely to be increased use of 'less lethal' weapons against disruptive inmates – preparations for this are already well in hand.

The information in this chapter has been drawn largely from the American experience. This is mainly because the developments in gaols there have preceded any major changes in the British prison system. We have cited a few instances where the new 'therapeutic' methods for dealing with dissent have come to light in Britain; but we have no way of knowing how widespread they are, since the Official Secrets Act effectively prevents such information becoming publicly known.* In addition, letters to and from prisoners are censored, and any adverse re-

---

*Some of the difficulties encountered in research in prisons are documented in Stanley Cohen and Laurie Taylor 'Prison Research: A Cautionary Tale'. *New Society*, 30 January 1975.

ferences to conditions in the gaols frequently result in the letter being returned, unsent, to the prisoner. References to earlier censorship too meet with the same fate. Prisoner's letters to organizations such as the NCCL are frequently suppressed, and prisoners are not allowed to write to any MP other than their own, or to private individuals they didn't know before they entered the prison.

The recent report of the workings of the prison service[54] reports a 'move away' from a 'medical model' of crime according to which persistent offending is a 'sickness'. But at the same time, the report states that the new types of treatment provide 'opportunities' for prisoners 'to learn to accept and deal responsibly with the consequences of their behaviour'. One example of such 'opportunities' are the new control units referred to earlier. The report says they 'create a framework which will help the prisoner to realize that it is in his own interest to mend his ways and that it is only by his own efforts in this direction that he will achieve his return to normal location'. Prisoners with 'personality abnormalities' or 'mental illness' are specifically *excluded* from the categories of prisoners who might be placed in a control unit – they are designed for a 'small hard core of really persistent and serious troublemakers who are reckoned to be capable of mending their ways'. This is precisely the type of prisoner who has been on the receiving end of many of the American 'therapeutic' techniques. It is also precisely that category into which those prisoners who attempted to organize politically would fall.

We are not arguing that the techniques described in this chapter will necessarily be adopted for use in British prisons; the British penal authorities will, of course, find their own solutions. Nevertheless, widespread knowledge of the possible implications of the 'therapeutic' model for prisons will be an important factor in ensuring that the 'therapeutic' solution is not adopted in Britain.

Conclusions

The technologies we reviewed in the last section are merely a sample of products from a vast and grim catalogue available to Western governments. Much technology is developed to cut the cost of manufacturing commodities or to create new ones. By contrast, the technology of political control has been developed or modified from existing technology to maintain the ruling class in power at times of economic, social and political crisis. It is no accident that many of these technologies have their origin – or their specific application to political control – in the Vietnam war, its backwash of political crisis in the USA, or in the Northern Irish war.

Western capitalism is now facing a crisis much greater than those which originally spawned these weapons. Their increasing introduction is a way of widening governments' scope for manoeuvre in this crisis. Yet at their present stage of development they would not be sufficient to prevent the growth of mass movements challenging the state. Political surveillance techniques are still extremely costly and labour-intensive. And it is simply not feasible to conduct the mass surveillance which would be necessary if large numbers of people began to participate in political action. The computer is at present not capable of performing the role of Big Brother. The arsenal of riot-control techniques is still almost as likely to politicize its victims as to deter them. And the political response in Northern Ireland to novel interrogation techniques, which has forced their abandonment, and in the United States to prisoner-control techniques, which led to their reduction, has left people rather more sensitive than previously to their dangers.

In other words, a satisfactory 'graduated response' is still far from being achieved. Despite their apparent suitability for the nightmare world of 1984, these present technologies are not capable of ensuring the political strait-jacket of Orwell's Oceania. Even so, the technology of political control should not be dismissed. It has the potential already to assist the state in isolating or neutralizing those people who seem most likely to lead widespread political and industrial protest. It may not prevent the growth of a movement which is gathering momentum – but it could help to weaken one which is already beset by divisions and uncertainties. Unless combated, this technology can help to tilt the balance of forces away from the working class at crucial moments. What measures can we take to prevent this?

One obvious way would be to combat the technologies on their own ground, by developing counter-measures. The more information we have about preparations being made by the state, the better able will we be to reduce their effectiveness. And in particular situations, such as demonstrations and occupations, there is clearly a need for wide knowledge of how to deal with riot-control agents. But this approach is necessarily limited. Consider the use of information technology: how do you prevent the state from amassing a secret file on your activities and even computerizing it? Interrogation and prisoner-control techniques, too, leave only narrow scope for counter-methods. And there is a certain danger in directing energy towards attempting to beat the state at its own game. On this terrain, the state will surely win. It has every means for technological development at its disposal. Its opponents have almost none.

Another approach which some scientists have adopted has been to refuse to collaborate in producing repressive technology. In the USA, demonstrations and campaigns against these types of technology and the scientists complicit in their development achieved some success in the later stages of the Vietnam war. More recently, a group of molecular biologists agreed a temporary moratorium on a whole area of research because of the possible accidental production of a lethal virus. This kind of action can have an important effect in alerting people to the dangers of new technologies and in demonstrating that scientists, too, have a political role and therefore a social responsibility. But such notions are making only very slow and uncertain headway among scientists. The British Association for the Advancement of Science is a case in point. Its meeting in 1970 was rudely interrupted by a BSSRS demonstration calling for greater attention to the social role of science. Now that the latter has become more fashionable, the BAAS has responded – by putting out a pamphlet on scientific development to help the police! Fortunately it was rather incompetent. But this demonstrates clearly the low level of understanding among scientists about the problem. It is certainly utopian to believe that military or police research will be seriously hampered by a massive refusal by scientists to help them with their problems – with all the advantages to career and pocket which can accrue.

Another possibility is that the security forces could be prevented from using the technology of political control if they were subject to more democratic control. There seems to be very little hope of this! Even if local police authorities were composed of people who were aware of the dangers, their power is very limited. As we have seen, the Home Office controls 50 per cent of local force budgets, and the police force is becoming increasingly centralized. In any case, much of the threat comes from those special squads which are directly under the control of the Home Secretary.

The absurdity of any idea that the security forces can be brought under democratic control is clearest with respect to the Army. It is an authoritarian instrument, isolated from civil life and headed by a reactionary élite. Its basic function is to protect the existing social order. Most advocates of working-class revolution from Marx onwards have stressed the importance of immediate disbandment of the capitalist army and its replacement by a workers' militia. Political organization within the Army completely, and within the police largely, are prohibited in Britain. Soldiers and police of the British democratic state do not even have the basic democratic right to form trade unions. Nor do they have unrestricted access to information – people have been prosecuted for handing soldiers a leaflet entitled 'Some Information for Discontented Soldiers'. So the rank-and-file are unlikely, except when the fabric of the state is being rent, to exercise any effective restraint on the repressive activities of their organizations.

In Britain, the Prime Minister and Cabinet have formal control over the police and Army. Is it possible that they would put a stop to the use of repressive technology by these forces? We have seen that Labour and Conservative governments alike have hosted the development of such instruments of repression as CS gas, rubber bullets and those special police squads whose basic purpose is to muzzle working-class action. Of course, under severe political pressure, the government can and has been forced to reduce its potential repressive armoury. But that need only be a temporary move, to be retracted later in secrecy.

Nevertheless, in a society like Britain, campaigns against the use of repressive technology and for democratic rights for the armed forces can have important political consequences. The anti-Vietnam war movement focused the attention of the whole world on the atrocities of American imperialism. A comparable movement against the British occupation of Northern Ireland could have similar political consequences. By disseminating information about the use of repressive technology and the activities of the security forces, it could help to counter the government's justifications for its policies. People who know about the effects of the technology of political control are much less likely to believe that these are harmless weapons. People who understand the relationship between political expediency and the use of repressive technology can no longer accept the argument that it is a 'technological fix' to solve a problem of 'law and order'. Through such campaigns, it is possible that people will come to realize that it is not simply repressive technology we are fighting, but the type of state which needs to use it.

It is important, however, to realize the limitations of such campaigns. It is impossible for the state to abolish the technology of political control while it still needs to use it. And capitalist states will always require their armies, their prisons and the rest of their repressive apparatus, to protect the privileged by keeping the majority down. The abolition of the capitalist state itself is the precondition for the abolition of the technology of political control.

This does not, of course, mean that post-capitalist states are automatically non-repressive. As we have seen, the Soviet Union led the way in psychological torture techniques and has been prominent in the political misuse of psychiatry. But the deep crisis after the 1917 revolution, coupled with the impossibility of establishing a socialist society in a capitalist world, led to the emergence of a bureaucracy which usurped political power from the working class. As we saw in Part Two, the development of a repressive state apparatus then became vital if the bureaucracy was to retain its power. Any new working-class revolution will have to ensure that ultimate power resides with the working class, in order to guard against the formation of a privileged section of society.

Under our existing system, the contradiction between the needs of capitalism and those of the working class can be relieved by some mixture of compromise and repression – but only temporarily. In a period of economic crisis, compromise becomes harder and harder to achieve and is replaced increasingly by repression. And, as the state changes, so does the working class. It demands more from its political representatives. Yet, in Britain, the Labour government is responding to the crisis by attempting to shore up capitalism. Such developments can only enhance the possibilities of the emergence of a mass party committed to socialism. In such a context, compromise would be a much less easy policy for the media to sell. Repression would be answered by revolutionary action. The victory of the Vietnamese people shows that, when that stage is reached, even the most vicious repression using the most advanced technology cannot safeguard the state.

However, severe economic crises and deep class conflict do not find an automatic resolution in socialist revolution. A drastic confrontation could lead, not to revolution, but to a massive defeat for the working class. Such a confrontation could also lead to very large increase in the investment by capitalist states in the technology of political control. Their potential might then become far greater than it is at present.

In the longer term, then, the technology of political control might help to fulfil the nightmare vision which Bukharin recorded as early as 1916 of the way in which capitalism might develop: 'Thus arises the final type of contemporary imperialist robber state, an iron organization which envelops the living body of society in its grasping paws. It is a new Leviathan before which the fantasy of Thomas Hobbes seems child's play.'

The events of the twentieth century are increasingly posing the question of socialism or barbarism. Only political action can answer it in our favour.

Afterword

We finished writing this book in January 1976. At that time it seemed that the new apparatus we described, the technology of political control, was passing almost unchallenged into the arsenals of Western governments intent on suppressing internal dissent. Continued economic crisis, with its accompanying social distress, would ensure that capitalist states would rely ever more heavily on technical means to replace ever less convincing political solutions.

Our rulers' appetite for modern counter-insurgency weapons has continued unabated. Scientists, technologists and other personnel in the weapons' industry have striven to satisfy it. Police forces, armies and intelligence services have reorganized and retrained themselves to use each new invention. State propaganda machines, assisted by compliant mass media, have attempted to legitimate the use and development of this new technology. Four years from 1984, it is becoming clear that any movement against the capitalist state must incorporate campaigns and demands aimed against this technology, and against the agencies which employ it. Oppositional movements in many countries are now beginning to investigate and act against the state organizations which infringe their democratic rights.

As we have seen in this book, formal democracy can be a smoke-screen behind which the state prepares its defence against its own population. But democracy is also the banner which identifies counter-movements working to defend human rights. Even a formal commitment to democracy by those who seek to pervert it allows us a framework, a set of laws and regulations, within which there is scope to fight.

By contrast in Northern Ireland, where few democratic rights existed for the Catholic minority, Army occupation and the suspension of civil liberties have fuelled the IRA campaign and granted a legitimacy to armed struggle. The channels through which democratic opposition could achieve political demands have become almost too narrow for passage. People imprisoned for armed opposition are still denied political status. A secret Army document published by the IRA in 1979 revealed that even the Army itself sees no end to the war, and no possibility of defeating the IRA.

The rise of urban guerrilla warfare in Germany and Italy has also had major political impact. But, despite state propaganda to the contrary, armed struggle is not the model for most oppositional movements. It is not within the power of a small, isolated group of armed men and women to shake the modern capitalist state by exposing its repressive nature. Far more has been achieved even by those who emerge from within the state to question its plans and actions – by the revelations of ex-intelligence agents, dissident soldiers, members of governments who are troubled by the decisions they are required to support, and by investigators plumbing the depths of state secrecy.

Such revelations are a very valuable means of exposing the nature of the capitalist state, but unless they act as catalysts for a movement, in the last resort they remain mere pin-pricks. And nowhere as yet has technological innovation for repressive ends been challenged in such a way as to throw into question its future development. But there are welcome indications that mass movements can arise on technological issues. The recent rapid change in consciousness on the nuclear power issue is the most obvious example. In this respect there have been far greater developments in other countries than in Britain. In the USA, Germany and Sweden there have been demonstrations over 100,000 strong opposed to nuclear power. In Germany, this movement has finally achieved a political voice with the election of 'Green Party' members to Parliament. In the United States, the Harrisburg disaster at Three Mile Island finally brought millions of citizens to the side of the anti-nuclear movement. In Denmark, the state has been obliged to stage a public debate for a referendum on nuclear energy.

The aspect of the technology of political control which seems most likely, in every advanced Western state, to generate widespread opposition, has been in the context of the issue of state secrecy as a whole. Of all the new technological means to suppress those who challenge state power, it is surveillance that has aroused most anxiety and scrutiny. The awareness of the state as Big Brother has passed into mass consciousness. In the area of secret personal records, every government must now justify its collection and computerization of information.

The fight against surveillance has been concentrated mainly on giving individuals access to secret records. In post-Watergate America, this has led to floods of information about the activities of the CIA and the FBI, and closer control on private data banks. Counter-surveillance has become an important political means of curbing the security services and secret agencies. A National Committee to Investigate the FBI has been established. And the CIA's covert operations around the world are everywhere being exposed as the hidden counterpart to the open warfare it no longer dares to wage. The 'counterspy' operation by world opponents of the CIA and US policy in the Third World has meant that in many countries every American diplomat, journalist and businessman is under suspicion. In Teheran, the occupation of the US embassy and the seizure of hostages in late 1979 led to the capture of documents proving that the Embassy was a centre for pro-Shah CIA operations. A decade of exposing CIA operations has meant that third world revolutionaries now know how to arm themselves against US intervention.

There are now movements to introduce Freedom of Information Acts in several Western countries. But Western governments looking across the Atlantic are naturally disturbed by the mass of 'dirty tricks' revelations which have discredited America's intelligence agencies and police forces. Far from legislating greater freedom of information, the 1979 Protection of Official Information Bill proposed by the Tory government would have introduced even greater restrictions in Britain, by making it an offence to disclose official information or to refuse to name the source of a disclosure. The Bill was designed specifically to protect the agencies who were mainly responsible for its drafting: MI5 and MI6. It was fortunately torpedoed in the wake of the

Blunt spy scandal. Successive British governments have opposed all attempts to bring in Freedom of Information laws through private members' bills. In Australia, a 'freedom of information' Bill introduced in 1978 by the Attorney-General was sharply criticized by civil rights campaigners who dubbed it the 'Secrecy Law' because it would actually strengthen state secrecy. France and Holland both passed laws in 1978, but, as with many other countries, the clauses give wide exemption to information the governments wish to keep secret.

Freedom of information is an essential, although far from foolproof, safeguard against the collection of information by the state. Since computer surveillance affects every citizen, it is also a vital lever for building campaigns against other aspects of state repression. For, as we have shown, watching and waiting are being carried out by secret agencies as pre-emptive measures to head off opposition before it becomes open and active.

Other elements of the technology of political control have received less scrutiny. As each new weapon is introduced, there is a momentary flurry in the media, followed by statements of justification by police and politicians; there is little comment when the new weapon is wheeled out for the second time. There is little public knowledge or debate about the new technological fixes, under development or technically feasible, which at some date in the 1980s may be employed to make street demonstrations too painful, or to produce personality breakdown in political prisoners, or whatever is to be released next from the chamber of horrors.

In the absence of mass movements challenging the state, opposition to these threatening technological developments will need to make use of conventional political organizations and processes. (How effective this can be will depend, of course, on the prevailing party political balance.) Party politicians and trade union leaders can play a leading role in heading movements to prevent or roll back the use of repressive techniques. But these bodies will not move unless stimulated by the left to question what is happening.

The late 1970s saw the founding in several countries of research agencies independent of the state determined to discover what the secret state was planning against its democratic opponents. In Britain, State Research, a group of journalists and investigators into the police, the Army, changes in the law and technology connected with counter-insurgency, was set up in 1977. Its role has been to provide briefings to all concerned with civil liberties in the West, and particularly to trade unionists, politicians and community groups who want to take action against the encroachments of the state. Groups like State Research have created a climate in which the state is sometimes forced to justify its activities.

In 1979, Tony Benn, then Energy Minister in the Labour government, made a widely-ignored speech in which he asked 'Could we back into a Police State because of high technology?' It was the first open admission by a Cabinet member that technology and politics were becoming inextricably interlinked to the detriment of democracy. Benn himself had become aware of this through being denied access to Cabinet briefings on sensitive questions like defence. He went on to point to the secrecy surrounding military technology and 'the vast machine of supervision created by the state to safeguard itself'. He called for greater control over the Army, whose influence extends 'far beyond the airfields, naval bases and barracks', and for the 'defence of individual freedom against erosions in the name of security and the need to win democratic control of all those services which have been set up to guarantee our security'.

Benn's speech was part of a sequence of labour movement responses to growing evidence that the security forces were acting without democratic control and retooling themselves in expectation of mass unrest. It has now been confirmed that a Civil Contingencies Committee of permanent civil servants has drawn up elaborate plans for troops to replace striking workers in essential industries and services. The police have secured temporary bans on political marches in a number of localities, including one extending over the whole of London for two months in 1978. They have launched propaganda campaigns on law-and-order to influence politicians in the run-up to elections.

Police corruption flourishes under the system where it is investigated only by the police themselves. No policemen were indicted for the murder of an anti-fascist demonstrator, Blair Peach, in Southall in May 1979. This, despite the eye-witness evidence of people who saw Special Patrol Group officers clubbing him, and despite the discovery of illegal weapons – clubs, lengths of chain, iron bars – in SPG lockers after the murder. In September 1978, the Trades Union Congress called for an independent inquiry into the activities and function of the Special Branch and the Special Patrol Group of the Metropolitan police. The immediate spur to this was the actions against trade union pickets at the Grunwick factory in North London during 1977; but there have also been numerous revelations of Special Branch surveillance of trade union activists. Workers occupying the Greenwich Reinforcement Steel Services in London discovered files showing that the works manager had been visisted by a Special Branch Officer retailing him highly inaccurate information on two trade union militants at the factory.

By late 1978 the accumulating weight of evidence that the security services were operating against a broad spectrum of left opposition groups pushed the Labour Party's National Executive into action. Prompted by Tony Benn, its Home Policy Committee set up a study group to investigate the workings of Britain's security services. The objective of the study group was to draw up proposals for the Labour manifesto. Benn's policy paper, 'Civil liberties and the Security Services', underlined the danger that the security services 'may drift into practices which actually undermine, or endanger, the freedom they are supposed to defend.' His proposal was that the study group would report on the relative credibility of the various external and internal dangers to the security of the state; on the technology now available to the state to counter these alleged dangers, and the use made of it in comparable countries; and on the possibility of publishing annually the budget and staffing of the security services, the names of those in charge of them, their guidelines for action, and the numbers of dossiers relating to political activities.

Without a wide movement within the Party and trade unions it is unlikely that a future Labour Party manifesto would include proposals to control these forces and their activities. Even if pledges for reform are written into the Manifesto very great pressure would be needed to ensure that a Labour government carries out this policy. For Benn's proposals and the work of the new committee to have even a chance of success, the campaign to reform the Labour Party and to make it answerable to its members when in government must be won first.

Democratic rights and the technology of political control are intimately interlinked. In every country where elements of democracy still exist, even in severely restricted forms, it is still possible to forge campaigns to bring the security forces, the secret police, the development of weaponry and the treatment of prisoners under democratic control. Such campaigns cannot abolish the threats to civil rights posed by states seeking to protect themselves against lawful opposition; but they can provide checks and obstacles which hinder the drift towards the strong state, and they can engender a consciousness that we have the ability to fight the state even in its most fearsome aspects.

January 1980   K.M.
J.R.
T.S.

References

1: Old and New Traditions of Violence (pp. 19–25)
1. C. Desmond Greaves, *The Irish Crisis*, Lawrence and Wishart, 1972, p. 19.

2: The Tory Offensive (pp. 26–31)
1. F. Kitson, *Low Intensity Operations*, Faber, 1971, p. 87.

3: Maximum Repression (pp. 32–7)
1. J. McGuffin, *Internment*, Anvil Books, Tralee, Co. Kerry, 1973, p. 87.
2. For a key report, see *The Times*, 9 June 1973.
3. M. McKeown, *The First Five Hundred* (pamphlet).

4: Sophisticated Counter-Insurgency (pp. 38–42)
1. Quoted in C. Harman, *The Struggle in Ireland*, International Socialists (pamphlet), 1973, p. 37.
2. Lieut.-Col. Graham, 'Low-Level Civil–Military Co-ordination, Belfast, 1970–1973', *RUSI Journal*, September 1974.
3. *Observer*, 11 August 1974.
4. *The Times*, 5 December 1974 and 6 December 1974.

5: The Significance of Northern Ireland (pp. 43–6)
1. *Hansard*, 14 December 1921.
2. See Liam De Paor, *Divided Ulster*, Penguin Books, 1972; and Greaves, op. cit.

6: Capitalism in Crisis (pp. 49–51)
1. For a detailed analysis of the crisis see Ernest Mandel, *Late Capitalism*, New Left Books, 1975. For a simpler discussion see E. Hobsbawm, 'The Crisis of Capitalism in Historical Perspective', *Marxism Today*, October 1975. For more facts on the British situation see also A. Glyn and B. Sutcliffe,

British Capitalism, Workers and the Profits Squeeze, Penguin Books, 1972.
2. *Crisis 1975*, Institute of Economic Affairs, 1975, p. 118.

7: The Fascist State (pp. 52–6)

1. D. Guerin, *Fascism and Big Business*, Pioneer Publishers, New York, 1939.
2. L. Trotsky, *The Struggle Against Fascism in Germany*, Penguin Books, 1975, pp. 112–13.

8: Military Intervention in Politics (pp. 57–67)

1. *The Times*, 11 January 1974.
2. *The Times*, 5 August 1974.
3. S. E. Finer, *The Man on Horseback*, Pall Mall Press, 1962.
4. T. Ali and G. Hedley, *Chile: Lessons of the Coup*, IMG pamphlet, 1974.
5. Stephen Fay, 'Britain's Schizophrenic Army', *Sunday Times*, 30 November 1975.
6. James H. Meisel, *The Fall of the Republic: Military Revolt in France*, University of Michigan Press, Ann Arbor, 1962, p. 16.
7. ibid., pp. 37–8.
8. *Hibernia*, 13 June 1975.
9. Finer, op. cit.
10. Fay, op. cit.
11. *Investors Chronicle*, 23 May 1975.
12. Robert Fisk, *The Point of No Return*, Cape, 1975.

9: Steps to the Strong State (pp. 68–77)

1. *The Times*, 6 November 1975.
2. Ralph Miliband, *The State in Capitalist Society*, Weidenfeld and Nicolson, 1969.
3. Christopher Farman, *The General Strike*, Panther, 1974.
4. Mike Kidron, *Western Capitalism Since the War*, Penguin Books, 1970.
5. *Police on the Homefront*, NARMIC, Philadelphia, 1971.
6. T. Roszak, *The Making of a Counter Culture*, Faber, 1970.

10: Small Steps' in the Law (pp. 78–86)

1. G. Robertson, *Whose Conspiracy?*, NCCL, 1974, p. 8.
2. ibid., p. 15.
3. ibid., p. 8.

4. NCCL, *Report of the First Four Months of the Prevention of Terrorism (Emergency Provisions) Act 1974*, 1975, p. 15.
5. *Sunday Times*, 30 November 1975.
6. D. Williams, *Not in the Public Interest*, Hutchinson, 1965.
7. See NCCL, *Northern Ireland (Emergency Provisions) Act, Memorandum on the First Year's Operation of the Act*, 1974.
8. *The Times*, 6 December 1974.
9. F. Kitson, *Low Intensity Operations*, Faber, 1971, p. 69.

11: From Counter-Insurgency to Internal Defence (pp. 89–114)

1. George Wilmers, 'Nato's Counter-Revolutionary Role', *Proceedings of the Bertrand Russell Memorial Logic Conference*, held in Denmark, 1971.
2. *The Times*, 17 December 1974.
3. R. G. S. Bidwell, in RUSI Seminar, 'The Role of the Armed Forces in Peacekeeping in the 1970s', 4 April 1973.
4. D. Horowitz, *From Yalta to Vietnam*, Penguin Books, 1969.
5. Lens, *The Military Industrial Complex*, Kahn and Averill, 1970.
6. Wilmers, op. cit. See also Cowling's paper given at the same conference.
7. Cited in Wilmers, op. cit.
8. RUSI Seminar, 'The Role of the Armed Forces in Peacekeeping in the 1970s', 4 April 1973.
9. Richard Clutterbuck, *Protest and the Urban Guerrilla*, Cassell, 1974, p. 224.
10. ibid.
11. Anthony Deane-Drummond, *Riot Control*, RUSI, 1975, p. 64.
12. ibid., p. 113.
13. Clutterbuck, op. cit., pp. 149–72.
14. Brian Crozier, *A Theory of Conflict*, Hamish Hamilton, 1974, p. 116.
15. ibid., p. 16.
16. Deane-Drummond, op. cit., pp. 42–3.
17. M. Calvert, article in *Mars et Minerva* (journal of the SAS), quoted in the *New Scientist*, 7 August 1975.
18. *Workers' Press*, 9 April 1974.
19. Robert Moss, *Urban Guerrillas*, Maurice Temple Smith, 1972, p. 94.
20. Deane-Drummond, op. cit., pp. 89–96.

References

21. Moss, op. cit.
22. *Daily Telegraph*, 11 December 1974.
23. Frank Kitson, *Low Intensity Operations*, Faber and Faber, 1971, p. 25.
24. *The Times*, 6 August 1974.
25. Clutterbuck, op. cit., p. 248.
26. Kitson, op. cit.
27. *The Times*, 23 June 1972.
28. *Sunday Times*, 14 May 1972.
29. Kitson, op. cit., pp. 55-6.
30. ibid., p. 68.
31. *Workers' Press*, 9 April 1974.
32. James H. Meisel, *Military Revolt in France: The Fall of the Republic*, University of Michigan Press, Ann Arbor, 1962.
33. *Army Land Operations Manual, Volume III: Counter-Revolutionary Operations*.
34. Kitson, op. cit., p. 87.
35. Deane-Drummond, op. cit., p. 117.
36. *Ireland: Rising in the North*, Big Flame pamphlet.
37. Crozier, op. cit., p. 152.
38. Deane-Drummond, op. cit., p. 106.
39. *The Times*, 6 November 1975.
40. Deane-Drummond, op. cit., p. 105.
41. Kitson, op. cit., p. 90.
42. See A. Neuberg, *Armed Insurrection*, originally published in 1928, published in England by New Left Books, 1970.
43. RUSI Seminar, 3 May 1971, p. 12.
44. ibid., p. 8.
45. Sir Robert Thompson, *Defeating Communist Insurgency*, Praeger, New York, 1966.
46. RUSI Seminar, 'The Role of the Armed Forces in Peace-keeping in the 1970s', 4 April 1973.
47. *Workers' Press*, 18 March 1975.
48. P. Laurie, 'Pig Ignorant about an Army Takeover', *New Scientist*, 19 September 1974.
49. Richard Clutterbuck, 'A Third Force?', *Army Quarterly*, October 1973, pp. 22-8.
50. J. Baynes, *The Soldier in Modern Society*, p. 79.
51. *The Times*, 14 January 1975.
52. I. Sitner, 'The President's Crime Commission Revisited', *New York University Law Review*, vol. 43, 1968.
53. *Sunday Times*, 30 November 1975.
54. *Sunday Times*, 13 July 1975.

References 305

12: Low-Intensity Operations in Britain (pp. 115–48)

1. J. Biggs Davison, in 'The Role of the Armed Forces in Peacekeeping in the 1970s', RUSI Seminar, 4 April 1973.
2. Figures from *Labour Research*, December 1974, p. 242.
3. *The Times*, 3 September 1974.
4. *Statement on the Defence Estimates*, HMSO, 1975.
5. *The Economist*, 21 December 1974 (our italics).
6. *Daily Telegraph*, 20 March 1975.
7. *Daily Telegraph*, 21 February 1975.
8. RUSI Seminar, 'The Role of the Armed Forces in Peacekeeping in the 1970s', 4 April 1973.
9. *The Times*, 21 October 1974.
10. *The Guardian*, 13 July 1974.
11. *Labour Research*, December 1974, p. 244.
12. Zoe Fairbairns, *Study War No More*, CND pamphlet, 1974.
13. WEA/Cobden Trust, *The Police*, August 1974.
14. *Report of the Commissioner of Police for the Metropolis, 1974*, HMSO, 1975.
15. Calculated from *Report of HM Chief Inspector of Constabulary for the Year 1974*, HMSO, 1975.
16. ibid., p. 13.
17. *Daily Telegraph*, 25 October 1974.
18. *Report of HM Chief Inspector of Constabulary for the Year 1974*, op. cit., p. 79.
19. *The Times*, 11 December 1974.
20. Calculated from data in *Social Trends*, no. 5, 1974, p. 205, Table 196.
21. P. Evans, *The Police Revolution*, Hutchinson, 1974, p. 165.
22. *The Times*, 11 December 1974.
23. *Report of HM Chief Inspector of Constabulary for the Year 1974*, op. cit., p. 96.
24. 'The Police and the State', *Labour Research*, February 1975.
25. WEA/Cobden Trust, op. cit., p. 7.
26. Letter to *Financial Times*, 18 July 1974.
27. Quoted in D. Madgwick and T. Smythe, *The Invasion of Privacy*, p. 69.
28. *The Times*, 30 October 1974.
29. *Daily Telegraph*, 18 April 1974.
30. *The Times*, 8 February 1975.
31. *Daily Telegraph*, 21 June 1974.
32. *Sunday Times*, 14 April 1974.
33. *Daily Telegraph*, 15 April 1974.

References

34. *Daily Telegraph*, 21 June 1974.
35. *The Times*, 10 October 1974.
36. H. Wilson, *The Labour Government 1964–70*, Penguin Books, 1971, p. 311.
37. *Sunday Times*, 14 April 1974.
38. *Time Out*, 17 May 1974.
39. *Time Out*, 13 September 1974.
40. G. Robertson, 'Lennon: A Case to Answer', *New Statesman*, 15 November 1974.
41. *Daily Telegraph*, 30 July 1974.
42. Robertson, op. cit.
43. *The Times*, 29 November 1974.
44. Quoted in *Workers' Press*, 29 November 1974.
45. *Daily Express*, 11 June 1975.
46. Quoted in *Sunday Times*, 23 May 1972.
47. *Sunday Times*, 13 July 1975.
48. WEA/Cobden Trust, op. cit., p. 8.
49. *Report of the Commissioner of Police for the Metropolis, 1974*, op. cit., p. 47.
50. *Essex Evening Echo*, 31 July 1974.
51. *The Times*, 17 October 1974.
52. WEA/Cobden Trust, op. cit., p. 7.
53. *Sunday Times*, 3 February 1974.
54. Quoted in T. Cliff, *The Crisis: Social Contract or Socialism*, Pluto Press, 1975, p. 100.
55. Information based on R. B. Pengelley, 'Internal Security – some recent British developments', *International Defence Review*, October 1973.
56. J. Harvey and K. Hood, *The British State*, 1958, pp. 111–12.
57. *Report of HM Chief Inspector of Constabulary for the Year 1974*, op. cit., p. 25.
58. ibid., p. 24.
59. *The Times*, 3 February 1975.
60. *The Times*, 25 January 1975.
61. *The Times*, 24 January 1975.
62. *Daily Telegraph*, 22 February 1975.
63. *The Times*, 3 February 1975.
64. *Time Out*, 10 May 1974.
65. *Workers' Press*, 15 August 1974.
66. *Sunday Telegraph*, 13 January 1974.
67. *Sunday Times*, 13 July 1975.
68. *The Times*, 7 January 1974.

69. 'The Heathrow Manoeuvres: Was There an Atomic Threat?' *Undercurrents*, no. 9, January–February 1975.
70. Quoted in 'The Police and the State', *Labour Research*, February 1975.
71. Quoted in *Socialist Worker*, 5 October 1974.
72. A. Deane-Drummond, *Riot Control*, RUSI, 1975, p. 132.
73. *Guardian*, 8 January 1974.
74. ibid.
75. *Guardian*, 25 January 1974.
76. *Guardian*, 9 January 1974.
77. *Report of the Commissioner of Police for the Metropolis, 1974*, op. cit., p. 48.
78. *The Times*, 3 July 1974.
79. *Guardian*, 16 August 1974.
80. *The Times*, 2 November 1974.
81. *The Times*, 23 October 1975.
82. *Socialist Worker*, 1 March 1974.
83. *Time Out*, 8 March 1974.
84. *Time Out*, 17 May 1974.
85. *Guardian*, 1 May 1974.

13: Watching and Waiting (pp. 151–81)

1. F. Donner, 'The Theory and Practice of American Political Intelligence', *New York Review of Books*, 22 April 1971; *Ramparts*, December 1970.
2. D. Madgwick and T. Smythe, *The Invasion of Privacy*, p. 102.
3. *New York Post*, 10 April 1975.
4. H. Schwartz, 'Six Years of Tapping and Bugging', *The Civil Liberties Review*, Summer 1974.
5. *New York Times*, 20 February 1975.
6. 'The Snoopers and the Peepers', *Undercurrents*, no. 7, July–August 1974.
7. Senator Edward Kennedy, Congressional Record, June 1972.
8. Schwartz, op. cit.
9. L. Friedman, quoted in *New York Times*, 7 February 1975.
10. *Daily Telegraph*, 6 June 1974.
11. *The Times*, 4 October 1974.
12. Quoted in J. H. F. Shattuck, 'National Security Wiretaps', *Criminal Law Bulletin*, vol. 11, no. 1, 1974.
13. *Standards Relating to Electronic Surveillance*, American Bar Association, New York, 1971.

14. *Equipment Systems Limitations in Surveillance Operations*, Mitre Corporation, Washington, DC, November 1973.
15. *DC Gazette*, December 1973, p. 21.
16. J. H. F. Shattuck, 'Tilting at the Surveillance Apparatus', *The Civil Liberties Review*, Summer 1974.
17. Donner, op. cit.
18. See *Equipment Systems Limitation in Surveillance Operations*, op. cit.
19. *New York Times*, 19 March 1975.
20. *Philadelphia Enquirer*, 13 February 1975.
21. *Ten More Years*, New Mexico Civil Liberties Union, 1974.
22. Hampstead Committee of 100, *Mail Interception and Telephone Tapping in Great Britain*, republished 1973.
23. *The Times*, 8 February 1975.
24. *Sunday Times Colour Magazine*, 20 June 1971.
25. *Washington Post*, 1 August 1973.
26. See *The Rape of American Privacy*, Communication Control Corporation, New York, NY, 1973.
27. See ibid; J. E. Cunningham, *Security Electronics*, Sams, Indianapolis, Ind., 1971; D. A. Pollock, *Methods of Electronic Audio Surveillance*, Charles Thomas, Springfield, Ill., 1973.
28. J. Hanlon, 'Boardroom Electronic Warfare', *New Scientist*, 10 July 1975.
29. J. Hanlon, 'The Telephone Tells All', *New Scientist*, 17 July 1975.
30. *New Scientist*, 30 January 1975.
31. *The Times*, 23 July 1974.
32. See *Daily Telegraph*, 13 September 1973; *Workers' Press*, 14 September 1973.
33. Hedley Voysey, 'Insecure at Any Price', *New Scientist*, 12 December 1974.
34. Quoted in *Realtime*, no. 7, 1973.
35. Figures from *The Times*, 13 December 1974.
36. *Report of HM Chief Inspector of Constabulary of the Year 1974*, HMSO, p. 4.
37. ibid., p. 4.
38. P. Baran, *Some Caveats on the Contribution of Technology to Law Enforcement*, Rand Corporation, 1967.
39. *Police Review*, 26 May 1972.
40. Edward Harriman, 'Computerizing the Police Notebook', *New Statesman*, 1 August 1974.

41. 'LEAA: Who Guards?' *Datamation*, 15 June 1971.
42. Information on SEARCH and FBI systems from Lawyers' Committee for Civil Rights under the Law, *Law and Disorder*, III, Chapter II, 1972.
43. 'The National Crime Information Centre', *FBI Law Enforcement Bulletin*, January 1974, p. 10.
44. Los Angeles Police Department, *LAPD and Computers*, 1975.
45. *Realtime*, no. 7, 1973.
46. *World Medicine*, 13 June 1973, pp. 22–9.
47. CSD Management Studies 2, *Computers in Central Government Ten Years Ahead*, HMSO, 1972.
48. See *New Scientist*, 19 August 1974, pp. 718–20; 'Computer Privacy', *New Society*, 31 August 1969.
49. OECD Informatics Studies 6, *The Evaluation of the Performance of Computer Systems*, 1974, p. 12.
50. *Data Banks, Privacy and Repression*, Computer People for Peace, New York, 1971, p. 17.
51. *Daily Telegraph Magazine*, 20 September 1974.
52. ibid.
53. *Data Banks, Privacy and Repression*, op. cit., p. 18.

14: Monitoring Militant Action (pp. 182–96)

1. *Report of HM Chief Inspector of Constabulary for the Year 1974*, HMSO, 1975, p. 52.
2. Alain Dural, 'Écouter la police', *Interférences*, no. 1, 1975.
3. *Report of HM Chief Inspector of Constabulary for the Year 1974*, op. cit., p. 53.
4. 'New Electronic Gadgets for the Police', *New Scientist*, 12 July 1973.
5. *Report of HM Chief Inspector of Constabulary for the Year 1974*, op. cit., p. 96.
6. Lawyers' Committee for Civil Rights under the Law, *Law and Disorder III*, 1972, p. 54.
7. Frost and Sullivan, Inc., *The Public Law Enforcement Market*, 1971, cited in *Law and Disorder III*, op. cit., p. 54.
8. *Police on the Homefront*, NARMIC, Philadelphia, 1971, pp. 95–6.
9. William O. Thomas, 'TV by Laser Beam Transmission', *FBI Law Enforcement Bulletin*, February 1974.
10. *Post Office Telecommunications Journal*, vol. 26, no. 1, Spring, 1974, p. 5.

11. *The Times*, 31 January 1973.
12. See A. H. Tickner and E. C. Poulton, 'Monitoring up to 16 Synthetic Television Pictures Showing a Great Deal of Movement', *Ergonomics*, 1973, vol. 16, no. 4, pp. 381–401.
13. *Indochina Information No. 1: Weapons of Imperialism*, published by Indochina Solidarity Conference, London, 1973, p. 16.
14. Quoted in Phil Stanford, 'The Automated Battlefield', *New York Times Magazine*, 23 February 1975.
15. David J. Duff, 'External Intrusion Detection Systems', *Proceedings of 1973 Carnahan Conference on Electronic Crime Countermeasures*, ed. J. S. Jackson, University of Kentucky, 1974.
16. *Equipment Systems Limitations in Surveillance Operations*, Mitre Corporation, Washington, DC, November 1973, pp. 23–4.
17. *The Times*, 19 August 1974.
18. P. A. Young, 'Thermal Viewers for Police Use', *Proceedings of the First International Electronic Crimes Countermeasures Conference*, Edinburgh, July 1973.
19. ibid.
20. ibid.
21. *LEAA Newsletter*, September–October 1971.
22. *The Police Chief*, May 1969, vol. 36, no. 5.
23. *Project Sky Knight: A Demonstration in Aerial Surveillance and Crime Control*, US Department of Justice, 1968.
24. *Law and Order*, November 1973, p. 85.
25. *New York Times*, 14 October 1973.
26. *LEAA Newsletter*, vol. 1, no. 12, September–October 1971.
27. *Police on the Homefront*, op. cit., p. 14.
28. Frost and Sullivan, 'The Public Law Enforcement Market', quoted in *Law and Disorder III*, op. cit.
29. Quoted in *Police on the Homefront*, op. cit., p. 14.
30. *Law and Order*, November 1973, p. 81.
31. *Report of the Commissioner of Police for the Metropolis*, 1974, p. 48.
32. Institute of Defense Analyses, *Task Force Report: Science and Technology*, US Government Printing Office, Washington, DC, 1967, p. 21.
33. ibid., p. 24.
34. Quoted in *Police on the Homefront*, op. cit., p. 16.
35. Los Angeles Police Department, *LAPD and Computers*, 1975, pp. 35–6.

36. *Police Review*, 22 March 1974, p. 356.
37. *Report of HM Chief Inspector of Constabulary for the Year 1974*, op. cit., p. 95.
38. *Daily Telegraph*, 16 October 1974.

15: Riot Control (pp. 197–228)

1. W. W. Herrmann, *Riot Prevention and Control: Operations Research Response*, System Development Corporation, Santa Monica, Calif., 1968.
2. *Non-Lethal Weapons for Law Enforcement*, Security Planning Corporation, Washington, DC, 1972.
3. I. B. C. MacLeod, letter to Jonathan Rosenhead, BSSRS, November 1973.
4. C. H. Henn, letter to Jonathan Rosenhead, BSSRS, August 1971.
5. *Non-Lethal Weapons for Law Enforcement*, op. cit.
6. ibid.
7. D. O. Egner, E. B. Shank, M. Wargovitch and A. F. Tiedemann, *A Multi-disciplinary Technique for the Evaluation of Less Lethal Weapons*, vol. 1, US Army Land Warfare Laboratory, Aberdeen, Md, 1973.
8. Institute of Defense Analyses, *Task Force Report: Science and Technology*, US Government Printing Office, Washington, DC, 1967.
9. D. O. Egner and L. W. Williams, *Standard Scenarios for the Less Lethal Weapons Evaluation Model*, US Army Human Engineering Laboratory, Aberdeen, Md, 1975.
10. A. Deane-Drummond, *Riot Control*, RUSI, London, 1975.
11. N. T. Callahan and R. L. Knoblauch, *Prevention and Control of Collective Violence Vol. 3 – Guidelines for Intelligence Personnel*, US Department of Justice, Washington, DC, 1973.
12. R. Applegate, *Riot Control – Materiel and Techniques*, Stackpole Books, Harrisburg, Pa, 1969.
13. *Prevention and Control of Mobs and Riots*, Federal Bureau of Investigation, Washington, DC, 1967.
14. ibid.
15. ibid.
16. Applegate, op. cit.
17. J. F. Coates, 'Some New Approaches to Riot, Mob, and Crowd Control', *Proceedings of the Second National Symposium on Law Enforcement Science and Technology*, ed. S. I. Cohn, Illinois Institute of Technology, Chicago, Ill., 1968.

18. This description is largely drawn from T. S. Crockett and J. A. F. Kelly (eds.), *Police Reference Notebook*, Professional Standards Division, International Association of Chiefs of Police, Gaithersburg, Md, 1970.
19. Deane-Drummond, op. cit.
20. ibid.
21. *Prevention and Control of Mobs and Riots*, op. cit.
22. Egner, Shank, et al., op. cit.
23. ibid.
24. B. K. Thein, E. B. Shank, M. Wargovich, *Analysis of a Bean-Bag-type Projectile as a Less Lethal Weapon* (Draft Report), US Army Land Warfare Laboratory, Aberdeen, Md, 1974.
25. *Non-Lethal Weapons for Law Enforcement*, op. cit.
26. Deane-Drummond, op. cit.
27. *ARCOM Laboratory Posture Report, FY 74*, US Army Armament Command, Rock Island, Ill., 1974.
28. Much technical detail for this section can be found in *The Problem of Chemical and Biological Warfare*, SIPRI, Stockholm, vol. 1, *The Rise of CB Weapons*, 1971; vol. 2, *CB Weapons Today*, 1973. Reference can also be made to: Applegate, op. cit.; J. F. Coates, 'Non-Lethal Police Weapons', *Technology Review*, vol. 74, no. 7, 1972; *Report to Ann Arbor Police Department on Chemical Mace*, University of Michigan Medical School, Ann Arbor, Mich., 1968.
29. This account of CS and its effects draws on: *The Problem of Chemical and Biological Warfare*, op. cit., vols. 1 and 2; *Report of the Enquiry into the Medical and Toxological Effects of CS (Orthochlorobenzylidene Malonitrite)*, Part II, HMSO, London, 1971 (Cmnd 4775); S. Rose (ed.), *Chemical and Biological Warfare*, Harrap, 1968; Egner, Campbell, et al., op. cit.
30. *Tactical Employment of Riot Control Agent CS (Field Manual 3–2)*, Department of the Army, Washington, DC, 1970.
31. Details of British weapons are drawn from: *Report of the Enquiry into the Medical and Toxological Effects of CS Gas*, op. cit.; *British Defence Equipment Catalogue*, 4th edn, Combined Services Publications, 1972; R. B. Pengelley, 'Internal Security – Some Recent British Developments', *International Defence Review*, October 1973; 'British Internal Security Equipment Survey', *International Defence Review*, October 1973.

32. Some hints can be found in *Beat the Heat: A Survival Handbook*, Ramparts Press, San Francisco, 1972; treatment details also from Crockett and Kelly, op. cit; H. J. Hucek, E. N. Wyler, G. A. Lutz, J. G. Dunleavy, and W. E. Jones, *Report of the Status of Riot Control Hardware*, US Army Limited Land Warfare Laboratory, Aberdeen, Md.
33. Quoted in the *Guardian*, 9 March 1974.
34. *Guardian*, 9 March 1974.
35. R. Applegate, 'Riot Control 1969', *Ordnance*, September–October 1969.
36. *The Times*, 24 January 1973.
37. Macleod, op. cit.
38. *Non-Lethal Weapons for Law Enforcement*, op. cit.
39. *Guardian*, 3 October 1973.
40. *The Times*, 3 October 1973.
41. Egner, Shank, et al., op. cit.
42. Quoted in *Police on the Homefront*, NARMIC, Philadelphia, 1971.

16: Torture and Interrogation (pp. 229–46)

1. *Report on Torture*, Amnesty International, 1973, p. 7.
2. Discussed in the World in Action film, 'Year of the Torturer', Granada TV, 1973.
3. *Report on Torture*, op. cit., p. 22.
4. R. Medvedev, *Let History Judge*, Knopf, New York, 1971, p. 286.
5. See R. J. Lifton, *Thought Reform and the Psychology of Totalism*, Norton, New York, 1961.
6. *Workshop on Human Rights: Reports and Recommendations*, Amnesty International, 1975, pp. 4, 5.
7. O. Fenichel, *The Psychoanalytic Theory of the Neuroses*, Norton, New York, 1945.
8. F. Hocking, 'Extreme Environmental Stress and Its Significance for Psychopathology', *American Journal of Psychotherapy*, vol. 24, 1970, pp. 4–26.
9. Frantz Fanon, *The Wretched of the Earth*, Penguin Books, 1967, pp. 225–32.
10. R. L. Swank and E. Marchand, 'Combat Neurosis: Development of Combat Exhaustion', *American Medical Association Archives of Neurology and Psychiatry*, vol. 55, 1946, pp. 236–47. There is an extensive literature on the relation

of such states to torture. See e.g. *Report on Torture*, op. cit., pp. 35–65.
11. L. E. Hinkle and H. G. Wolff, 'Communist Interrogation and Indoctrination of "Enemies of the State" ', *American Medical Association Archives of Neurology and Psychiatry*, 1956, vol. 76, pp. 115–74.
12. *Workshop on Human Rights*, op. cit., p. 5.
13. C. Dickens, *American Notes and Pictures from Italy*, Oxford, 1957, pp. 99–100.
14. For a detailed analysis of the use of sensory deprivation in torture, see T. Shallice, 'The Ulster Depth Interrogation Techniques and Sensory Deprivation Research', *Cognition*, vol. 1, 1973, pp. 385–405.
15. A. Sachs, *The Jail Diaries of Albie Sachs*, Harrill Press, 1966, p. 252.
16. ibid., pp. 219–20.
17. P. Suedfeld, 'The Benefits of Boredom: Sensory Deprivation Reconsidered', *American Scientist*, 1975, vol. 63, pp. 60–69.
18. *Sunday Times*, 14 July 1974.
19. *Guardian*, 3 May 1974.
20. I. Oswald, *Sleep*, Penguin Books, 1966.
21. *Sunday Times*, 6 October 1974.
22. *The Times*, 25 February 1975.
23. *Workshop on Human Rights*, op. cit., p. 4.
24. *Sunday Times*, 6 July 1975.

17: Scientific Interrogation (pp. 247–53)

1. J. F. Kubis, 'Comparison of Voice Analysis and Polygraph Lie Detection Procedures', paper prepared for the US Army Land Warfare Laboratory, Aberdeen, Md, August 1973.
2. *Workers' Press*, 14 August 1974.
3. British Association for the Advancement of Science, 'Science and the Police' (pamphlet), 1974, no. 3.
4. *Police Review*, 10 May 1974.
5. *Psychology Today*, no. 1, April 1974.
6. R. C. Davis, 'Physiological Responses as a Means of Evaluating Information', in A. D. Biderman and H. Zimmer (eds.), *The Manipulation of Human Behaviour*, Wiley, New York, 1961.
7. J. McGuffin, *The Guinea Pigs*, Penguin Books, 1974, p. 137.
8. Cited in J. Rolin, *Police Drugs*, Hollis and Carter, 1955, p. 18.

9. For a description of these techniques see W. Sargant and E. Slater, *Introduction to Physical Methods of Treatment in Psychiatry*; 5th edn, Churchill and Livingstone, 1972.
10. L. A. Gottschalk, 'The Use of Drugs in Interrogation', in Biderman and Zimmer, op. cit.
11. *Psychology Today*, April 1975.
12. M. T. Orne, 'The Potential Uses of Hypnosis in Interrogation', in Biderman and Zimmer, op. cit.

18: Prisoners of the Strong State (pp. 254–84)

1. D. Morrison and M. A. Waters, *Attica: Why Prisoners are Rebeling*, Pathfinder, 1972 (pamphlet).
2. Edward M. Opton Jr, 'Psychiatric Violence against Prisoners', *Mississippi Law Journal*, vol. 45, no. 3, 1974.
3. *Report of the Work of the Prison Department 1974*, HMSO, Cmnd. 6148.
4. Cited in L. Coleman, 'Prisons the Crime of Treatment', *Psychiatric Opinion*, vol. 2, no. 3, June 1974.
5. S. Cohen, pre-publication draft of 'A Futuristic Scenario for the Prison System', in Basaglia (ed.), *The Crimes of Peace*, Einaudi, Turin, 1974.
6. Kendell et al., 'Psychiatric Diagnosis in Britain and the United States', *British Journal of Hospital Medicine*, vol 6, no. 2, 1971, p. 147.
7. Cooper, 'Diagnostic Changes in a Longitudinal Study of Psychiatric Practice', *British Journal of Psychiatry*, 1967, 113, pp. 129–42.
8. Cornelia Mee, *The Internment of Soviet Dissenters in Mental Hospitals* (pamphlet), 1971, p. 1.
9. G. Low-Beer, cited in 'Sinister Psychiatry', *World Medicine*, 3 October 1973, p. 18.
10. Zhores and Roy Medvedev, *A Question of Madness*, Penguin Books, 1974, p. 98.
11. Letter to the *British Medical Journal*, 9 November 1974.
12. Medvedev and Medvedev, op. cit., p. 181.
13. *Sunday Times*, 19 August 1973.
14. S. M. Silverman, 'A Symbolic Element in the PFLP Hijackings', *International Journal of Social Psychiatry*, 1973, p. 284.
15. Cited in Jessica Mitford, *The American Prison Business*, Allen and Unwin, 1974.

316 References

16. W. J. Gray, 'The English Prison Medical Service', in *Medical Care of Prisoners and Detainees*, Ciba Foundation Symposium 16, 1973, pp. 132–3.
17. P. Stanford, 'A Model Clockwork Orange Prison', *The New York Times Magazine*, 17 September 1972.
18. Opton, op. cit., p. 640, citing the Ciba Foundation symposium on the medical care of prisoners.
19. Cohen, op. cit.
20. *Interim Report of the Committee on Mentally Abnormal Offenders*, HMSO, Cmnd. 5698, July 1974.
21. Cohen, op. cit.
22. Coleman, op. cit.
23. Cohen, op. cit.
24. Opton, op. cit.
25. *New York Times*, 19 September 1971.
26. J. A. Meyer, 'Crime Deterrent Transponder System', *IEEE Transactions on Aerospace and Electronic Systems*, vol. AES-7, no. 1, January 1971 (USA). See also R. K. Schwitzgebel, 'Limitations on the Coercive Treatment of Offenders', *Criminal Law Bulletin*, vol. 8, no. 4, 1972.
27. J. McConnell, 'Criminals Can Be Brainwashed Now', *Psychology Today*, April 1970.
28. M. P. Dumont, 'The Politics of Drugs', *Social Policy*, July/August 1972, p. 32.
29. *Science for the People*, May 1974.
30. ibid.
31. ibid.
32. Cited in Opton, op. cit., p. 627.
33. *Science for the People*, op. cit.
34. *World Medicine*, 14 November 1973.
35. Cotter, 'Operant Conditioning in a Vietnamese Mental Hospital', in Ulrich, Stachnik and Mabry (eds.), *Control of Human Behaviour*, 1970.
36. *Science for the People*, op. cit.
37. V. H. Mark, W. H. Sweet and F. R. Ervin, letter in *Journal of the American Medical Association*, vol. 201, 1967, p. 895.
38. Cited in *Human Events*, 5 May 1973.
39. Cited by S. Chorover in 'Pacification and the Brain,' *Psychology Today*, May 1974.
40. For a detailed account of the history and techniques, uses and misuses of psychosurgery see E. S. Valenstein, *Brain Control*, Wiley, New York, 1973. See also P. Breggin, 'The Return of

Lobotomy and Psychosurgery', *Congressional Record*, 24 February 1972.
41. V. H. Mark and F. R. Ervin, *Violence and the Brain*, Harper and Row, New York, 1970.
42. Breggin, op. cit.
43. See, for example, H. Narabayasin et al., 'Stereotactic Amygdalectomies for Behaviour Disorders', *Archives of Neurology*, 1963, pp. 9–16.
44. Gloor, in *The Neurobiology of the Amygdala*, Basil E. Eleftheriou (ed.), Plenum Press, New York, 1972, p. 446. See also the paper by A. Kling in the same book.
45. Cited in Valenstein, op. cit., p. 231.
46. *Interneurone*, transcript of a discussion of the Southampton Brain Research Association, February 1973, p. 8.
47. See José M. R. Delgado, *Physical Control of the Mind: Towards a Psychocivilised Society*, Harper and Row, New York, 1969.
48. *Special Treatment and Destructive Imprisonment against Political Prisoners in the BRD* (pamphlet), published on behalf of the Red Army Fraction prisoners, September 1974.
49. B. Beaumont, 'Forced Feeding, Medicine and Torture', *Science for the People*, no. 27.
50. ibid.
51. *Science*, vol. 188, p. 816.
52. *Evening Standard*, 14 May 1975.
53. Cited in Opton, op. cit., p. 606.
54. *Report of the Work of the Prison Department 1974*, op. cit.

Additional References

Since the first edition in 1977, there has been a great increase in relevant literature. This is a list of the sources we have found most useful, especially books and articles which further illuminate points we were trying to make, or which forced us to rethink some of our previous conclusions.

General Sources

Two new periodicals have significantly extended the work we began in this book:

State Research is the bi-monthly bulletin of the State Research Group. It covers the fields of law, espionage, policing, the military, technology, and internal security operations, together with international material and monitoring of right-wing organizations. Available from State Research, 9 Poland Street, London W1; or in book form as *The Review of Security and the State* (1978 and 1979), Julian Friedmann Books.

CILIP, a thrice-yearly newsletter on civil liberties and police development in the West, is produced by the West Berlin Institute for Conflict Studies. Available from Berghof Stiftung für Konfliktforschung, Winklerstr. 4a, 1000 Berlin 33.

The Leveller, *Time Out*, *New Society* and the *New Statesman* regularly publish useful material.

Ireland

P. Chalk, 'Surveillance, the law and military rule', *Ireland Socialist Review*, Spring 1979. Documents the continuation of the Army/RUC campaign of sophisticated counter-insurgency in Northern Ireland through 1978.

The British Media and Ireland, published by Information on Ireland, 1 North End Road, London W14.

Fascism

D. Edgar, 'Racism, fascism and the politics of the National Front', *Race and Class*, Autumn 1977. Examination of the NF's fascist ideology.

M. Walker, *The National Front*, Fontana 1977. The development of the British far right since Mosley, with details on the NF's structure and policies.

P. Rees, *Fascism in Britain: an annotated bibliography*, Harvester Press 1979. Useful for its list of 839 publications by and about fascism in Britain, rather than for its political analysis.

Military Intervention

W. Gutheridge, 'Could it happen here?', *The Police Journal*, Jan-Mar 1979, Vol. LII No. 1. Possibility of a *coup d'état* in Britain.

P. Hennessy, 'Whitehall brief I–VIII', *The Times*, Oct.–Nov. 1979. A series of articles investigating government planning for civil defence and internal counter-subversion, including the role of the Army.

G. Marshall, 'The armed forces and industrial disputes in the UK', *Armed Forces and Society*, February 1979.

A. Roberts, 'The British armed forces and politics', *Armed Forces and Society*, August 1977. Historical summary of the changing role of the military in British politics from the seventeenth century to the mid-1970s.

Steps to the Strong State

T. Benn, *The Democratic Control of Science and Technology*, Spokesman Press pamphlet, 1979. Analysis from a left-labour perspective of the threats to civil liberties from reliance on advanced technology, especially nuclear power.

T. Benn, *The Right to Know*, Institute for Workers' Control pamphlet, 1978. Benn wrote this text on open government and freedom of information while he was still Energy Secretary.

Disclosure of Official Information: A Report on Overseas Practice, HMSO 1978. A detailed review covering nine Western countries.

R. Jungk, *The Nuclear State*, John Calder 1979. Argues that the security required by a nuclear state is incompatible with democracy.

JUSTICE, *Plutonium and Liberty*. Report by British Section of International Commission of Jurists, 1978. Some possible consequences of nuclear reprocessing for an open society.

Report of the Windscale Inquiry (Parker Report), HMSO March 1979.

E. P. Thompson, Introduction to *The Review of Security and the State*, Julian Friedmann 1978. A controversial essay on the growth of the strong state and the historical response to it. Reprinted as a pamphlet by State Research.

Civil Liberties and the Law

Review of the Operation of the Prevention of Terrorism (Temporary Provisions) Acts, 1974 and 1976 (Shackleton Report) HMSO 1978, Cmnd. 7324.

B. Rose-Smith, 'Police powers and terrorism legislation', in P. Hain (ed.) *Policing the Police*, John Calder 1979. A critical survey of the use of the PTA.

H. Harman and J. Griffith, *Justice Deserted*, National Council for Civil Liberties pamphlet, 1979. Jury vetting in political trials.

E. P. Thompson, *The State versus its 'Enemies'*, Merlin Press 1979. A pamphlet on the history of jury vetting. Thompson wrote a series of articles in *New Society* and the *New Statesman* during 1978 and 1979 dealing with state secrecy and civil liberty.

T. Harper, 'Emergency powers', *New Law Journal*, 15 March 1979. A summary of emergency powers legislation.

From Counter-Insurgency to Internal Defence

Col. R. Eveleigh, *Peacekeeping in a Democratic Society: The Lessons of Northern Ireland*, C. Hurst & Co. 1978. An extension of Kitson's argument that the military should be prepared to intervene in Britain, and should base their operations on the lessons of Northern Ireland.

Low-Intensity Operations in Britain

The Secret Services

C. Pincher, *Inside Story*, Sidgwick and Jackson 1978. A source of important factual information about the operations of MI5 and MI6, especially their international connections; but written with an underlying right-wing ideology.

P. Hamilton, *Espionage, Terrorism and Subversion in an Industrial Society*, Peter A. Heims 1979. A right-wing account written by an ex-spy.

Additional References

The Police

Blood on the Streets, Bethnal Green and Stepney Trades Council 1979. The actions of police in relation to racist attacks in London's East End since 1976.

T. Bowden, *Beyond the Limits of the Law*, Penguin 1978. A comparative study of the police in crisis politics.

P. Hain (ed.), *Policing the Police*, Vol. 1, John Calder 1979. Three essays on the growing power of the police and their lack of accountability.

R. Mark, *In the Office of Constable*, Collins 1978. Revealing memoirs of a highly influential Chief Commissioner of Metropolitan Police.

K. Sloan, *Public Order and the Police*, Police Review Publishing Co. 1979. A manual of basic public order law with a survey of left and right political groups and a significant section on police riot control, written by a police officer.

State Research carries reviews and surveys of literature on the police, as well as the other areas covered by this book.

The Technology of Political Control

General

Counter Information Services, *The New Technology*, pamphlet, 1979. Social and economic effects of the 'microchip revolution'.

S. Wright, 'An assessment of the new technologies of repression', in *Repression and Repressive Violence*, Amsterdam, Swets and Zeitlinger 1977.

S. Wright, *New Police Technologies*, Journal of Peace Research, Vol. XV No. 4, 1978. An exploration of the social implications and unforeseen impacts of some recent developments. Appendix lists some weapons manufacturers.

Watching and Waiting

National Academy of Science, USA, *On The Theory and Practice of Voice Identification*, National Research Council 1979. Authoritative review of state-of-the-art, stressing unreliability of current methods.

R. McKay, S. Peak, K. Margolis, 'Terminal Surveillance', *Time Out* 13–19 April 1979. Details of the Northern Ireland Army computer at Lisburn.

Additional References

D. Campbell, 'Lifting the veil on police computers', *New Scientist*, 18 Jan. 1979. Summarizes available information on the Police National Computer and the Metropolitan Police computer.

Report of the Committee on Data Protection, (Lindop Report), HMSO, 1978. Cmnd. 7341. Includes information about police and military computers and the secrecy surrounding them.

Campaign against the Model West Germany, *Under Observation: The Computer and Political Control*. Details of the West German police intelligence computer. From Evangelische Studenten-gemeinde, Querenburger Hohe 287, 4360 Bochum, West Germany.

Monitoring Militant Action

P. Kelly, 'Heli-Tele is watching you', *The Leveller*, Dec. 1979. Documents the British use of sophisticated helicopter-borne TV cameras, night vision cameras etc.

Securitech, Unisaf Publications Ltd. Annual consisting of advertisements for purveyors of private security services and technology, including night vision devices, intrusion detectors etc. From 32–6 Dudley Road, Tunbridge Wells, Kent.

Riot Control

'Impact weapons – the shape of things to come?', *Police*, Vol. XI No. 4, Dec. 1978. New and future developments in riot control technology.

Stockholm International Peace Research Institute (SIPRI), *Anti-Personnel Weapons*, Taylor and Francis 1978. Along with consideration of fragmentation bombs and the like, contains authoritative account of known capabilities and effects of electric, acoustic and impact weapons.

J. Rosenhead, 'A new look at less lethal weapons', *New Scientist*, 16 December 1976. Contains further information on the effects of plastic and rubber bullets. Hansard, 21 January 1977, shows that Parliamentary questions revealed that the energy levels – hence dangers – of these weapons was even higher than the article had supposed.

J. Rosenhead and T. Shallice, 'Lewisham', *Science for People* No. 37, Autumn 1977. Brief analysis of police tactics at this demonstration, and of the introduction of riot shields.

Council for Science and Society, *Harmless Weapons*, 1978. Analysis of police riot control systems from a liberal standpoint, arguing against them in terms of public loss of support for the police. An appendix summarizes available weaponry.

Interrogation, Torture and Prisoner Control

General

P. Watson, *War on the Mind: The Military Uses and Abuses of Psychology*, Hutchinson, 1978. An extensive but politically confused view of all types of military psychology.

P. Schrag, *Mind Control*, Marion Boyars, 1979. The use of advanced technology to control behaviour, particularly in the US mental health system.

P. Greenfield, in *American Psychological Association Monitor*, Dec. 1977. Detailed account of the CIA's penetration of American academic psychology.

J. Marks, *The Search for the Manchurian Candidate*, Allen Lane 1979. The story of the CIA's secret efforts to control human behaviour.

Interrogation

W. E. Lucas, 'Solitary confinement isolation as coercion to conform', *Australian and New Zealand Journal of Criminology*, No. 9, 1976. A detailed and definitive account of modern solitary confinement procedures and their effects.

W. Ristow and T. Shallice, 'Taking the hood off British torture', *New Scientist*, 5 August 1976. The further history of the Northern Ireland torture methods.

Report of the Committee of Inquiry into Police Interrogation Procedures in Northern Ireland, (Bennett Report), HMSO 1979. Cmnd. 7497. Bennett found that RUC members had ill-treated suspects under interrogation and placed heavy reliance on confessions in order to convict suspected terrorists. Some of his proposals for changes in procedure have since been adopted. See also T. Harper's commentary on the Report in *New Law Journal*, 29 March 1979.

Prisons

M. Fitzgerald, *Prisoners in Revolt*, Penguin 1977. The history of prison protest in Britain with important information on present British prison conditions.

324 Additional References

M. Fitzgerald and J. Sim, *British Prisons*, Blackwell 1978. A comprehensive account of the British penal system with emphasis on the rights of prisoners.

D. MacDonald and J. Sim, *Scottish Prisons and the Special Unit*, Scottish Council for Civil Liberties pamphlet, 1979. The use of 'control units' in Scottish prisons.

T. Whitehead, 'Drugs in prison', *The Abolitionist: Journal of Radical Alternatives to Prison*, Summer 1979. Information on the use of drugs in prisons. From 182 Pentonville Road, London N1.

K. Margolis, 'The exile of Astrid Proll', *Time Out*, 29 June 1979. The experiences of an ex-Red Army Fraction member who was tortured in a German prison and spent a year in British prisons fighting extradition.

International

N. Chomsky and E. S. Herman, *The Washington Connection and Third World Fascism*, Spokesman Books 1979. Extensive information on state repression by the United States' client states.

M. Klare, *Supplying Repression*, Field Foundation Pamphlet 1977. The export of new repressive technology by the US to the third world. See also: M. Klare, 'Le Commerce International des Moyens de Repression', *Le Monde Diplomatique*, June 1979.

M. Halperin, J. Berman, R. Borosage and C. Marwick, *The Lawless State*, Penguin USA. Documented report on the crimes of the US intelligence agencies, the CIA abroad and the FBI at home.

P. Agee and L. Wolf (eds), *Dirty Work: The CIA in Western Europe*, Lyle Stuart Inc., Secaucus, New Jersey, 1978. The CIA's role in guarding internal European security.

Covert Action Information Bulletin. Bi-monthly bulletin uncovering CIA activities and personnel around the world. From Covert Action Publications, PO Box 50272, F Street Station, Washington DC 20004.

C. Ross and K. Lawrence, *The Politics of Repression in the United States 1939–76*. Documents the routine surveillance of subversives and record-keeping by the FBI. From American Friends Service Committee, 513 North State Street, Jackson, Mississippi, 39201 USA.

S. Cobler, *Law, Order and Politics in West Germany*, Penguin 1978. Charts and criticizes the German state's response to urban guerrillas and active political movements.

N. Brown, *The future global challenge: a predictive study of world security, 1977–1990*, Royal United Services Institute for Defence Studies 1977. Future trends in internal security as a response to continuing challenges to Western states.

Index

Aden, 229
Agee, Philip, 153
agents provocateurs, 129, 153
Algerian war, 58, 59–60; torture in, 229, 233
Allen International, 225–6
Allende, Salvador, 58–9
Amnesty International, 229, 231, 233–4, 245, 249–50
Anderson, Ruth, 278–9
'Angry Brigade', 80
Anti-Picket Squad, 135, 145
anxiety neurosis, 232–3, 234, 236; see also Torture
Applegate, Colonel, 203
army: as part of state apparatus, 58; restrictions on democratic rights of soldiers, 289–90
Army Land Operations Manual (ALOM), 90, 92, 100, 102–6, 107, 111, 113, 133, 143, 186, 188, 201, 246
Arrowsmith, Pat, 83
Asklepeion programme, 267–8
Attica prison rebellion, 255, 268
Attlee, Clement, 127, 138

'B Specials', 23–5, 45; disbandment, 26
Bad Debt Act, 35–6, 71
Baldwin, Stanley, 73
Balniel, Lord, 99
Baran, Paul, 174
'baton round', 209–10; see also Rubber bullets
Battle of Algiers, 233
Baynes, Lieutenant-Colonel, 111

Belfast, 23, 25, 28, 40, 219
Belgium, 91, 112, 179
Bidwell, Brigadier R. G. S., 91–2
Birmingham bombing (1974), 70, 81–2, 246
Birmingham University, 223–4
Birtles, Bill, 85
Black Panthers, 158
Bloody Sunday, 36–7, 197
Bomb Disposal Squad, 133
Bone, Edith, 240
Bovill, Charles, 225–6
Bow Group, 143
Brazil, 68, 229, 235
Brice, J., 279
brine, cold, 227
Britain, 69–70; colonial wars, tactics in, 19–21, 229; fascism in, 51, 52–6, 99; General Strike, 49, 73, 103, 110, 138, 148; government and data banks, 168, 178–80; harassment of Irish militants, 82–3; legal system, 78–86; miners' strike (1972), 135–6, 137; miners' strike (1974), 14, 57, 136, 144–5; obstacles to military coup, 57–64, 98; seamen's strike (1966), 127; social conflict in, 46, 50–51; strength of working class, 54; 'strong state', 51, 67, 70–73, 78–86, 92; torture in, 230, 237, 243–6; trade unions, 51, 54; and world capitalist crisis, 50–51
British Army: defence against 'Soviet threat', 90–93, 116, 197; exercises in public, 141–7;

British Army – *contd*
independent telephone system, 167; and internal security, 84–6, 89–90, 92–109, 111–14, 137–48; and politics, 57–67, 73, 84–6, 119; strength of, 116–19; in strike-breaking, 138, 145, 148; training for policing roles, 103; *see also* Northern Ireland; British Army

British Association for the Advancement of Science, 247, 249, 252, 289

British Broadcasting Corporation, 71, 106

British Society for Social Responsibility in Science, 219, 289; development of, 12–14

Brooke, Henry, 123

brutalization techniques, 245–6

Buckley, William, 57

bugging: cost, 165; counter-measures, 165–7; 'infinity bug', 164, 167; and 'spike' microphone, 164–5; and telephone, 163–4; in UK, 155–6, 165; in USA, 155, 165

Bukharin, Nikolai, 292

Bunyan, Tony, 115, 147, 159

Bureau of State Security (BOSS), 125

Burntollet Bridge incident, 23, 24

business intelligence organizations, 128

Butner Federal Research Center, 268, 283

Cable Street (1936), 53

Caetano visit (1973), 125

Callaghan, James, 223

Calvert, Brigadier Michael, 93, 95, 117

Canard Enchaîné, Le, 156

Carr, Robert, 282

Carver, Sir Michael, 99

Central Integrated Traffic Control (CITRAC), 122, 184–5

Central Intelligence Agency (CIA), 76, 135, 153, 159, 169, 250

Chalfont, Lord, 57, 116–17

Che Guevara, 97

Chemical Mace, 200, 212–13, 222

Chicago Seven trial, 153

Chichester-Clark, Major, 24, 30, 32

Chile, 56, 58–9, 63, 68, 229

China, 93, 232, 266

Churchill, Winston, 225

Civil Contingencies Committee, 137, 147–8

Civil Protection Ltd, 215

civil-military-police co-ordination, 67, 100, 102, 119, 131–2, 138–9, 141–8

Clark, Ramsay, 230

Clausewitz, C. von, 91

Clay Cross, 79, 102

Clutterbuck, Major-General Richard, 39, 93–4, 98, 111, 143, 148

CN gas, 212–14, 215

Cohen, Professor Stanley, 225, 257, 264, 265, 267, 283

Committee on Mentally Abnormal Offenders, 264

Commonwealth Immigration Act, 84

communications interception, 125, 152–67

communism, threat to imperialism, 19, 45, 91–2

Communist Party of Great Britain (CPGB), 94, 127; bugging of HQ, 156

Compton, Sir Edmund, 35, 44

conscription, 111–13

Conspiracy Act (1875), 79–81, 85

'Control Units', 244–5, 267, 284

'conveyor' system of interrogation, 242

counter-insurgency campaign, in military theory: 'preparatory period', 100–103, 152–81; 'non-

violent phase', 103–7, 114, 182–292 *passim*; 'open insurgency', 107–8
Copeland, Miles, 145
Cotter, William J., 159
Coutinho, Carlos, 242–3
CR gas, 206, 221–3
Creggan, Army barracks, 29
Criminal Investigation Department (CID), 170, 175
Criminal Justice Act (1970), 30
crowd control, 139; and computers, 194–5; and helicopters, 192; and TV surveillance, 183–5; *see also* Riot control
crowd dispersal, 202–5
Crozier, Brian, 94, 106
CS gas (orthochlorobenzylidene malonitrile), 19, 102, 210, 212–21, 222, 223; as means of collective punishment, 27; in Cyprus, 24; development of, 214; effects on health, 217–20; in House of Commons, 214; use in Northern Ireland, 12–13, 22, 24–5, 26–30, 42, 43–4, 215–21; protective measures, 220–21; public reaction to, 29, 218; supply to British police, 217; superiority over CN gas, 213–15; tactical disadvantages, 28, 43; use in Paris (1968), 29, 219; in Vietnam, 13, 24, 29, 215–17, 219
curfews, 104
Cyprus campaign, 24, 100, 206, 215
Czechoslovakia, 69, 242, 259

D-notice system, 83
dart gun, 227
De Albuquerque, Afonso, 243
Deane Drummond, Anthony, 94, 97, 104, 105, 106, 143, 198, 203, 227
Deedes, William, 101
De Gaulle, Charles, 62, 113

Denmark, 162, 179
Department of Health and Social Security, use of computers, 178–9
Department of Intelligence (Home Office), 124
Derry, 22, 23, 29, 36, 40, 205, 216, 219; Battle of Bogside (1969), 12, 23, 24, 221; *see also* Bloody Sunday
Dickens, Charles, 237
Diplomatic Protection Group, 133
Douglas-Home, Charles, 98
drugs, as instrument of repression, 260, 270–74
Dulles, John Foster, 91
Dumont, Matthew, 268, 271

Economic League, 119, 128
Ehrenburg, Ilya, 231
electro-convulsive treatment (ECT), 271, 274–5
electronic battlefield, 12, 19
Elliott-Bateman, Michael, 144
Emergency Powers Act, 40, 84, 85
Ensslin, Gudrun, 239
Ervin, Frank, 275–6, 278, 279
European Commission on Human Rights, 35n
European Economic Community, and security cooperation, 76–7

Fairbairns, Zoe, 119
Fanon, Frantz, 233
fascism, roots of, 52–6, 63, 68, 70, 99
Faulkner, Brian, 32, 37
Federal Bureau of Investigation (FBI), 176–7, 180, 205; COINTELPRO programme, 153–4, 158, 159, 163, 169
Fenichel, O., 232–3
Finland, 61, 179
First Circle, The, 158
Fisk, Robert, 41–2, 66, 106

FLAIR (Fleet Location and Information Reckoning), system, 196
'flying pickets', 80, 135, 137, 202
Foot, Professor M. R. D., 101
forced feeding, 281–2
Ford, General, 37
France, 91, 156; Army and Algeria, 59–60, 229, 233; *coup d'état* (1958), 58, 62; CRS riot police, 110; Communist Party, 62; and Indochina, 60; May 1968, 29, 97, 113, 188, 206, 219; repression in, 71; Socialist Party, 62; unrest in army, 112
Freeland, General, 26

Gandhi, Indira, 69
Gardiner, Lord, 35
Gartree Prison protests (1972), 264
gas, in riot control, 197–200, 204–5, 212–23
Gaughan, Michael, 282
Geneva Protocols (1925), 212, 216
Germany: fascism in, 52–6, 68; Kapp putsch, 59, 61–2; revolution in, 61, 96, 108, 113; West Germany, 50, 91, 116, 206; torture, 230, 238–9
Gerrard, John, 134, 135, 137, 145
Giap, General, 97
Gilmour, Ian, 137
Glasgow: dustmen's strike (1975), 67, 138; firemen's strike (1973), 138
Gluzman, Semyon, 259
Goldwater, Barry, 260–61
Gottschalk, L. A., 251–2
Graebe, Carl, 212
Grant, Larry, 130
Gray, W. J., 262
Greece, 76, 91, 250; torture, 232, 234, 245
Gregory, Ronald, 140
Grendon Underwood Psychiatric Prison, 262

Grigorenko, Pyotr, 259–60
Groves, Emily, 29
guerrilla warfare, urban, 95–7, 102, 103, 115, 137, 198; Hythe school, 137–8
Guyana, 215

Hampstead Committee of 100, 160
Hattersley, Roy, 230
Heath, Edward, 132
Heathrow airport exercises, 67, 141–6
helicopters, 188, 191–3
Himsworth Committee on CS gas, 29, 44, 218–20, 223
Hinkle, L. E., 235
Hitler, Adolf, 52, 53, 55, 99
Hobbes, Thomas, 292
Home Defence and Emergency Planning Committees, 136
Home Office, 76
Hong Kong, 209–10
hooding torture, 33–4, 236, 237, 245
Housing Finance Act (1972), opposition to, 79
Huckfield, Leslie, 42
hunger strikes, 281–2
Hunter-Brown, M., 276
hypnosis, 252–3

identity cards, 136–7, 170
image-intensifiers, 189
imprisonment, as a means of political repression, 229
Incitement to Disaffection Act, 71, 81
Indeterminate Sentence, 265
India, 69; Amritsar massacre, 197
India House incident (1973), 134
industrial espionage, 155
Industrial Relations Act, 79
infiltration, 124, 125, 128–30, 153
information, techniques for extraction of, 247–53
infra-red viewers, 189–90

Ingraham, Barton, 279
'instant banana', 227; 'instant mud', 227
Institute of Conflict Studies (ICS), 90
Institute of Defence Analysis, 12, 175, 194
intelligence, political and operational, 152-3, 182
intelligence computer, 22, 41-2, 123, 153, 180-81; limitations on use in 'preparatory period', 169-71; *see also* Police National Computer; Police, and computers
intelligence reports, importance of, 40-42, 102, 104, 123, 125-8
International Civil War, theory of, 93
International Socialism group (IS), 127
internment, 32-3, 35, 36, 39, 64, 82, 280
interrogation techniques, 242, 246, 247-53; in Northern Ireland, 32-6, 230, 233, 234, 243, 245, 246, 250, 287; *see also* Torture
Irish Republican Army, 26, 30, 34-5, 37, 38, 41, 60, 66, 95-6, 147; ban on, 81; in Britain, 124, 281-2; Provisionals, 104-5, 129-30, 167, bombing campaign, 30, 32, 81, growing support for, 30, 31, 36, 96; split in, 30; 1956-62 campaign, 32
isolation, prolonged, 237-41, 243-5; *see also* Sensory deprivation
Israel, 249, 252-3
Italy, 49, 91; Carabinieri, 110; fascism in, 52-5, 68

Jackson, George, 254, 262, 268
Jellicoe, Lord, 132, 137n
Jenkins, Roy, 83, 244, 282
Johnson, Professor Harry, 50
Johnson, Lyndon B., 75, 230
Johnson-Smith, Geoffrey, 101
Joint Intelligence Committee, 131

Kapp, Wolfgang, *see* Germany, Kapp putsch
Kennedy, John F., 201
Kenya, 40, 100
'key word' detection, 158
KGB, torture techniques, 33, 235, 236-7, 242
Khrushchev, Nikita, 259
King, Cecil, 83
King, Sir Frank, 64
Kitson, Major-General Frank, 31, 39, 67, 85-6, 97-107, 115, 137, 152, 175, 198

Labour Party: and capitalism, 72-3, 90, 112, 290-91: tapping of telephones at HQ of, 156
laser-guidance of bombs, 12, 19
Latin America, police and army, 76, 229
law, and political control: command of respect, 79, 86; flexibility, 78-9; and intensification of repression, 79-86
Law Enforcement Assistance Administration (LEAA), 75-6, 152, 168, 175-6, 192, 198, 206-7
Lawless, Gerry, 14
Lenin, Vladimir Ilyich, 97
Lennon, Kenneth, 128-31, 153
Lennox, Gordon, 214
lie-detector, *see* Polygraph
Ligue Communiste, ban on, 71
Lindemann, Professor, 225, 226
liquid irritants, 227-8
Lisburn, British Army HQ, 41, 167, 224
Litterick, Tom, 126
Littlejohn brothers, 153
Lloyd George, David, 45
Long Kesh, 167, 189, 222

332 Index

McClean, Ray, 219
McConnell, James, 271
McGuffin, J., 33, 34
McKearney, Joseph, 40
MacNamara, Robert, 12, 201
mail interception, 159–61
Malaya, 40, 100
'man-stopper' bullets, 139–40
Manual of Military Law, 84–5
Mao Tse-tung, 97, 102
Mark, Sir Robert, 109, 134, 143
Mark, Vernon, 275–6, 278, 279
Martinson, Robert, 257
Mason, Roy, 65, 117, 223
Massu, General, 113, 233
Masterson, John, 244
Matthews, Ralph, 156
media, state control of, 68, 71–2, 106, 202
Medvedev, Roy, 231
Medvedev, Zhores, 260
Meinhof, Ulrike, 239–41, 276n
Meisel, James H., 59–60
Mendershausen, Horst, 93
Messinger, Sheldon, 266
Meyer, J. A., 269–70
MI5, 131 174; MI6, 131
Miliband, Ralph, 72
Military Aid to Civil Ministries (MACM), 148
Military Aid to the Civil Power (MACP), 91, 92, 103, 148
military dictatorship, 57–64, 68
military spending: reduction in, 116–17; role in economy, 73
Ministry of Defence, 24, 29, 116, 119, 139, 144, 146, 148, 199, 225; operations room, 133; use of computers, 178
Mitchell, John, 176
Mitre Corporation, 187
Monday Club, 66, 101, 115
Montgomery, Field-Marshal, 64
Moscow trials, 231
Moss, Robert, 97, 101–2
Mussolini, Benito, 53, 55

Narut, Dr, 246
National Association of Local Government Officers (NALGO), 55, 121
National Council for Civil Liberties (NCCL), 40, 71, 81–3, 85, 126, 128, 130, 284
National Front, 53–4
National Industrial Relations Court, imprisonment of five dockers, 79, 135, 254
National Security Plan, 147–8
Newell, Mollie, 244
night-vision devices, 188–91
Nixon, Richard, 164
Northern Ireland, 13–14, 117, 135, 139, 188, 224; anti-internment movement, 36–7; arrests, 40–41; 'carrot and stick' policy, 38; Civil Rights Movement, 22–5, 35, 43; civilian deaths, 36–7; creation of statelet, 45–6; discrimination against Catholics, 22, 26, 38, 45–6; house searches, 38; Orange marches, 23; Protestant paramilitary groups, 39, *see also* UDA, UVF; rent and rates strike, 35–6, 71; sectarian assassinations, 39; solidarity movement in Britain, 37, 44, 290; SAS involvement, 133; 'strong state' in, 45–6; Sunningdale agreement, strike against, 64–6; war as testing-ground, 21, 46, 115, 137; *see also* Derry; CS gas; Internment; Interrogation techniques; Irish Republican Army; Rubber bullets
Northern Ireland, British Army intervention, 23–5; anti-guerrilla strategy, 31–42, 95–6, 107, 115, 137; armoured vehicles, 27; black propaganda, 104; casualties, 30; collusion with UDA, 39, 60, 66; collusion with Unionists, 26; curfew, 27; use of firearms, 27,

31, 43–4, 199; links with civil
  service, 39, 59, 101, 104;
  repression, 26–42, 108–9, 112;
  and Tory government, 26; and
  UWC strike, 64–6
Northern Ireland Act (1972), 84
Northern Ireland (Emergency
  Provisions) Act (1973), 81, 84
number plates, 'electronic', 187–8

Official Secrets Act, 72, 83, 90,
  283
Oldfield, Sir Maurice, 131
O'Neill, Terence, 22, 23
Opton, Edward, 270n, 272
Orne, M. T., 252–3
Orwell, George, 273, 288
Oswald, Ian, 243

Paisley, Ian, 60
Parker, Lord Chief Justice, 13, 35,
  44, 230, 233
parliamentary democracy, mass
  allegiance to, 60–61, 63, 68
Paton, Lori, 159
Pentagon, 12, 74, 157
Peterloo massacre, 197
photic driver, 225–6; and epilepsy,
  226
PIDE, 125; use of torture, 232,
  236, 242–3
plastic bullet, 211
Pluysch, Leonid, 273
police, 20; and civilians, 120–21;
  and compu ers, 171–8, 194–6;
  and firearms, 139–41; use of
  helicopters, 191–3; increase in
  size, 120–22; internal security,
  109, 111–14, 120, 122–3, 138–48;
  international cooperation, 76–7,
  135, 152; use of night-vision
  devices, 189–91; 'special support
  units', 134–6; and advanced
  technology, 75, 119, 122, 152,
  247–53; telecomunications,
  182–3; TV surveillance, 183–5;

trend to centralization, 120, 123,
  152, 289; 1974 restructuring, 120
Police National Computer, 123,
  171–4
Police Review, 174, 248
Police Scientific Development
  Branch, 122, 190, 195
political groups: files on, 125–6;
  harassment, 153–4, 158, 159,
  170, 174; and mass action, 93–8
political prisoners, 280–82;
  isolation of, 281; and prisoner
  control, 255–7, 264–5, 281; status
  of, 281
polygraph, 247–9; counter-
  measures, 249
Porton, chemical warfare
  establishment, 206, 213–14, 218,
  221, 222
Portugal, 63, 232, 236, 242–3, 250
Post Office Act (1969), 159
Post Office Investigation Branch,
  160, 161, 162
Powell, Enoch, 101
Prevention of Terrorism Act
  (1974), 70, 73, 81–4, 85, 170, 246
Price sisters, 246, 281–2
printometer, 162
Prior, Jim, 137n
prison: use of drugs, 264, 271–4;
  use of ECT, 264, 271, 274–5;
  mail censorship, 283–4; revolts,
  255, 264–5, 267, 268–9;
  segregation of inmates, 266–7;
  'therapeutic model', 255–7,
  264–8, 271, 284; 'therapeutic
  techniques', 264–8, 271–80,
  282–4; use of surgery on brain,
  275–80; *see also* Prisoners;
  Political prisoners
prisoners, radicalization of
  'criminal', 254–6, 264–5
Prisoners' Code, 262
private armies, 110, 121
private data banks, 180
projectiles, blunt, 207–12

psychiatry, use of in political repression, 257–64, 268, 280; 'diagnosis' of political non-conformists, 260–62
psychiatric prisons, 262–3
'psychological operations,' ('psyops'), 102, 104–6
psychosurgery, 275–80

Rand Corporation, 93
Raytag tracking device, 188
Red Army Faction, 238–41, 281
Red Lion Square demonstration (1974), 134, 141, 204
Rees, Merlyn, 42, 64–6, 223
Regional Crime Squad, 123
riot control, organization, 201–5
riot control, technology, 197–228, 287; inherent dangers of, 199–200, 207–28; need for constant innovation, 201, 227; official justifications of use, 198–200; principle of 'graduated response', 201
Robertson, G., 80n
Roche, Frank, 214
Rodgers, William, 245
Rose, Hilary, 14
Rose, Steven, 14
Roszak, T., 75
Rowntree, Francis, 29
Royal Ulster Constabulary (RUC), 12, 112, 215; violence against Catholics, 22–5, 45
Royal United Services Institute (RUSI), 90, 91–2, 101, 108–9, 115
rubber bullets: Belfast surgeons' report, 210–11, suppression of, 30; as cause of death, 29, 199, 211; description of, 28, 209; development of, 27–8, 43, 208–10; in Northern Ireland, 13, 20, 22, 27–31, 42, 43, 199, 209–10; use at short range, 28–9, 209; stiffening of, 28–9

Russian revolution, 69–70, 96, 113, 291

Sachs, Albie, 239–41
Safe Streets Act (US, 1968), 165
Sales, Rosemary, 14
Saltley coke depot, 135
Scarman tribunal, 134, 141
Schermuly Limited, 210, 211, 215
Scheuer, James 193, 228
schizophrenia, diagnosis of, 257–8
Schwitzgebel, R. K., 270
science: and the state, 11–13; of management, 74–5; ideology of 'neutrality' of, 12
scientists: and army, 119; radicalization of, 11–13, 288–9
secret police, function of, 68
sensors, electronic, 186–8
sensory-deprivation, 19; in Northern Ireland, 13, 22, 33–5, 42, 236–9; psychological effects, 33, 44, 237–41
Serbsky Institute, 260
Short Service Commissions, 118
Shrewsbury building workers, 79–81, 135, 205, 254
Sinn Fein, 128–30
sleep-deprivation, 33, 235, 242–3
Smith, Gerald, 279
'snatch squads', 205
Socialist Labour Party, 159
Socialist Workers' Party (US), 154, 159
Solzhenitsyn, Alexander, 158
sonic devices, 223–5
Sound Curdler, 224, 225
South Africa, 45–6, 215, 239, 241, 244; *see also* BOSS
Southern Ireland: anti-British reaction, 37; Dublin car bombs (1972), 105; growing economic importance for Britain, 22, 25, 46
Spain, 50, 63, 68

Special Air Services (SAS), 102, 114, 133, 142, 145, 147; use of torture, 245–6
Special Branch, 123–31, 139, 144, 159, 170, 174, 175; and industrial disputes, 126–7; and Irish community, 128–31; Irish Squad, 125; Personal Protection Squad, 125
Special Constables, 111, 121
Special Police Radio Inquiry Network (SPRINT), 194–5
Special Powers Act (1922), 45, 84
'squawk box', 224–6
Stalin, Josef, 231, 237, 258
Stansted airport operation (1975), 145
Starritt, Deputy Commissioner, 128–31
'state élite': and capitalism, 72; and technocracy, 74
stench weapons, 227
Sting-RAG projectile, 211
Stirling, Colonel David, 110
Strong State: in Eastern Europe, 69; introduction by 'small steps', 70–77; and political crisis, 68–9, 92; and Social-Democratic parties, 72–3; and socialist revolution, 69–70
Stun-Bag, 208–10
Sunday Times, 30, 35
Special Weapons and Tactics (SWAT), 198
Sweden, data bank system in, 168, 179
Sweet, William, 275
Symbionese Liberation Army, 198, 273
Synanon Games, 232
Szasz, Thomas, 260

'tailing', 157; electronic devices, 187–8
taser paralysis, 227
tear gas, 212–23

technology, repressive: and capitalist state, 11, 14–15, 21, 22, 43–4, 46, 287, 290–91; limitations to use, 287–8; not used for humanitarian reasons, 43–4, 199; political fight against, 288–92; purpose of, 11, 20–21; range of, 11; social character of, 20–21; US supremacy, 151
Technology of Repression, The New, 14
telephone tapping: automatic monitoring, 157–8, 161–2; counter-measures, 166–7; location of, 162–3; in USA, 153, 154–5, 163; in UK, 154, 155, 156, 161–2
television surveillance, closed-circuit, 183–5; in London, 185
Territorial Army Volunteer Reserve (TAVR), 111, 116, 117, 136, 146, 147
Thames Valley computer project, 174–5, 178
thermal viewers, 189, 190–91
'third force', 110–11, 133
Thompson, E. P., 90
Thompson, Sir Robert, 109, 124
Thompson, Brigadier, 101, 109
'Thought Reform', 231–2, 266
torture: commissions on use of, 35, 44; in destroying political effectiveness, 231–3, 234–43; exposure to noise, 33; growing use of, 229–30; in extraction of information, 230–31, 248; as means of terror, 233–4; and production of stress, 234–43, *see also* Anxiety neurosis, psycho-physiological, 235–43; 'stoika' position, 33; in trial preparations, 231
Tory government (1970–74): introduction of direct rule in Northern Ireland, and repression in Northern Ireland, 26–38, 43;

Tory government (1970–74) – *contd*
  preparations for showdown, 136–7, 144–5
Tote Trakt, 236, 238–41
transponders, 269–70
Tribune Group, 117
Troops Out Movement (TOM), 14
Trotsky, Leon, 55–6
Trotskyism, 94, 105–6, 154
Truman Doctrine, 91–2, 93
truth drugs, 249–52
Tuzo, General, 32

Ulster Defence Association (UDA), 39, 60, 66
Ulster Defence Regiment (UDR), 116
Ulster Volunteer Force (UVF), 30
Ulster Workers' Council, strike, 64–6
unemployment, and army recruitment, 118
Unionist Party: collusion with British Army, 26; opposition to reform, 26
United States: Attica revolt, 255; Berkeley riots, 192; black movement, 14, 158, 199, 229, 255, 275–6; counter-insurgency, 74; computerized law enforcement, 175–80, 194–6; industrial militancy, 50; military industries, 73; National Science Foundation report, 199, 210, 224, 227; press, 71–2; torture, 229–30, 237, 246; Watts riots, 75; as world policeman, 76, 152; *see also* Vietnam war
USSR, 14, 69, 291; 'cultural opposition', 259; psychiatric repression of dissidents, 258–60, 273, 291; and the west, 90–93; *see also* KGB
Vacaville psychiatric prison, 273, 275
vehicle registration, computerization, 172–4
Vietnam war, 21, 75, 76, 151, 199, 291; civic action programmes, 39, 40; CS gas in, 13, 24; electronic sensors in, 186–7; helicopters in, 191, 193; and inflation, 50; movement against, 14, 255, 290; and scientists, 12; 'technological fix', 19, 74; torture, 229
violence, of the state, 20–21, 45
'voice prints', 157–8
Von Seeckt, General, 61
Vorster, John, 45
Vowles, Jeffrey, 101

Wakefield prison, 224–5, 267
Waldron, Sir John, 101, 108, 109
Walker, Sir Walter, 110
Warren, Des, 80
water-cannon, 205–7; limited effectiveness, 22–3, 24, 207; electrically charged, 227
Watergate, 155
Watkins, Brigadier Brian, 132
Wedgwood, Josiah, 73
Welfare State, and social control, 71
Widgery, Lord, 129
Wilson, Harold, 65
Wolff, H. G., 235
Workers' Revolutionary Party: raid on education centre, 134; shadowing of demonstration, 147
working class, and military strategy, 94–9, 103, 107–8, 110, 113–14, 138, 145–8
Wormwood Scrubs, 244, 267